AND GOD SAID

ALSO BY DR. JOEL M. HOFFMAN

⊶AND GOD SAID⊷

HOW TRANSLATIONS

CONCEAL

THE BIBLE'S

ORIGINAL MEANING

Dr. Joel M. Hoffman

THOMAS DUNNE BOOKS

ST. MARTIN'S PRESS ⌇ NEW YORK

THOMAS DUNNE BOOKS.

An imprint of St. Martin's Press.

AND GOD SAID. Copyright © 2010 by Joel M. Hoffman. All rights reserved. Printed in the
United States of America. For information, address St. Martin's Press, 175 Fifth Avenue,
New York, N.Y. 10010.

www.thomasdunnebooks.com

www.stmartins.com

www.AndGodSaid.com

Library of Congress Cataloging-in-Publication Data

Hoffman, Joel M., 1968-

And God said : how translations conceal the Bible's original meaning / Joel M.
Hoffman. — 1st ed.

p. cm.

"Thomas Dunne books."

Includes bibliographical references and index.

ISBN 978-0-312-56558-9

1. Bible. O.T. English—Versions.   2. Bible. O.T.—Translating.   I. Title.

BS1133.H64 2010

221'.052—dc22   2009040037

First Edition: February 2010

10   9   8   7   6   5   4   3   2   1

Jonah Maccabee Dreskin had a contagious curiosity about the world, a devious sense of humor, and an intolerance for mediocrity that helped bring out the best in those who knew him. I'd like to believe that he would have enjoyed this book—I know I would have had fun discussing it with him—but I'll never know, because his life came to a sudden, tragic end while I was finishing up the manuscript. This book is dedicated to Jonah's memory.

CONTENTS

LIST OF TABLES

ACKNOWLEDGMENTS

This book began, though we did not know it at the time, during a class I taught on translation some years ago at HUC-JIR in New York City. One of my students, Marci Bellows, graduated and became Rabbi Marci Bellows. Then Irene Goodman, now my agent, spoke to Rabbi Bellows about a book on Bible translation, and Rabbi Bellows gave Irene my name. Thank you, Marci, for putting us in touch with each other.

Once we started working together, Irene Goodman stubbornly insisted that I do things her way. Without exception she has been right and this book is much the better for it. Irene has taught me an enormous amount about how to write and about now to navigate the world of publishing. Irene is also a fun person to work with and a kind soul. I've been lucky. Thank you, Irene.

Irene put me in touch with Peter Joseph, at Thomas Dunne Books, and working with Peter and his team has been a sheer delight. The folks at Thomas Dunne Books, and Peter in particular, have helped make the writing and publishing of this book a pleasure. I have also learned more from Peter than I would have thought possible. I'm glad my next book will benefit from his wisdom, and I can't help but wish I had met him earlier. Thank you, Peter.

Also in terms of putting this book together, thank you to Elizabeth Curione, for overseeing production; to Cheryl Krementz, copyeditor, and Julie Gutin, proofreader, for their attention to detail in their work on my manuscript; and to Robert Grom, for the beautiful cover that so wonderfully captures the spirit of this book.

I am grateful to Father Dennis McManus, who took the time to read a draft of this book and offered invaluable detailed suggestions.

This book took me five months and fifteen years to write: five months of actual writing, and fifteen years of exploration, discovery, learning, teaching, and grappling with the holy text of the Bible. Irene and Peter were my primary partners during the five months. I've been fortunate to have wonderful friends, teachers, and students during the fifteen years. I can't possibly single out everyone who has been helpful along the way, but I must start by mentioning my father, Rabbi Lawrence Hoffman, Ph.D., who in addition to everything else has been my study partner for as long as I can remember.

Rare are the environments that truly value learning and creativity while also recognizing the inherent worth of each individual. I've been lucky enough to spend time at three such places, and I'm grateful to the people who helped each one thrive.

From Kutz Camp in Warwick, New York, thank you in particular to Rabbi Allen "Smitty" Smith, whose vision it was to build the place; to Rabbi Stuart Geller, a master teacher and now dear friend; and to the literally thousands of students and fellow teachers whom I met along the way.

From HUC-JIR in New York City, I must single out Rabbi Dr. Eugene Borowitz and Rabbi Dr. Leonard Kravitz. I can hardly believe my good fortune at having been able to sit at a table with them.

And from SWFS, also in New York City, I am most grateful to Rabbi Gary Bretton-Granatoor and Rabbi Manny Gold, who created one of my favorite places in the world. I am equally indebted to my many students there—I wish I had space to list them all—who, like the other members of the faculty, have become my teachers. Also from SWFS, I am particularly grateful to Rabbi Ammi Hirsch and Cantor Dan Singer. Thank you for the happiness and celebration.

In addition, my thanks go to Rabbi Billy and Cantor Ellen Dreskin, for their support, honesty, and wisdom; Danny Maseng, for expanding my horizons; David and Karen Frank, for their kindness and thoughtfulness, and for opening so many doors; Douglas Hofstadter (though I've never met him), for introducing me to the challenge of translation; Rabbi Jaimee Shalhevet, for her insight; Janet Walton, for being on clear on what matters; Jennifer Hammer at New York University Press, for publishing my first book in a way that made me want to continue; Lauren Rose, for her support and enthusiasm; Marc Brettler, for his compassion and knowledge; Stuart Matlins at JLP, for bringing so many of my translations into print; and Tal Varon, who by personal example reminds me to walk humbly.

Finally and mostly, my thanks go to my parents, Sally and Larry, who gave me everything.

PREFACE

The Biblical book Songs of Songs, frequently quoted at weddings, is about romantic love. Yet most translations speak of "my sister, my spouse" or "my sister, my bride," practices that are not only unromantic but quite illegal in most places.

How did this happen? How did well-meaning translators throughout history so distort the original meaning of the Bible that, in this case, courtship ended up as a felony?

Song of Songs is but one example of a common pattern of mistranslation that prompted me to write this book, even knowing that passions run high when it comes to Bible translation.

For example, in the fall of 1993, a Yale student named Kevin Wilson began a project to translate the Bible into Klingon. (Klingon is the make-believe language that aliens in the popular *Star Trek* series would speak if they were real.) Wilson's team included nearly a dozen scholars, among them Dr. Lawrence M. Schoen, who had already earned a Ph.D. in cognitive psychology, and the Reverend Professor Glen Proechel, then a Spanish instructor at the University of Minnesota.

But Professor Proechel ended up quitting the translation project in protest, arguing that *Dr. Schoen was doing it wrong.* "It's not going to make any sense" the way Wilson's gang was doing it, he told *The Wall Street Journal* in June of 1994, explaining that the Klingons' "mode of thought is quite different."

There are no Klingons, there is no Klingon thought, and, except for what linguist Dr. Marc Okrand invented for the 1984 movie *Star Trek III: The Search for Spock*, there is no Klingon language. But that didn't stop two qualified academicians from taking their vehement disagreement to the media.

Not surprisingly, disputes about translating the Bible into real languages spoken by real people run even deeper. Accordingly, there have been numerous failed attempts to fix the broken translations.

So why would I enter an arena so full of disagreement?

Because the fields of Bible study and translation theory have historically been kept separate, with Bible scholars often only partially aware of research into translation and, similarly, translation experts unwilling to turn their attention to the Bible. My background is in both.

It's been a lot of fun applying honest translation theory to the Bible.

My hope is that you will enjoy learning what the Bible really means as much as I have enjoyed researching it and writing about it.

⤛⤛ PART ONE ⤜⤜

Getting Started

1

THE KING'S ENGLISH:
WHY WE'RE ALL STUCK IN THE
MIDDLE AGES

"If the King's English was good enough for Jesus, it's good enough for me."

That quip by Miriam Amanda "Ma" Ferguson to her Texas constituents last century actually reflects a common attitude toward the Bible. While of course most people know that it wasn't originally written in English, they also think that the ancient text is conveyed pretty accurately in the familiar English quotations: "The Lord is my shepherd . . . ," "In the beginning, God created heaven and earth . . . ," "Thou shalt not covet . . . ," "Let my people go . . . ," and so forth. Most people think they know what the Bible says because they've read it in English.

But they're wrong.

Sometimes the familiar English is just misleading, obscuring the focus of the original or misrepresenting an ancient nuance. Other times, the mistakes are more substantial. But the errors are significant and widespread.

This book is a straightforward exploration of where things went awry, how we can recover the original meaning of the Bible, and what we learn from better translations. As we work toward answers, we'll travel a fascinating path that meanders through history, metaphor, sociology, ethics, the law, and even such obscure topics as zoology and Babylonian mathematics, in addition to our primary tools of linguistics and translation theory. Modern linguistics will guide our understanding of ancient Hebrew, and translation theory will help us render what we understand in English.

Because the familiar English translations are, well, familiar, we'll use them as a reference point, looking at where they succeed and, perhaps more importantly, where they fail, starting with an appreciation of the magnitude of the problem.

The majority of English translations stem from the King James Version of the Bible (KJV), first published about four hundred years ago. Named for King James of England, who commissioned it in 1604, the KJV is a literary classic, a volume so central that, like Shakespeare's works, it helped shape the very language in which it was written. But a lot has happened since the early 1600s. English has changed over four centuries. Our understanding of the past has improved. And advances in translation theory and linguistics have opened new doors into antiquity.

Like medieval scholars trying to understand Egypt without carbon dating, or a doctor two hundred years ago trying to fathom the Black Plague, Bible translators throughout most of history have been working blind, struggling—though of course they did not know it—without the numerous benefits of twenty-first century knowledge.

Some people initially don't like the idea of mixing modernity and the Bible, because, as they correctly point out, the Bible isn't modern. Nor, they observe, is the Bible scientific, and they therefore wonder why a book like this one introduces linguistics, history, archaeology, and other modern approaches as we probe the Bible. But the matter is more nuanced than that. Even though the prophets who commented on the Five Books of Moses were unaware of modern literary theory, for example, we can still use that framework to help us understand what the prophets were doing and how they wrote. For that matter, they may not even have known about the rhetorical devices they used in the poetry, but we can nonetheless use our modern understanding to understand their ancient work.

We might compare the situation to that of a Renoir painting found languishing in a garage somewhere. Even though the painting is a non-scientific work of art, we'd use science to determine its authenticity. And if it were authentic, we'd use more science to clean it up and to recover as much of the original as possible. Depending on the state of the painting, we might want cleansing agents, infrared photography, or even a complete reconstruction. These modern nonartistic steps would restore the older art. Similarly, modern science, rather than turning the Bible into what it was not, helps us retrieve what it was.

Because the KJV is so widely used, and because it has been so central in English translations of the Bible, we'll start by looking at that translation more closely. When we do, we'll find three main sorts of short-comings. The first problem is that English has changed in 400 years. The second is that the authors misunderstood some of the Hebrew, so they didn't always appreciate the meaning of some parts of the Bible. And third, their conception of translation was seriously flawed, so that even when they did understand the Hebrew, they were not always able to convey it properly in English.

These problems are not limited to the KJV. They afflict other translations, too. The proportions differ, with more modern versions from last century offering (obviously) more modern English but frequently and surprisingly sometimes doing an even poorer job of translation. First things first, though. Let's look at the KJV and see how it actually blurs and distorts the meaning and beauty of the Bible.

THUS SPAKE KING JAMES

Not surprisingly, the English of the twenty-first century differs from that of the seventeenth century.

Some of the changes in English are obvious, such as the verbs in "Abraham clave the wood for the burnt offering" (modern English demands "cleaved" or, better, "split"), "The LORD God of heaven . . . which spake unto me and that sware unto me" ("spoke" and "swore"), or "God hath shewed Pharaoh what he is about to do" ("has" and "shown"). Similarly, the fifth plague in Egypt is called "a very grievous murrain" ("murrain" is a disease of cattle and sheep) and the sixth "blains upon man" ("boils," perhaps), both times using terminology that modern readers find foreign. Isaiah 31:3 warns, "He that is holpen shall fall down" ("helped").

While these obsolete words give the modern reader the mistaken impression that the Bible, too, is obsolete, they also red-flag their own shortcomings. Words like "clave," "blains," and "holpen"—and many more like them—don't mean anything in modern English. So they don't convey the wrong meaning of the Hebrew so much as they sometimes fail to convey any meaning at all.

Other changes in English are more subtle and insidious, because the older words still exist in modern English but with different meanings. The KJV translation "I shall not want" had nothing to do with desire but rather with lacking, so "I will lack nothing" is the real point. Moses is called "meek," but to indicate humility, not powerlessness. The "vail under the taches" that adorns the Tabernacle might now be called a "curtain." (And "taches" are clasps.) On its face, Proverbs 28:21 seems odd: "To have respect of persons is not good." But "respect" meant "to be partial," and the point was to avoid favoritism.

Similar changes include "let," as from Isaiah 43:13, "[God] works; who can let it?" The text there uses "let" not in the modern sense of "allow" but, rather, its opposite, "hinder" (a term preserved in tennis but otherwise rare nowadays). "Prevent" (from the Latin *praevenire*) used to mean "go before" or "precede," which is why Psalm 59:10 reads "The God of my mercy shall prevent me" in the KJV, while now we would say, ". . . will go before me." The beautiful imagery of Song of Songs, "the flowers appear on the earth . . . the voice of the turtle is heard," now wrongly suggests a turtle; the animal is in fact a bird, now called a "dove" or a "turtledove." And modern readers do not immediately think that a talking donkey is the same as a talking ass.

In addition to changes in the meanings of English words, we find differences in what linguists call "register," such as how formal language differs from informal, spoken from written, casual from stiff, etc. (We cover this more in Chapter 3.) The authors of the KJV purposely chose formal but not archaic English, English they would have called modern (though now linguists classify it as "Middle English" or "Early Modern English"). Twenty-first-century readers who encounter the lofty, archaic English of the KJV wrongly conclude that it was meant to reflect lofty, archaic Hebrew. It was not. Back then, "I shall" was standard, while "I will" was used only for emphasis. The word "thou" was intimate, sometimes used in contrast to "ye." Verbs like "goest" were commonplace. The effects of these changes combine in sentences like "Who told thee that thou wast naked?" which was originally no more formal than "Who told you that you were naked?" Similarly, "draw not nigh hither" is just "come no closer."

So far, we've seen cases where the KJV had the right translation for its time, but English has changed enough to make that translation wrong for our time. But while the scholars and theologians who worked on the KJV did a surprisingly good job, they were not perfect, and sometimes even in the seventeenth century the English in the KJV was wrong.

For example, Leviticus 25 deals extensively with the "jubile year," now spelled "jubilee." It's the fiftieth year of a cycle, a year in which to "proclaim liberty throughout all the land." (The concept proved so compelling that the forgers of the Liberty Bell in Philadelphia co-opted the line.)

The Hebrew for 'jubile(e)" year is *yovel*, a word that refers to a kind of horn, perhaps a ram's horn, and, presumably, is associated with the fiftieth year because a horn is to be blown in that year. (In Chapter 2 we learn how we know what the Hebrew means.) The Latin form of *yovel*, based on the Greek, is *iobileus*. By pure chance, that Latin word sounds like *iubileus*, connected to the verb *iubilare*, "to celebrate." That is, the Latin words for "*yovel* horn" and "jubilation" sound almost the same. Based on this Latin coincidence, the Hebrew word for a kind of horn turned into an English word that suggests celebration. The KJV translation is simply wrong.

(A similar process gave us the myth that the fruit Eve eats in Genesis is an apple. It's never called that, but the Latin word for "apple" is *malum*, a word that also happens to mean "evil." Because the tree from which the fruit comes is the tree of "knowing good [*bonum* in Latin] and evil [*malum*]," some people assumed that the fruit, too, must be a *malum*—that is, an apple. At least that mistake never made it into the KJV, but the coincidence still caused enough widespread confusion that most people think the Bible calls the fruit an "apple.")

The KJV didn't get just individual words wrong. The translators made mistakes about Hebrew grammar, too. The very common Hebrew word *leimor*, literally "to say," introduced direct quotation in an era that predated punctuation. But the authors of the KJV, not knowing that the word was the equivalent of quotation marks, translated the word as "saying." That's how we get the common but wrong "God blessed them, saying . . ." or "God spake . . . saying . . . ," etc. It's so common that people who read the Bible find it familiar, but it's a mistake. (We talk more about "saying" on page 37.)

Another aspect of grammar is syntax—that is, word order. In every language tiny differences of word order can make a huge difference ("working hard" is not "hardly working"), but until last century researchers lacked a solid understanding of these matters. So it should come as no surprise that the KJV translators erred here as well, misunderstanding subtle clues with far-reaching implications. We'll see examples in Part II, particularly when we look at poetry and imagery.

Sometimes the KJV translators understood the Hebrew but rendered it incorrectly in English. One clear example comes from the snake in Genesis. The snake tells Eve that eating the fruit won't kill her. But the English reads, "Ye shall not surely die," rather than the correct "[You] surely will not die." That is, the KJV leaves open the possibility that Eve could die (you won't surely die, but you might die), while the Hebrew is more reassuring.

Another example comes from Ezekiel's famous vision of the dry bones, in which God tells Ezekiel to prophesy to dry bones in a valley, commanding them to re-form into people. Describing part of the reassembling, Ezekiel 37:7 in the KJV reads, "The bones came together, bone to his bone." Whose bone is "his bone"? The Hebrew simply means "one bone to another," a fact the authors of the KJV must have known, but—and again, we go into more detail in Chapter 3—the primitive state of translation theory (combined with the near lack of the word "its" back then) blocked an accurate translation.

Sometimes the point of the Hebrew was not merely to convey information but to do so poetically. While the KJV certainly possesses a certain poetry, it does not match the original Hebrew very well. Take for instance Job's humble admission that he is but "dust and ashes." Thanks to the KJV, that phrase has become an English expression. But the original Hebrew had two nearly identical words. The question of exactly how the words were pronounced when the Book of Job was written is a complicated one, but we can see for sure that the words for "dust" and for "ash" (it's singular in Hebrew) both have three letters, and the final two pairs are identical: *ayin-peh-resh* for "dust" and *aleph-peh-resh* for "ashes." The effect in Hebrew is difficult to reproduce in English, but a pair like "oil"/"soil" gives the right idea. "Rhyme"/"reason" is also similar to the original Hebrew effect. "Dust"/"ashes" is not.

We've seen examples of three kinds of problems in the KJV: The Hebrew was misunderstood. The English didn't represent the Hebrew.

And the English, even though it used to match the Hebrew, no longer does because English has changed. Unfortunately, the KJV is not the only edition that suffers from these common problems.

NEW AND IMPROVED

The Bible shelf of most bookstores offers dozens of choices for the potential Bible reader. That's because we are not the first to think about the KJV or about translation, and many others have tried to improve on the flawed but familiar renderings, to correct the antiquated English of the KJV, to apply new theories, or to promulgate religious doctrine.

But even as newer tools to understand the original Hebrew became available, translators generally worked in the shadow of the KJV, either trying to emulate it or, occasionally, specifically trying not to. Some Biblical scholars grew up with the KJV, so they knew it best and unwittingly relied on it. Others, like Ma Ferguson, saw God's own work in King James's mission. And still others simply bowed to economic realities, betting that a KJV-based translation was more likely to sell copies. (The Bible remains the all-time bestselling book ever written.)

In other words, the general methodology has been to start with the KJV and either purposely keep as much as possible or (rarely) change as much as possible. But neither approach makes much sense. There's no sound reason to start translating ancient Hebrew by using a four-hundred-year-old English translation any more than, say, a study of a fifteenth-century Ming vase should start with a photograph instead of with the original.

So in the end, even though more modern translations address some of the shortcomings in the KJV, they are still tainted by it, and even suffer problems of their own. We discuss and evaluate various translations in detail in the Appendix, but for now here's a sample of what's available and why none of the current translations is satisfactory.

The widely used New Revised Standard Version (NRSV) was

published in 1989, following the Revised Standard Version, itself a revision of the 1901 American Standard Version. But the American Standard Version was based on the KJV. So even though the English in the NRSV has largely been modernized, a lot of confusing language remains in the translation. The NRSV replaces "draw not nigh hither" from the KJV with "do not come closer," but, for example, it keeps "want" in Psalm 23, hoping the reader will understand that the verb means "lack."

The history of the NRSV also demonstrates how even modern translators base their work on the KJV. The introduction to the 1971 edition of the Revised Standard Version not only refers to the original introduction to the KJV (published with the original edition of the KJV); it actually quotes the part of that introduction that denies creating a new translation: "We never thought from the beginning, that we should need to make a new Translation . . . but to make a good one better." That attitude pervades most of the translations.

Similar to the Revised Standard Version is the New American Bible (NAB). A 1943 encyclical by Pope Pius XII put the project in motion, but it wasn't published until 1970. As in other modern Bibles, the text, though still based on the KJV, is generally readable. Instead of the KJV's "draw not nigh hither," we find "come no nearer," which is comparable to the NRSV's "do not come closer." The end of the first line of Psalm 23 in the NAB reads, "There is nothing I lack." Though it claims to be "a completely new translation throughout," the NAB frequently mirrors the flawed text of the KJV, sometimes only approximately and sometimes exactly.

While the NRSV and the NAB try to modernize the KJV, the New Living Translation (NLT) has a different approach based on a different agenda. The year 1971 saw the publication of the Living Bible, an attempt by Mr. Kenneth Taylor to paraphrase the Bible. The NLT is a 1996 rewrite of Taylor's 1971 publication, and it goes even further in coercing the ancient Hebrew into colloquial English. Instead of "I shall not want," it offers "I have everything I need." The translation is marked by other chatty phrases like "do not come any closer," "you won't get a single bite of meat" (Deuteronomy. 28:31), etc. While this idiomatic phrasing frequently captures the general point of the original Hebrew, it completely fails to convey the tone, poetry, imagery, etc.

The year 1978 brought yet another modern, popular translation: the New International Version (NIV). It falls very loosely between the KJV-based NRSV and the free-flowing NLT. According to its committee on Bible translation, the NIV strives to be "idiomatic but not idiosyncratic." (Its rendering of Psalm 23 reads, ". . . I shall not be in want.") Unfortunately, the decision to produce "idiomatic" English even when the Hebrew might have been idiosyncratic is a fundamental mistake. When the Hebrew is idiomatic, the NIV does a reasonably good job with its English renderings. But, like the NLT, the NIV destroys the poetry and much of the imagery of the original Bible.

While the NRSV, the NIV, and in particular the NLT are generally more readable than the KJV, and while they solve some of its problems, they are not always more accurate. As we just saw, one fundamental problem is represented by the NIV's goal of a translation that is idiomatic. The problem is that the Bible contains a great variety of writing styles, and only some are idiomatic in Hebrew.

The modern translations—particularly the NLT, but others as well—and, for that matter, the KJV, all dull down the text by assuming that it should all sound more or less the same in English. So the NLT's translation of the direct prose of Genesis ("God created the heavens and the earth") sounds the same as the lofty poetry of Job 38:36 ("Who gives intuition and instinct?"). The NRSV recognizes that Job is poetry, but rather than giving us poetry in English, it follows the KJV and offers the barely comprehensible "Who has put wisdom in the inward parts, or given understanding to the mind?" The NIV does better with the poetry—"Who endowed the heart with wisdom or gave understanding to the mind?"—but still uses "heavens" in Genesis for what should be "sky."

In short, to homogenize the English is a fundamental mistake. In spite of the authors' intentions, the KJV is now uniformly formal and frequently archaic. The NIV is, by design, idiomatic. The NRSV walks a middle ground. These three represent the translations that are available, and none of them does justice to the varied nature of the original Hebrew.

We thus add to our growing list of translation deficiencies.

BROKEN TELEPHONE

Modern linguistics has proven extremely useful in decoding the ancient message of the Bible, because the science sheds new light on all languages, including ancient ones. And the modern field of translation has been invaluable in providing English renditions of foreign texts. Unfortunately, there are no English translations of the Bible that fully take advantage of these advances.

English speakers who read Ovid or Aristotle or Pushkin in translation have a better sense of the original texts than do readers of any existing English translation of the Bible. But there is no reason that English speakers can't have the same access to the Bible that they do to other great works.

This book demonstrates, step by step, how linguistics and translation theory combine to make the Bible clearer than it has been since the days it was first penned.

In a game called "broken telephone" or sometimes just "telephone," children sit in a circle and pass a secret to one another. One child thinks of a word or sentence and whispers it to his or her neighbor. The neighbor follows suit, again whispering the message and passing it on. As the message makes its way around the circle, it mutates. Some people don't speak clearly. Others don't hear so well. And some players can't resist the temptation to change the message into what they want it to be. By the time the message returns to the person who first started it, it is all but unrecognizable.

Latecomers to a global and millennial game of "broken telephone," we, too, rely on revisions of modifications to outmoded and ill-conceived approximations of an original message first committed to parchment more than two thousand years ago. Like the children playing "telephone," some generations made translation mistakes. Others changed the message into what they wanted it to be. And sometimes generations, speaking slightly different dialects, just misunderstood one another.

But unlike the children playing "telephone," we still have the original.

And it's time to recover the initial message.

2

RECAPTURING THE PAST:
WHAT DOES THE HEBREW MEAN?

GETTING STARTED

"Why do you drive on a parkway and park on a driveway?"

"When a house burns up why does it also burn down?"

"If the ice-cream man brings ice cream in the ice-cream truck, shouldn't we fear the fireman in the fire truck?"

Wordplays like these—and many more like them—show us something important about how language works. We see that the most straightforward way to understand words and phrases just doesn't work. It's a mistake to think that a "parkway" must be a place for parking just because it includes the word "park." (In fact, a "parkway" used to be a "way" that traversed a "park.") It's a mistake to conclude that just because "up" and "down" are opposites, "burn up" and "burn down" must also mean different things. And it's a mistake to use "ice-cream truck" to figure out exactly what "fire truck" must mean.

Unfortunately, these sorts of basic errors mar many Bible translations and obscure the real meaning of the ancient text.

The first step in translating the Hebrew Bible is to understand the Hebrew words in which it was written. Starting right at the beginning, for example, we have the word *breshit*, usually translated "in the beginning." How do we know what the word means?

Just a bit later in Genesis, Eve gets punished for eating from the "tree of knowledge of good and evil." The usual translations are mostly right, but how do we know what the words mean? What about Eve's punishment? According to the KJV, women for all time will experience "sorrow" in childbirth. Others translations give us "pain." Which is it? Is childbirth sorrowful or painful?

In *The Dragons of Eden*, Carl Sagan observes that childbirth is accompanied by actual physical pain. He claims that humans more than any other animal experience pain in childbirth, and that the source of this added pain is the disproportionately large size of a newborn's head. Dr. Sagan then connects this scientific fact to the Genesis account. After all, why is the human head so large? Because people are so smart. Scientifically, human intelligence requires a large human head, which causes pain in childbirth. Biblically, eating from the tree of knowledge caused pain in childbirth. Science and the Bible match in this case, Dr. Sagan says, but only if the text really means "tree of knowledge," and only if *etzev* (the Hebrew word here) means "pain" and not "sorrow." How can we be sure what the words mean?

We find ourselves in the unfortunate situation that Dr. Sagan's observation makes sense only if we are working from the right translation, even though he meant to bridge the gap between science and the Bible, not a particular translation of it.

Too frequently, Bible translators choose the straightforward but wrong approach that we saw at the beginning of the chapter, one that would make us think that a parkway is for parking on. This widespread fundamental mistake forces us to question almost everything we read in translation. Carl Sagan's conclusion is still valid (probably), but, as we will see, others are not.

Perhaps surprisingly, modern translations are frequently worse in this regard than older ones. For example, Exodus 31 describes the Sabbath using two words for the seventh day: *shabat* and *shabaton*. The word *shabaton* looks a lot like *shabat*, but it is a mistake to conclude that the meaning of the longer word *shabaton* necessarily includes the meaning of the shorter word. Still, Everett Fox's 1995 translation *The Five Books of Moses* gives us "Sabbath, Sabbath-Ceasing," as though the English translation for *shabaton* must include the English translation for *shabat*. (In Modern Hebrew, *shabaton* is a sabbatical, the paid time off given to professors. In the Bible, it probably served to emphasize the word *shabat*.)

A couple of verses later, Fox translates "[on the seventh day, God] paused-for-breath" where most other translations prefer "was refreshed" or just "rested." Fox thinks the verb is related to a noun that means "breath" (he may be right—we'll have more to say about this very interesting word in Chapter 4), but then he wrongly concludes that the verb's translation must be directly and simply related to the meaning of the noun. It does not. As we see in the English noun/verb pair "chair" (people sit on chairs, and someone chairs a meeting), nouns and verbs can be related in very complicated ways. And as we see with the noun and verb "count" (on *Sesame Street*, Coun Von Count teaches children to count), nouns and verbs need not be directly related at all. "Paused-for-breath" happens to have the word "breath" in it, and the Hebrew words for "breath" and "rested" are related. But that coincidence does not make "paused-for-breath" the right translation. The Hebrew just means "rested."

Though this sort of mistake creeps into the KJV less frequently, we still find it. For example, in Leviticus 13 we read of skin ailments and what to do about them. One of many maladies is something called in Hebrew a *baheret*. Because that word is related to one that means "clear" or "bright," the KJV jumps to the conclusion that *baheret* means "bright spot." The NIV uses that same translation, while the NRSV opts for the less specific but probably less wrong "spot." The NAB gives us "blotch." The text offers specific remedies for specific problems, one of these problems being the *baheret*. If we are to understand the text, it's important to know whether it means "bright spot," just any old "spot," or, as the Jewish Publication Society (JPS) translation offers, "discoloration." Technical words like this are exceedingly difficult to understand fully, so we don't know for sure what the word means. For all we know, *baheret* is acne. Or it might not even be a real disease.

For our current purposes, though, we care less about the skin disease from the KJV, or the Sabbath and resting from Fox, and more about general techniques. That's because there are, in fact, two questions: What does the Hebrew mean? And how do we figure out what the Hebrew means?

Before we can turn to the first question, we have to address the second. We have to have a sense of how we are going to go about recovering what the ancient Hebrew words meant.

In general, the most obvious way to understand what foreign words mean is to ask a native speaker, but, clearly, we don't have that option for ancient Hebrew. Unfortunately, some of the methods that have commonly been used instead, while more practical, are also unreliable. And these unreliable approaches to figuring out what words mean have led to unreliable translations.

We also have to recognize that most people who care about the Bible already have a sense of what they want it to mean. Whether taking cues from the New Testament, later commentaries, religious leaders, childhood religious instruction, or personal spirituality, we all have baggage when it comes to the Bible. An honest inquiry demands that we leave that baggage behind.

So our next task is to forge a more sound way of investigating the past. Our first step will involve some general background about languages, starting with the question of whether all languages are the same.

IT'S ALL GREEK TO US

As we move forward, we need to evaluate a variety of potential ways to understand Hebrew, decode its vocabulary, interpret its grammar, and so forth. We want to know which investigative techniques give us the most reliable information about ancient Hebrew. Unfortunately, the only truly sure way of knowing which theory is most accurate is already knowing the answer. If we knew what the Hebrew meant, we could compare different theories and see which one gave us the answer that we already know is right. (Though if we knew what the Hebrew meant we wouldn't need the theory in the first place.)

But even though we don't know what the Hebrew meant, because we can't ask native speakers, we have much more information about modern languages. So our basic approach as we evaluate each bit of linguistic theory will be to apply the theory to modern languages, languages that we know much more about. If a particular theory gives us the wrong answer for modern languages, we conclude that the theory is unreliable. And if, by contrast, the theory always gives us the right answer for modern languages, we conclude that the theory is sound.

We tacitly adopted this approach at the beginning of the chapter. We used the English words "driveway" and "parkway" to show that words don't always mean what their parts would suggest. We used the phrases "burn up" and "burn down" to show that phrases that look like opposites might mean the same thing. and so forth. In this section, we're going to use some other modern languages, and in Chapter 3, when we test translation approaches, we're going to use modern foreign languages a lot more.

If we have a guess about what an ancient Hebrew word means, in the end it will always be a guess. Hopefully it will be an educated guess—one in which we have a lot of confidence, one that is almost certainly correct—but as with any other endeavor, it's hard to know with absolute certainty that we have not made a mistake. By contrast, if we have a guess about what an English word means, we can just ask one of the hundreds of millions of English speakers to see if we're right.

So we can use English and other modern languages to test our theories about how to understand a language. If we think that words that rhyme—that is, words that sound almost the same—usually mean almost the same thing, all we have to do is look at English (say, "fate" and "gate") to see that we're wrong. If we think that two words that sound exactly the same must mean the same thing, again, English ("blue" and "blew") demonstrates otherwise. Jumping ahead a little, if we think that two words in two different languages that sound the same must mean the same thing, we immediately see that we're wrong. Modern Hebrew has a word that sounds like "dog"—that is, a word pronounced /dahg/—but it means "fish."

This general approach assumes that to some extent all languages are the same. But are they?

The answer is very clearly yes. One of the most important results of modern linguistics has been the discovery that certain elements of all human languages work basically the same way. Even though literally thousands of details can differ—everything from what the words sound like to what order they go in—human language is fundamentally the same.

Noam Chomsky's theory of universal grammar is one way of understanding this similarity among languages. Chomsky's position is that language is like other things for which humans are suited. Just as the human lung can breathe only air and not water, so too the human brain can learn only certain language patterns. Other researchers, like Hilary Putnam, explain the similarity among languages differently. But the debate tends to focus on why languages are the same, not whether they are the same.

This is good news for us, because it means that we can safely use modern languages like English or Modern Hebrew or even Swahili to help us probe various ways of understanding ancient Hebrew and, ultimately, to find a method that works well.

WORDS MISUNDERSTOOD

Words are the most fundamental unit of language. If we don't understand the ancient Hebrew words, we have no hope of understanding anything more complicated, like sentences. Unfortunately, three common methods of understanding Hebrew are rampant among translators, and none of them works very well. The three methods are **internal word structure**, **etymology**, and **cognate languages**. Though these three approaches are ultimately unreliable, we learn about how language works (and how it doesn't) by looking at them in detail and, in particular, by seeing examples of where they fail. So before we look at a fourth method that really does tell us what the Ancient Hebrew words mean, we turn to the wrong approaches.

Internal Word Structure

The first common but incorrect way to figure out what a word means is to look at its internal structure.

Again, using the methodology we agreed on earlier, we'll look at modern languages to see if internal word structure is a good guide to what a word means, and we'll see that it is not.

The "parkway" demonstration we just saw is weak, because in the end a "parkway" does have something to do with a "park," even if the relationship isn't as obvious as it first seems. It's tricky to use the parts of that word to understand the full word, but we'd like clearer examples. Here's one.

By definition, a "patent" in English is a "non-obvious art." "Art" here is also used technically, and it refers to science as well as what most of us think of as "art." The important part is the "non-obvious" provision. In fact, Section 103 of Title 35 of the U.S. Code, the part of U.S. law that deals with patents, specifically notes that "non-obvious subject matter" is a "condition for patentability." Something that is obvious cannot be patented. (Or, at least, it shouldn't be patentable. From time to time the patent office grants patents for things that seem obvious, as in patent #6360693, granted in March 2002 for "an apparatus for use as a toy by an animal, for example a dog, to either fetch, carry, or chew . . . formed of wood . . ." Someone practically patented the stick.)

The suffix "-ly" in English often marks an adverb. One might think, therefore, that "patently" would mean "in a patent-like way" or, perhaps, "in a non-obvious way." But it does not. It means just the opposite. It means "obviously!" Even though the word "patently" is, well, patently made of the two parts "patent" and "-ly," and even though a patent must be non-obvious, "patently" does not mean "non-obviously."

We see another demonstration in the word "host," someone who welcomes guests at a party, for example, or at an inn. Yet someone who is "hostile" is just the opposite. To be a "host" is to be warm and welcoming. To be "hostile" is not. Even though "infantile" means "like an infant," "hostile" does not mean "like a host."

Knowing what an intern is does not shed light on what internal means. A hospital is not necessarily a place where people are hospitable. Police officers don't work in offices. Sweetbread is not sweet and it's not bread. An old joke notes that "pro" is the opposite of "con," and therefore asks what the opposite is of "progress."

The point is that words don't get their meanings from their parts. Language doesn't work that way.

At least, language doesn't *always* work that way, and that's the catch. It is, of course, true that some words mean what we would expect based on their parts. "Calmly," for example, means just what one would think based on the word "calm" and the suffix "-ly." But only some words get their meaning from their parts. Unless we can figure out which words follow the pattern and which ones do not, we cannot use word structure to figure out what words mean.

Unfortunately, the nature of Hebrew makes this errant approach very appealing. To really understand the temptation to use internal word structure in Hebrew we have to know a little more about Hebrew.

So we'll spend a few pages looking at how Hebrew words are made. Hebrew internal word structure is as complicated as it gets, but the pages that follow will give you a basic introduction to it (and the Appendix has suggestions for where you can find more).

Hebrew Roots

Hebrew words usually have three parts: a **root**, consisting of two or three consonants; a **pattern**; and **prefixes** and **suffixes**. All three contribute to the meaning.

English has prefixes (like "pre-") and suffixes (like "-ly" or "-s"), so these are the easiest part of Hebrew words for English speakers to understand. Parallel to the plural suffix "-s" in English we find the plural suffix -*im* in Hebrew. A *migdal* in Hebrew is a "tower," and *migdalim* are "towers."

But unlike English, the Hebrew word *migdal* can be broken down into smaller parts, specifically, a root and a pattern. The consonants G.D.L form the root. And the *m* and the vowels form the pattern, which, for convenience, we can mark as *miXXaX*. The *X*'s are placeholders for root consonants. If we change the root from G.D.L to K.D.Sh, we get *mikdash*, which is a temple. From Z.R.Ch we get *mizrach*, "east."

So *miXXaX* is one pattern. Another pattern is *XaXoX*. Using the same three roots we just saw—G.D.L, K.D.Sh, and Z.R.Ch—we get *gadol*, *kadosh*, and *zaroch*. The first two mean "big" and "holy," respectively, and the third isn't a word.

If we use the pattern *XaXaX*, we get past-tense verbs: *gadal* ("grew") and *zarach* ("shone").

From this we see two things. First, not every root can pair with every pattern. Second, the patterns can be used to create nouns, adjectives, verbs, whatever.

The fun part is to find the connections between the various patterns and roots. For example, the first pattern we saw, *miXXaX*, frequently denotes a place, and the second pattern (*XaXoX*) an adjective. *Mikdash* is a "temple" and *kadosh* is "holy." The connection is clear. A temple is a holy place. It looks like Q.D.Sh always has something to do with holiness. Similarly, *migdal* is a "tower," *gadol* is "big," and a tower is a big place. The sun shines (*zarach* is "shone") in the east, which in Hebrew is *mizrach*. "Shone" and "east" share the root Z.R.Ch.

But not all words that share a root have a common meaning. For example, the pattern *hiXXiX* often has to do with making something happen. From the root K.T.N, we find *katon*, which means "small," and *hiktin*, which means "to make something small" or, more colloquially, "to shrink." The opposite of *katon* is *gadol*. It means "big," and it comes from the root G.D.L. Not surprisingly, if we put the root G.D.L into the pattern *hiXXiX* and create the word *higdil*, we get the word for "enlarge." Like *katon/hiktin* and *gadol/higdil,* we find *rachok* (from the root R.Ch.K) and *karov* (from K.R.V). *Rachok* means "far" and *karov* means "near." So we follow the pattern and create two more words: *hirchik* and *hikriv.* The former, as we expect, does mean "make far away," that is, "distance." But the second one means "sacrifice"!

What happened? Nothing. It's just a methodological error to think that internal word structure can tell us what words mean. That's not how words work. (As it happens, there are two words *hikriv* in Biblical Hebrew, and one of them, the rarer of the two, does mean "make near.")

However, the tempting nature of a simplistic system that would tell us what words mean leads many people down one of two wrong paths. The more obviously wrong path is to completely misunderstand what *hikriv* means, thinking that it means "make near"—no more and no less. With very common words like "sacrifice," not a lot of people make this error. After all, the numerous and detailed descriptions of the sacrifices in the Old Testament are hardly compatible with "make near." It's hard to imagine a context in which a translator cannot tell if the slaughter and resulting guts and gore have to do with animal sacrifice or just moving things closer.

But many people make a more subtle mistake. They assume that even though *hikriv* means "sacrifice," it still must have *something* to do with "make near." Perhaps, they wrongly guess, the point of a sacrifice was to bring the sacrificer closer to God. Or perhaps the point was simply to make the sacrificed animal closer to God. Or to bring us closer to the animal. (I hope not.) One of these is a lovely idea, in my mind, and only the third is ridiculous, but all three are wrong. Or, at least, the reasoning is flawed, because as we have seen, words don't get their meaning from their internal word structure. It's just a mistake to think that Biblical sacrifice had more to do with nearness than modern sacrifice does.

How do we know that internal word structure doesn't indicate shades of meaning? We've seen that internal word structure doesn't dictate meaning, but maybe it influences nuance.

It does not. Once again, we can look at modern languages to understand the situation. In this case, we've already seen counterexamples. A "host" is not someone who "holds a party, but in a somewhat hostile way," and someone who is "hostile" is not "combative, but in a way that reminds us of the people who held that party Saturday night." "Host" and "hostile" just don't mean the same thing, and using one to understand the other is a mistake.

Another wrong hypothesis is that Hebrew is fundamentally different than other languages, and that even though most languages don't use internal word structure to add nuance to words, Hebrew, because of its root system, works differently.

To disprove this notion we only have to look at Modern Hebrew or Arabic.

Modern Hebrew, also called Israeli Hebrew, is the Hebrew spoken natively by most Israelis. Though it is based on the Hebrew of the Bible, it has been a spoken language for less than two hundred years. Because Hebrew wasn't spoken for almost two thousand years and was then reborn in the nineteenth century, it has changed less than a language otherwise would over so much time. But also, because a conscious effort was made to get people to speak the language anew,

Hebrew has changed in ways that are not entirely typical. Roughly speaking, Biblical Hebrew is to Modern Hebrew what Shakespearian English is to modern English.

(A thumbnail sketch of Hebrew goes something like this: The language was spoken in and around Jerusalem during the first millennium B.C. and for the first seventy years of the first millennium A.D., until the exile of the Jews from Jerusalem in the year 70. Aramaic and other languages quickly replaced Hebrew as the spoken language of the Jews. Hebrew assumed a religious role, written and read but not generally spoken except during prayer services and ritual readings of Scripture. By A.D. 200, most Jews no longer spoke Hebrew. It wasn't until the second half of the nineteenth century that people forced themselves to speak Hebrew again, and, when their kids started speaking Hebrew natively, the modern language was born. My book, *In the Beginning: A Short History of the Hebrew Language*, listed in the Appendix, has much more detail.)

The word "Arabic," too, is a short form for a variety of languages, including the highly stylized dialect in which the Quran is written, the formal language of discourse in the Arabic-speaking world, and a host of local dialects that are sometimes quite different from one another.

Modern Hebrew and Arabic are useful for our current purposes because, like Biblical Hebrew, they have a root system of the sort we saw starting on page 23.

It's usually a mistake to use Modern Hebrew directly to understand Biblical Hebrew, because of the differences between the two, but we can nonetheless use the nature of Modern Hebrew to help us understand how root-based languages work.

At it happens, the four pairs "big"/"enlarge," "small"/"shrink," "far"/"distance," and "near"/"sacrifice" exist in Modern Hebrew (though the pronunciations have changed) as well as in Biblical Hebrew, though the second meaning for *hikriv*—that is, "make near"—no longer exists in Modern Hebrew. The related *kirev* is used instead. This shows us that the root K.R.V is still used to create verbs having to do with "near."

While animal sacrifice is illegal in Israel, the word *hikriv* has survived, and it's a simple matter to ask Israelis whether that word implies some sort of nearness based on the root it shares with the word "near." Israelis universally agree that it does not.

We shouldn't be surprised by this. Languages are basically the same, and words don't get their meanings from their internal structure.

Commentary

At least, internal word structure doesn't tell us what the words *originally* meant. Religious communities, and particularly Jews, tend to read the text of the Bible on at least two levels.

We're looking at one level here, the level of words in a language that are used to put sentences together. These words have meanings, and if we are to correctly translate the Bible we have to know what the words mean. And if we want our translation to help us retrieve the original meaning of the Bible, we have to know what the words originally meant.

But words can be used in many ways. One traditional way of reading the Bible relates not to what the original authors intended—that is, not to what the Hebrew words meant when they were penned—but rather to what they can be made to mean. We might call this a derived meaning, in that we derive a meaning from the original meaning of the words.

We care about this derived meaning because one way of making the religious leap from the original meaning to the derived meaning is to use internal word structure.

And again, we can look at modern language to see some examples.

We might suppose that one reason to "atone" for mistakes is to develop a sense of "oneness." And we know it works, because "atonement" is also "at-one-ment." This may or may not be interesting, and it may or may not tell us more about the human condition, but two things are certain:

First, even though this process tells us more about how (some) modern people think of atonement, it does not tell us what the *word* "atonement" means. That is, it may tell us more about the process, but it doesn't tell us more about the word. Many people don't bother to keep the two separate—and we'll have more to say on this shortly—but it's important. It's possible that atonement has something to do with becoming one with yourself, but even if that's true, it's not because of what the word "atonement" looks like. In fact, we can't even talk about the impact of atonement, how people do it, what it's for, etc., until we know what the word means.

Second, and more importantly, something about this process of breaking up a word and looking at its parts resonates deeply with many people. When most people hear that "apologizing is important because it leads to a feeling of unity," they evaluate the proposition with their head. Does it makes sense? Why? Who is making the claim? What is the evidence? By contrast, many people evaluate "atonement is at-one-ment" with their heart. It's cool. It's a neat wordplay. And, surprisingly, even rational thinkers sometimes give the statement more weight because of the wordplay.

Similarly, even the most rational people in modern society tend, unknowingly, to believe things that rhyme more than they otherwise would. "A stitch in time saves nine." It (nearly) rhymes. It must be true. Even people who don't know what it means think it's probably accurate. (It means that mending clothing with one stitch before a small rip becomes worse will save more stitches later. Take care of things before they get out of hand.)

In the infamous O. J. Simpson trial, defense attorney Johnnie Cochran tried to put a glove on Mr. Simpson's hand. The glove was too small. "If it doesn't fit, you must acquit," Cochran told the jury. "Fit." "Aquit." It rhymes, so it must be true. The strategy was incredibly effective, even though it mixed rational thought with, in this case, poetry.

In Matthew 16:2–3, Jesus offers some meteorological advice: "When it is evening, you say, 'It will be fair weather, for the sky is red.' And in the morning, 'It will be stormy today, for the sky is red and threaten-ing'" (NRSV). Well, maybe, maybe not, most people think. By con-trast, an old bit of seafarers' advice seems much more convincing: "Red sky at night is a sailor's delight. Red sky in the morning is a sailor's sure warning." It rhymes. And people, unknowingly, take it more seriously. (As it happens, where weather systems tend to move from west to east—a common pattern—the saying has some truth behind it.)

Bible interpretation frequently involves this sort of wordplay, so we should be careful to distinguish the scientific meaning of a word from its traditional religious meaning.

In 1040 a man named Solomon, son of Isaac, was born in Troyes, France. His Hebrew name forms the acronym Rashi, and it is by that one-word name that he is usually known. He left the province of his birth to study in Worms (now part of Germany) for a while, learning what was then the accumulated wisdom of nearly one thousand years of Jewish exile. By the time Rashi died in 1105, crusaders had destroyed the schools of his youth, leaving Rashi as one of the primary sources of knowledge about what had been taught there. For this and other rea-sons, Rashi is widely regarded in Jewish and some Christian circles as a preeminent Biblical commentator. (And because he wrote in Hebrew but sometimes referred to his native language of what we would now call Old French, Rashi is one key way French scholars learn about the history of French.)

Rashi, like other commentators, freely mixes what we might call the scientific meaning of words—what they originally meant to the people who wrote them—with interpretive, religious meaning.

For example, Exodus 25:18 describes two cherubs—Biblical an-gelic creatures—that are to adorn the Tabernacle. Rashi points out that the cherubs have "the image of a child's face." His reasoning? The Hebrew word for cherubs is *kruvim*, a word that happens to sound like the Aramaic word *k'ravya*. (The similarity is more pronounced in He-brew than in the English transliterations here, because in Hebrew vowels are generally less important than they are in English.) The

Aramaic prefix *k-* means "like," and the word *ravya* means "child" or "apprentice." So *k'ravya* means "like a child" in Aramaic. Rashi, basing his decision on the mid-first-millennium Babylonian Talmud, concludes that the *kruvim* must be *k'ravya*—that is, the cherubs must be "like a child."

This type of reasoning is typical of Biblical interpretation.

By way of further example, we might look at Genesis 47:29. Describing Jacob's final moments on Earth, the text reads: "When the time of Israel's [that is, Jacob's] death drew near . . ." (NRSV). Rashi points out that "time of death drawing near" is a phrase that's used only for men who didn't live as long as their father. (Jacob was 147. Isaac, his father, lived to be 180 years old.) While this is true—Rashi knew his Bible—it doesn't follow that the phrase "time of death drew near" means "to live fewer years than one's father."

We will soon see that phrases are essentially the same as words. As with *kruvim*, Rashi assigns a meaning to a phrase here based on his religious bent, not scientific linguistics. Our point is not to deny Rashi (or others) their right to do this but rather to point out that they are engaged in interpretation, not translation.

In short, we see that internal word structure is interesting, and it has a solid foundation as a cool way to look at words. But it doesn't tell us what words mean.

Etymology

The next popular but wrong way to figure out what ancient words mean is etymology.

Basically, etymology is "where a word comes from." Etymology therefore often tells us what a word *used to mean*. But, as with internal word structure, etymology does not tell us what a word *does* mean. (In a lovely bit of irony that demonstrates our point, the word "etymology" comes from the Greek for "true meaning.")

Once again, we look at English. A favorite example among linguists is the pair of words "glamour" and "grammar." It turns out they come from the same source. But very few people (linguists excluded) would agree that grammar is glamorous. And even to the extent that there is glamour in grammar, it's not because of those two words.

A slightly longer example involves medieval monks who were tasked with copying ancient religious manuscripts. The manuscripts had to be copied by hand because printing had yet to be invented, and the job had to be done by monks because most laypeople were illiterate.

So some monks would spend their days copying Greek and Latin manuscripts, preserving the ancient texts by writing them anew. It turns out that due to its architecture, the interior of the typical monastery is an ill-advised place to read and write. There's not enough light. So the monks put tables just outside their dark buildings and used these tables as copying desks. Because these fixtures were immobile, they were called stationary booths.

As the general population in Europe grew more literate, more and more people needed writing supplies: paper or parchment, quill pens, blotters, and so forth. Before specialized stores arose to fill this consumer need, people had two choices: They could make their own supplies, or they could try to buy them.

Buying was easier, and the most convenient place to find writing supplies was one of the monks' stationary booths. By association, then, the supplies themselves came to be called stationary supplies. (The technical name for this sort of expansion of meaning is "metonymy." It will come up again later.) Only afterward did an arbitrary spelling decision assign the ending "-ary" to the word that means "immobile" and the ending "-ery" to "writing supplies." Both words actually have the same etymology.

This true story demonstrates etymology perfectly. It is frequently interesting, but it does not tell us what words mean. In this case, knowing that "stationary" and "stationery" have a shared etymology would not help someone trying to decode English figure out what the words actually mean.

A third example comes from the word "wife"—that is, "female spouse." As chance would have it, Old English, and Germanic languages in general, had two words for "woman," one more complimentary than the other. The genteel word was *frau*. The less polite word was *wyf*. (The words may have had the same connotations that "woman" and "broad" do in some English dialects.) But it would be a terrible mistake to think that "wife" is a derogatory term just because it comes from what used to be a less-than-complimentary way of referring to a woman.

A bit of folk wisdom attributes "rule of thumb" to an ancient English law that allowed a man to hit his wife with a strap not bigger than his thumb. There's no evidence to support this probably wrong etymology, but even if it's true, people who use the phrase aren't wife beaters.

Etymology in the Bible

Like internal word structure, etymology has intuitive appeal. It just seems obvious (even though it's not true) that a word's history ought to determine, or at least influence, its meaning.

Perhaps this is why the Bible itself has so much etymological detail. In fact, many of the stories seem to have been written to explain why a certain name exists. They end with "that is why the name of the place is called . . ." or "that is why he is called . . . ," etc. (The translation "the name of the place is called" is wrong. More accurate would be simply, "the place is called . . ." or "the name of the place is. . . .")

Genesis explains why Adam and Eve have the names that they do. *Adam* in Hebrew means "person," and *Chava*, the Hebrew version of "Eve," shares a root with "life." Genesis 3:20 tells us, "Adam called his wife's name Eve; because she was the mother of all living" (KJV). Adam and Eve's names are both based on wordplay.

Isaac's Hebrew name is *Yitzchak*, which means "he will laugh," creating a wordplay with Abraham's reaction when he hears that his ninety-year-old wife, Sarah, will conceive and bear Isaac: Abraham laughed. (The wordplay is closer in Hebrew, because "he will laugh" can also mean "he laughed.") Isaac's name is also based on wordplay.

Jacob's Hebrew name is *Ya'akov*, which means "he will follow," from the Hebrew root A.K.V, which also gives us the word *ekev*, "heel." When Jacob and his twin, Esau, are born in Genesis 25:26, we read: "Afterward his [Esau's] brother came out, with his hand gripping Esau's heel [*ekev*]; so he was named Jacob ['he will follow']" (NRSV). Jacob's name is a double pun, playing on "heel" and "he will follow."

Jacob has a dream at a certain spot, and he calls the place Bethel, or, in Hebrew, *Beit El. Beit* means "house of" and *el* means "God," so Bethel means "House of God." Jacob encounters God there and calls the place "house of God."

The place called "Beersheba" (now the name of a town at the northern edge of the Negev desert in modern Israel and now sometimes spelled "Beersheba") is composed of two words in Hebrew: *be'er* and *sheva*. The first word means "[water] well." The second one sounds the same as the Hebrew word for "seven" (also pronounced *sheva*) but may mean "oath," because the word for "seven" is the source of the word for "oath" in Hebrew. The verb for "to swear [an oath]," for example, comes from the root of the word "seven," as does a more common word for oath, *shvu'ah*. (Numbers are commonly used to create other words. In Hebrew "armed" is literally "fived," presumably because the metaphor in Hebrew comes not from the human arm but from the five-fingered hand. To "decimate" in English—that is, to "destroy most of"—comes from the Latin *decem*, "ten." It originally meant "to destroy one tenth of.")

So Beersheba is either the "well of seven" or the "well of oath." In Genesis 21, Abraham and Abimelech argue over a well. By the end of the chapter, they conclude a pact and swear an oath at a place that gets named *Be'er Sheva*. According to Genesis 21:30–31: "[Abraham] said, 'These seven ewe lambs you shall accept from my hand, in order that you may be a witness for me that I dug this well.' Therefore that place

was called Beer-sheba; because there both of them swore an oath"
(NRSV). It's a triple pun. The text connects the first half of the proper
noun Beersheva to the Hebrew word *be'er*, "well." It connects the second half of the proper noun both to "seven" and to "oath."

Numbers 11:3 tells us, "So that place was called Taberah, because
the fire of the LORD burned against them" (NRSV). The Hebrew for
"burned" is *ba'arah*, from the same root (B.A.R) from which the name
Taberah is formed.

In Joshua 5:9 we read of a place called Gilgal: "The LORD said to
Joshua, 'Today I have rolled away from you the disgrace of Egypt.'
And so that place is called Gilgal to this day." *Gilgal* means "rolled."

We don't know whether these are the real origins of the names (that
is, really etymology) or whether the names came first and the stories
afterward (perhaps as puns), but either way, it's clear that etymology of
some sort is popular in the Bible itself. We must therefore be particularly careful about our position on etymology: Etymology is what a
word used to mean or where a word comes from. It does not tell us
what a word *does* mean—at least, not necessarily.

So as with the internal structure of words, we cannot use etymology to figure out what the ancient Hebrew words meant when the Bible
was written.

Cognate Languages

The final popular but wrong way of trying to decode ancient Hebrew
is cognate languages. Frequently, the same word will appear in two
related languages. Sometimes a word will start in one language and
then get used in another. In the first case, the word that appears in each
language is called a **cognate**. The second case, really a subcase of the
first, is called "borrowing" (even though the word is never given back).

It stands to reason but isn't true that knowing what a word means
in one language will tell us what it means in another.

Once again we look at modern languages to illustrate the point.

Once (then) French President François Mitterrand came to visit the United States, he declared, through a translator, that he demanded the U.S. president come visit France.

What happened?

The French president used the French verb *demander* when he wanted to invite his American counterpart to Paris. The French *demander* and the English "demand" are clearly cognate. (The -*er* ending in French, pronounced "ay," marks an infinitive.) But unlike the English "demand," which implies force, the French *demander* means "to ask," and Mitterrand meant to "ask if the American president would come visit France."

While clearly "ask" and "demand" have something in common, it would be a terrible mistake for English speakers to try to deduce the meaning of the French based on their own language, or vice versa. The words are different enough that confusion between them almost caused an international incident.

This French/English pair is representative of one of the ways that cognate words differ between languages. They can have very different nuances.

Equally, words change meaning when they travel ("get borrowed") from one language to another. The English word "sombrero" means "Mexican hat," but in Spanish it just means "hat." A baseball cap in Spanish is a *sombrero*. In Modern Hebrew, the word *kontzert*, borrowed from the English "concert," means "classical music concert."

A particularly interesting case of borrowing and the risks of relying on cognate languages can be seen in the Modern Hebrew word *ekspres*, which refers to a type of bus route. The word was recently borrowed from the English word "express," but, unlike the English, the Hebrew word *ekspres* means "local." It's the bus that stops at every station between two points.

What happened is this: Originally, the Israeli bus company had three kinds of bus routes. One stopped at every stop between two points—say, between the port city of Haifa and the northern Kiryat Shmona. Another stopped at only a few select stops. But a third route took the bus into almost every village between the two cities, stopping not only at all the main stops but also weaving through a variety of towns. This third route was called the *m'asef*—literally, "collector" route. In contrast to the collector, the first bus, which stopped at every stop, was called the *ekspres*—that is, "local." The "express" bus was called *mahir*, "speedy." (The Israeli bus company that created the terms, Egged, has since abandoned the term *ekspres*, fearing it might be confusing.)

This true story is yet another example of the dangers of using cognate languages to figure out what a word means. So we add cognate languages to etymology and internal word structure, completing our list of three ways that words do not get their meaning.

PUTTING WORDS IN THEIR PLACE

So if looking at internal word structure, etymology, and cognate languages doesn't work, what does? How do scholars figure out what the ancient Hebrew words meant?

The most reliable way of determining what a word in a dead language means is to see how the word is used in context. Once again, we'll look at some modern examples, where we can test the results, before we look at ancient Hebrew.

Suppose we want to know what "driveway" means, and we can't ask an English speaker. If we can find enough sentences where "driveway" is used, we'll learn that driveways are frequently paved (and that driveway-paving services frequently do the paving) and that they are used for parking on. "Park in the driveway" is one very common context for the word "driveway." We almost never find the phrase "drive in the driveway." We do find "drive up the driveway" and "drive into the driveway," but again, in the context of then parking. Unlike internal word structure, which leads us in the wrong direction, context points immediately to the right answer.

"Ice-cream truck" and "fire truck" work the same way. A look at both words in context shows us that ice-cream trucks are vehicles where people buy ice cream, while fire trucks are summoned to put out fires.

We can look at the English word "opposite" for a slightly more complex example. A naive definition of the word "opposite" might be "completely unlike" or "altogether different." Yet when asked for the opposite of "dog," most people will suggest "cat," even though cats and dogs are certainly not altogether different. If the naive definition of "opposite" were right, the opposite of "dog" might be "yesterday." But context ("cat is the opposite of dog") shows us that the word "opposite" is more nuanced. It can mean "completely unlike" but also "complementary" or "the other of a pair."

Because context is so useful, Biblical scholars long ago got the idea of compiling what's called a **concordance**—that is, a list of the contexts of every word in the Bible. In these days of computers and the Internet, finding every context of a word is a trivial matter, but it wasn't always so. People spent their lives painstakingly recording every Hebrew word in the Bible and compiling a list of the contexts in which the word appeared. Shlomo Mandelkorn created such a compilation in the nineteenth century. More recently, others have created similar works. And today, the "search" function of most electronic editions of the Hebrew Bible does the same thing as a concordance.

Let's look at a Hebrew example. One of the most common words in the Hebrew Bible is *leimor*. The word literally means "to say," and it's most commonly translated as "saying." This is where we get (terrible) translations like, "God spoke unto Moses, saying . . ." Let's look at the context of *leimor* and see if we can figure out what it really means.

The first thing we see about *leimor* is that it is indeed used for things that are said. It's used for what people say, as in Genesis 27:6 (to pick one of many examples at random): "And Rebekah spake unto Jacob her son, saying [*leimor*], Behold, I heard thy father speak unto Esau thy brother, saying [*leimor*] . . ." (KJV) or, more colloquially (and accurately), "Rebekah said to her son Jacob, 'I heard your father say to your brother Esau . . .'" (NRSV). The word is also used for what God says, as in Genesis 1:22: "And God blessed them, saying [*leimor*], Be fruitful, and multiply . . ." (KJV) or "God blessed them, saying [*leimor*], 'Be fruitful . . .'" (NRSV and NAB).

But it's also used for songs, as in Exodus 15:1: "Then sang Moses and the children of Israel this song unto the LORD, and spake, saying [*leimor*], I will sing . . ." (KJV). Here the KJV has a problem, because in English songs aren't "said"; they're sung. The NRSV and NAB do better: "Then Moses and the Israelites sang this song to the LORD: 'I will sing. . . .'"

The word is also used for questions, as in Genesis 37:15: "And the man asked him, saying [*leimor*], What seekest thou?" (KJV). Again the KJV has a problem, because in English one doesn't say questions; one asks them.

But a picture begins to emerge. The word *leimor* is used for questions, statements, songs, blessings, commandments, etc. In fact, *leimor* is used for anything that involves *direct quotation*. Indeed, it *introduces direct quotation*. We don't have a word like that in English, but we have something just as good. We have punctuation. The role of quotation marks is to mark direct quotations. This is why the NRSV correctly uses quotation marks where the KJV has the misleading (that is, wrong) translation "saying." (Surprisingly, the authors of the NRSV, who seem to have understood *leimor*, still get it wrong sometimes in translation, as we just saw in Genesis 1:22.)

English quotation marks can be used for words of a speech, question, song, whatever. So, too, the Hebrew *leimor* was used for any direct quotation. So *leimor* doesn't mean "saying . . ." at all. It means, "comma, quote. . . ." (In the next chapter we'll take a more detailed look at how to transform our knowledge of ancient Hebrew words into successful translations.)

This quick look at how to use context has already shown us something important about ancient Hebrew, something that the authors of the KJV didn't appreciate. The KJV translators looked at the internal structure of *leimor* and jumped to the wrong conclusion.

In this case, the wrong translation in the KJV just leaves the reader with the misimpression that songs were said, not sung. But in other cases with other words, the results are more fundamental.

WORDS SIDE BY SIDE

Every so often, we are lucky enough to find a context that is particularly helpful. The most helpful context, of course, is one that defines a word. This is rare in the Bible.

But as we will see in the next chapter, Biblical poetry often consisted of putting synonyms in parallel. These synonyms are one of the best ways of making sure that we have correctly understood the ancient Hebrew words. For example, we find the word *rozen* half a dozen times in the Bible, and it's never defined. But Proverbs 31:4 is typical of how the word is used. Kings and *rozen*s should drink wine, the verse tells us in poetry. In our modern context, we would expect that *rozen*s are very different than kings, because we are supposed to eschew redundancy, particularly in poetry. But ancient poetry worked differently. Good poetry frequently consisted of finding synonyms. Because *rozen* is almost always used in parallel with "king," we have good reason to believe that *rozen* means something like "king."

When in Isaiah 40:23 we further see that *rozen* is used in parallel with "judges," we learn more about *rozen*s and about judges. From other sources, we know a lot about kings and judges. Isaiah 40:23 shows us that all three have something in common. Very roughly, they were related in the way that "senators" and "governors" are in the modern United States. They were both important parts of the government of ancient Israel. (We go into much more depth about "kings" in Chapter 5.)

Though we know less about what a *rozen* was—"prince" is a typical translation—we know that he was someone in a high position, like a king and like a judge. We don't have an exact word for that (or, really, for "king" and "judge," again as we'll see in Chapter 5), and the word isn't important enough to warrant more discussion here, but it still serves to demonstrate the general point that the parallelisms common in Biblical poetry are particularly helpful in decoding words. Even though it didn't help us understand *rozen* perfectly, we have a good sense of the approximate meaning of the word.

WORD COMBINATIONS

Everything that we have seen about words applies to combinations of words, too. Just as we cannot use internal structure, etymology, or cognate languages to understand a single word, we shouldn't use these three methods with combinations of words. We've already seen one example. Knowing what "fire," "truck," and "fire truck" mean won't help us know what "ice-cream truck" means.

A more detailed example highlights the issue. English has a verb "pick" and two words "on" and "up" that can be added to verbs. "Pick" (as in "pick a lock") means "open stealthily without a key." "Up" means "away from gravity," and "on" means "touching and located in the direction of open space." (All of these definitions are approximate.) This knowledge, however, doesn't explain why "pick on" means "annoy," "pick up" means "increase" (as in, "pick up the tempo"), and "pick up on" means "discern."

For that matter, "serving on the faculty at Harvard" is a prestigious appointment, while the seemingly similar but very different "serving the faculty at Harvard" is a description of a waiter. Yet even though the word "on" indicates an academic position versus a menial one with the word "serve," it has just the opposite role in the phrase "to wait on." This is true even though the waiter is the server.

A severe example is the common modern American phrase "I could care less," which, it turns out, means the same thing as "I couldn't care less."

These demonstrate that phrases, just like words, don't get their meanings from their internal structure. This means that even once we've understood two words, we may not understand what they mean when they are used together.

Once again, the only reliable way to understand phrases is to look at context.

By way of further demonstration, let's look at the phrase "tree of the field" in the Bible and try to figure out what it means. For example, Isaiah 55:12 offers a beautiful image of celebration: "For you shall go out in joy, and be led back in peace; the mountains and the hills before you shall burst into song, and all the trees of the field shall clap their hands" (NRSV).

But a field is an odd place for a tree. (And clapping hands is an odd thing for a tree to do, but we assume that that's part of Isaiah's poetic imagery.) The literal translation "trees of the field" is wrong.

So we look at context. Curious readers may wish to look at the complete list of where the phrase "tree(s) of the field" appears: Exodus 9:25; Leviticus 26:4; Isaiah 55:12; Jeremiah 7:20; Ezekiel 17:24, 31:4, 31:5, 31:15, and 34:27; and Joel 1:12 and 1:19. Based on this, what does "trees of the field" really mean?

The book of Joel (in verse 1:12) offers some initial help: "The vine withers, the fig tree droops. Pomegranate, palm, and apple—all the trees of the field are dried up; surely, joy withers away among the people" (NRSV). It seems that the phrase "trees of the field" summarizes "grape vines, fig trees, pomegranate trees, palm trees, and apple trees" (except that "apple" is probably wrong as a translation, too).

Leviticus 26:4 gives us more help: "I will give you your rains in their season, and the land shall yield its produce, and the trees of the field shall yield their fruit" (NRSV).

Jeremiah 7:20 warns that God's wrath "will be poured out on this place, on man and beast, on the trees of the field and on the fruit of the ground" (NRSV).

All of these contexts point in the same direction. A "tree of the field" was a fruit-bearing tree. At first glance, the suggestion seems preposterous. After all, the phrase "tree of the field" has the word "field" right in it. Surely it must have something to do with fields, right? Wrong. We've learned in this chapter that phrases don't get their meanings from the words used to make them. There's nothing odd about "field" indicating "fruit" in this context.

"Strawberries" don't grow in straw. "Wild animals" can be calm. And in Hebrew, as we just learned from context, "field trees" are fruit trees.

MORE ON MEANING

So far, we've skipped over the really important question of what it means for a word to mean something. Sources for more detailed answers appear in the Appendix, but for now we need to consider two aspects of "meaning": Words can mean more than one thing, and the meaning of a word can be extended. We'll start with the first one.

Homonyms

Homonyms are words that are spelled the same way but mean different things. (The term is also used for words that are spelled differently but still sound the same.) We have to be aware of homonyms when using the context method to figure out what a word means.

For example, if we want to figure out what the English word "bank" means, and if a search of how the word is used in context tells us that "money is kept in a bank" and "a bank is where a river meets the shore," we have to be careful to recognize that "bank" means two completely different things. In the case of "financial institution" and "riverside," it's pretty easy to figure out that we have two words that just happen to sound the same. But other cases are more difficult.

In the first Gulf War, the United States sent some 500,000 troops to the Middle East. A reasonable but wrong conclusion would have been that those troops contained several million individual soldiers. After all, a boy-scout troop, a girl-scout troop, or, for that matter, the F-Troop (from the television series) usually has more than a dozen members. The confusion comes because the word "troop" at once means "group of people" and "person." Without external supporting evidence, it might be difficult for a researcher in several hundred years to figure out when the word means what.

We have to be careful not to make the same mistake when we look at ancient Hebrew. For example, the word *elef* pretty clearly means "thousand." The book of Numbers, among other things, deals with a census of the Israelite people. (That's why it's called "Numbers" in English.) It describes the populations of each tribe in thousands (*elef*), hundreds, and tens. It then gives a grand total, also in thousands, hundreds, and tens. The math works only if *elef* means "thousand."

But then in Numbers 31:4–6, we find the word *elef* in reference to what would be a military delegation. Each tribe must send one *elef*. While the word may mean "thousand" there, the phrasing would be odd. In Numbers 31:5 we read in the NRSV: "So out of the thousands [*elef*] of Israel, a thousand [*elef*] from each tribe were conscripted, twelve thousand [*elef*] armed for battle." Why would the text mention "the thousands of Israel" rather than any number of much more reasonable choices: "people of Israel," "sons of Israel," "soldiers," "fighters," etc.? One good possibility is that *elef* means more than one thing. It means "thousand," but it also means "fighting unit."

But here's the thing. The other possibility is that *elef* always means "thousand," and the text in Numbers 31:4–6 is either purposely oblique or it's normal text and there's something else about ancient Hebrew that we've misunderstood. Sometimes, even our best investigation leads only to a pretty good guess.

There are lots of ways a word might have two meanings.

The meanings might reflect two completely unrelated words (like the two words "bank"). It's usually pretty easy to identify this scenario, especially if the word is used often, because one of the word's meanings won't make any sense when the word is used in its second sense. It's hard to imagine a plausible scenario where "financial institution" and "riverside" might be confused.

Or there might be two related words (like "troop"). This case is harder to identify, because when the words are related, there's a greater chance that the wrong meaning will seem plausible. Only a detailed analysis of the first Gulf War could distinguish the two meanings, teasing apart "500,000 people" and "several million people."

Another possibility is that a word might have different meanings in different dialects.

A British high-school student came to an American summer camp. One evening during a group discussion about war, he and an American learned that they disagreed vehemently about the appropriate use of military force. One student thought the military was a good thing; the other was shocked even to hear such a suggestion. After a bitter exchange of words, the British kid and the American found themselves walking side by side. The Brit asked the American if he wanted "to work things out." The American, glad to have a peaceful conclusion to the tension, quickly agreed. So the British kid hit him.

What went wrong? In America, "work things out" usually means "talk things out." In England it usually means "fight things out."

Another British/American example is more subtle and, therefore, more likely to cause confusion. American author John Steinbeck's book *Of Mice and Men* takes its name from a line in a poem by Robert Burns. Many Americans are familiar with the quotation: "The best laid plans of mice and men [often go awry]." But that's not actually the original. The poem really reads, "the best laid schemes of mice and men. . . ." The problem is that in Scottish English, a "scheme" is any old plan, while in American English it's a plan to do something wrong or illegal. (Consider a "scheme to get money" versus a "plan to get money.")

In America, "tabling" an issue at a meeting means agreeing not to vote on the issue. In England, it means the opposite.

Certainly the Bible contains more than one dialect of Hebrew. For example, essentially the same passage appears in I Kings 8 and II Chronicles 6. But even though the meaning is the same, minor differences in the Hebrew grammar reflect different dialects. (The dialect in Chronicles is commonly called "Late Biblical Hebrew," but the term

"Biblical Hebrew," rather than "Early Biblical Hebrew," is usually employed for the more widely used dialect in Kings.) In I Kings 8, a verb has two parts and no subject, while in II Chronicles 6 the same meaning is conveyed with a one-part verb in conjunction with a subject. Details about both grammatical constructions are complicated, so we won't analyze them here, but it is still important to see that the Hebrew is different.

Frequently, as in the difference between Kings and Chronicles that we just saw, scholars can identify and isolate the various dialects, at least warning translators when more work is needed—but not always. So when we look at a word in context, we must remember that even context can be misleading if we're not careful.

In addition to cases like these, another major way a word can mean more than one thing is through various systematic extensions of a word's meaning, as we see next.

Extensions

When a captain shouts, "All hands on deck," presumably he wants his sailors in their entirety, not just their hands, on the deck. Are we to conclude, based on this, that "hand" also means "person"? Not necessarily, because languages have a variety of ways in which the meanings of words can be extended.

The extension we've just seen is technically called metonymy—that is, using a word to refer to something related to that word. It's widespread in English and, in general, across the languages of the world. Similarly, if a man wearing a sombrero (in the English sense) arrives at a baseball game, people might comment, "Get a load of the sombrero," meaning, "Get a load of the guy wearing the sombrero." That's metonymy. So is "the White House denied accusations that . . ." when the point is "the accusations were denied by someone in the White House." Similarly, if a guy at a restaurant orders a corned-beef sandwich and then asks for a glass of milk, his waitress might remark: "The corned-beef sandwich in the back needs more milk." In an example we'll come back to in Chapter 4, the sentence "Not a soul was left in the room" doesn't mean that the room contained a bunch of corpses. Rather, "soul" is used metonymically to mean "human being that has a soul."

It's important to keep track of these things, because we don't want to get confused when we look at how a word is used in context. For example, we wouldn't want to think that "corned-beef sandwich" means "person eating a sandwich." Equally, once we know what a word means, we want to understand how it is used. (On the other hand, a full description of English would have to include the fact that "hand" usually means "person" in reference to workers on a ship. We'll return to that point shortly.)

For example, the Hebrew word *eretz* means "land," and, just like its English counterpart, the word refers at once to the physical earth and to the area under control of a ruler. So in Genesis 1:10, God calls the dry land *"eretz."* The word means the soil itself. But later on, the *"eretz* of Egypt" will refer not to the soil but to the region under the control of Egypt. Because our English word "land" works just as well in both cases, it's a bit tricky to see both meanings.

As an example that doesn't work so well in English, we can consider the words *negev* and *teiman*, literally "Negev (region)" and "Yemen." But in the Bible, they frequently just mean "south." "Toward the Negev" (*negba*) is the opposite of "toward the north." Again, we see metonymy.

Metonymy is just one of a variety of ways words assume non-literal meaning. Similes, metaphors, and other poetic devices all extend the meanings of words. For convenience, we can call all of these—including metonymy—poetic, but that doesn't mean that they are used only in poetry. In fact, they are just as common in ordinary prose.

Color words are a good way to get a sense of what's going on.

The German word *blau* means "blue." So a "blue sky" in German is *"blau."* But here's the problem. A *blaumark* in German—literally, a "blue letter"—is not a "blue letter" at all in English. A *blaumark* in

German is the letter that a school sends home to parents when their child misses school. The German *blaumachen*—literally, "to make blue" or "to do blue"—means "to skip school." In general, *blau* in German refers to truancy.

But in English, "blue" most often refers to sorrow. We don't have an expression "to make blue" or "to do blue," but we can "feel blue"— that is, "be sad."

It's not hard to imagine translators with only a partial knowledge of German or, perhaps, with a knowledge of academic German but not colloquial German, going through the following steps: They come across the phrase *blaumachen*. They translate it literally as "make blue." They know that "make blue" isn't good English, so they tweak it a bit and end up with "feel blue," congratulating themselves on having avoided a stilted literal translation and coming up with something modern and colloquial while still capturing the essence of the original. They are completely wrong.

Similarly, "to be blue" in modern Russian means "to be gay."

In Modern Hebrew a "blue movie" is a pornographic film. Apparently, "blue movie" means the same thing in some dialects of English, too. But in English we also have "blue laws," which have (almost) nothing to do with pornography. They are regulations about commerce on the Sabbath, forbidding the sale of alcohol, requiring stores to close in some municipalities, and even in some places invalidating personal checks written on Sunday. In addition, we have blue (and red) states, which have nothing to do with sorrow ("feeling blue"), keeping the Sabbath ("blue laws"), or pornography ("blue movies"). Blue states are states that tend to vote Democratic. Then there's "blue blood," which is associated with nobility, notwithstanding the anatomical fact that everyone's blood is blue when it returns to the heart, and "blue blood" literally is blood with no oxygen. A candle that "burns blue" is an omen of death. And "blueberries" are actually purple.

In English, "green" is associated with envy ("green with envy"), but also inexperience ("greenhorn"), nature ("green thumb"), and conservationism ("going green"). Paradoxically, when "green" applies to plants, it can mean both "unripe" and its opposite, "flourishing." In at least one instance, "green" is the same as "blue." "Green in the face," as in "shouting until you're green in the face," is the same as "shouting until you're blue in the face." Like "blue," "green" is used to refer to things that are not green. Similarly, we use other color words for some things that are actually typically green, like blackboards.

The description of the Tabernacle in Exodus includes what the King James Version translates as "rams' skins dyed red." That description may be right. But the NRSV translation, "tanned rams' skins," is more likely. "Red" (*adom* in Hebrew, or, as a verb, *m'odam*) here may not literally mean "red." Just as the English "tan" is both a color and a process, "red" in Hebrew means more than just a color.

In Genesis 25:30, Esau begs his brother Jacob for "that same red pottage" (KJV). The Hebrew word *adom* ("red") appears twice (and the word "pottage" is implied but doesn't appear in the Hebrew—the Hebrew refers simply to something red). The KJV uses "that same" in an attempt to capture the double word. But, like the hypothetical translators of German who think that *blaumachen* means "to feel blue," have the translators of the KJV missed the whole point? Does "red" imply something in Hebrew that it does not in English?

The answer is almost certainly "yes." "Red" in ancient Hebrew was connected to the ground. Even the words are similar. "Red" is *adom* and "ground" is *adama*. Esau was born "red" (Genesis 25:25—where the Hebrew word is the related *admoni*, perhaps "reddish"), and he is a man of the field (Genesis 25:27). Clearly, Esau wasn't literally "red." Though he may have had a red tint to his skin, more likely the point of the passage is to make a connection between Esau's complexion and the nature of his character. Like an American baby born green who grew up to be jealous, Esau was born red and grew up to work the field. The connection between "red" and "field" is as obvious in Hebrew as in the English pair "green" and "envy." In fact, the Hebrew words are even more closely related. Their meanings overlap, and, in addition, they share the root A.D.M. The standard English translation "red"/"field" misses the entire wordplay.

When Esau asks for his brother's "red," and, in particular, when the text doesn't explicitly indicate what red thing Esau wants, the scene transcends its seemingly mundane content of a man asking his brother for food that just happens to be red. It is instead a symbol-laden image of thinking you have what you need but, in fact, not having it at all. Esau, a hunter—seemingly able to fend for himself, born "red" and working "red" (images that work in Hebrew but not English)— suddenly finds himself not having enough "red" and having therefore to rely on his seemingly less powerful brother Jacob.

The original story is about the limits of physical power (Esau) and the power of God (Jacob). The reader gets a hint of the theme when Jacob and Esau are still in their mother Rebekkah's womb, and God tells her that she will give birth to two peoples, and "the mighty will serve the younger." Esau is the mighty one, but his seemingly weaker brother really has the power. The meek shall inherit the earth, some might say.

In this case, the text even contains a clue about the poetic nature of the Hebrew word "red." The continuation of Genesis 25:30 tells us, "Therefore he [Esau] was called Edom" (NRSV). Notice the similarity of sound. "Red" is *adom*, and Esau is *edom*. The Edomites are the "Red People." And Esau is their father (Genesis 36:9, e.g.).

All of this complexity, beauty, and imagery is lost in the seemingly obvious translations: "feed me [. . .] with that same red pottage" (KJV) or "let me eat some of that red stuff" (NRSV).

The same word "red" shows up in the erotic poetry of Song of Songs, where "my beloved" (Song of Songs 5:10) is called *adom*. The KJV and most later translations choose "ruddy" for *adom* here, precisely because "my beloved is red" doesn't make any sense in English. But, in fact, hedging and using "ruddy" doesn't help matters. We have no Hallmark cards for "my ruddy one."

The translators ought to have noticed that something was amiss because the first part of the line reads, in English, "My beloved is white," giving us the silly "my beloved is white and red," more reminiscent of a children's riddle about a newspaper than of romance. We will leave "white"—*tzach* in Hebrew—for another time, noting now that we don't have a good word in English for it. (There's another word in Hebrew, *lavan*, which means simply "white." The Hebrew word we see here is more poetic. Other English translations range from "radiant" to "dazzling" to "clear-skinned," and these are closer.) But we want to focus on "red," which, we now understand, has little to do with color here and everything to do with earthiness.

Adom is a good thing, perhaps along the lines of "rugged" in English, an image destroyed by "red" and "ruddy," neither of which is generally considered desirable in English. We know that *adom* is a positive trait because it is just the first in a litany of beautiful images. Many of the words are even more difficult to translate than *adom*, but the point is that "my beloved" is better than everyone else, a once-in-a-lifetime find, precious and rare like gold with jet-black hair and lips begging to be kissed. "Red" has no place on this list in English. Unfortunately, we don't have a really good translation option here.

It's not just colors that are used "poetically." For example, "sweet" has a variety of very different meanings in English: sugary, kind, etc.; and as we saw earlier, "sweet" even turns "bread" into "sweetbread"— that is, animal brains. In Hebrew, "sweet" modifies water to mean what we call in English "freshwater," so in Hebrew the opposite of "saltwater" is "sweet water." (Surprisingly, the KJV translates "sweet water" literally in James 3:11, even though it correctly gives us "freshwater" just one verse later.)

The English word "great" represents positive traits, usually meaning "better than just good." A great idea, for example, is better than just a good idea. Yet the Great Depression was not better than any good depression; it wasn't good at all.

The technique that we used earlier—looking at a word in context— will help us understand not just the core meaning of a word but also the broader ways in which it is used. We just have to be careful not to jump to conclusions about a Hebrew word. It would be easy to stop investigating once we learn that *adom* means "red," but it would be a mistake. This mistake, perhaps more than any other, contributes to the faulty translations so widely available.

Two Kinds of Extension

The careful reader may have noticed that at this point we're actually talking about two things at once.

On the one hand, as we just saw, words mean more than what they might at first appear. "Green" in English sometimes invokes "envy," sometimes "inexperience," plus many more concepts that, in the end, don't have much to do with the actual color green. "Hands," to the captain of a ship, means "workers."

And on the other hand, a word or phrase can be used inventively to give it a meaning it doesn't normally have. "Corned-beef sandwich," instead of "the person eating that corned-beef sandwich," is an example. So is the first time that "hands" was used for "workers," or "stationary supplies" for "supplies that I plan to get from the stationary booth."

Over time, extensions can actually create new words and phrases, so words and phrases can migrate from the second category to the first. Even though "stationery" started off as a case of metonymy, now it's a whole new word.

When this process applies to phrases, we call them "idioms."

IDIOMS

"There's more than one way to skin a cat."

It's an interesting expression. It means not just that there's more than one way of doing things; it means that there's more than one good way of doing things. But more to the point, it has nothing to do with cats, skinned or otherwise.

We might imagine an ancient cat-worshipping Egyptian trying to make sense of this line if it were translated into Egyptian. It would be like an American reading, say, that "There's more than one way to burn a church"—only it would be even worse for the Egyptian. Egyptians worshipped cats, making cats not only symbols of God but living instantiations of God.

Still, we can use the parallel of "There's more than one way to burn a church" as a potential English translation of something. Is there anything we could do to get past the churchness and burningness of the expression? Probably not. Any expression in English that seems to involve church-burning, not surprisingly, does form an association with burning churches in the minds of the people who hear the phrase.

Surprisingly, though, there's a similar two-word expression in English: barn burner. What's surprising is that it has nothing to do with burning barns. The word connotes something impressive or successful, which is why when then-CEO of Chrysler, Lee Iacocca, wanted to warn that sales figures for his car company would not be impressive, he cautioned that the upcoming month "will not be any barn burner."

Going back to "There's more than one way to skin a cat," we might compare that expression to a phrase that someone makes up, say, "It would be like skinning a cat." What's important is that "like skinning a cat" is a comparison, not an expression. (It's an odd comparision, but that isn't the point.) As speakers of English, we automatically know that the expression has nothing to do with cats, and the comparison has everything to do with cats.

Augmenting our examples just a bit, we have five potential English sentences:

1. There's more than one way to skin a cat.
2. There's more than one way to burn a church.
3. The party Saturday night was a real barn burner.
4. At the party Saturday night the frat boys burned a barn.
5. It's a felony to skin a live cat.

The problem is that (1) and (2) look like they're almost the same thing. So do (1) and (5), (2) and (3), and (3) and (4). But it would quite obviously be a mistake to translate (4) as (3) or to mix up any of the other pairs.

When we look at the Hebrew of the Bible, we want to make sure we avoid that kind of error. We don't want Hebrew that essentially means "There's more than one way to skin a cat" to end up in translation as anything other than what it really is. So far we've seen that the first step to producing a good translation is figuring out what the ancient Hebrew words mean. In the next chapter, we'll see how to turn those words into an accurate translation.

3

BRIDGING THE GAP:
WRITING HEBREW IN ENGLISH

BLIND IDIOTS

"Out of sight, out of mind" sounds as if it might be paraphrased as "blind idiot," but of course it cannot. Yet many translations of the Bible make this sort of basic mistake when they render ancient Hebrew into modern English.

That's because knowing what the Hebrew words mean is only one half of translating the Bible. The second and more difficult half is finding English words that do the same thing as the original Hebrew. More generally, translation consists of two parts: decoding the original language (Hebrew, in our case), and finding a translation in a new language (English, for us) that does the same thing as the original.

In Chapter 2 we used examples from modern languages to get a sense of how the first half of translation works. We'll use the same approach now to understand the second half. And, as before, some examples will help pave the way for a discussion of the underlying theory.

In 1992, Laura Esquivel wrote a book in Spanish called *Como agua para chocolate*. In this case, the Spanish words are so familiar and easy to translate that we don't even need the techniques of the last chapter to figure out what they mean: *Como* is "like," *agua* is "water," *para* is "for," and *chocolate* is "chocolate." Accordingly, the English-language version of the book (and then movie) was called *Like Water for Chocolate*.

Esquivel's quirky story centers around a woman who cannot marry the man she wants because she is the youngest daughter and a family tradition insists that she therefore be the one to care for her mother. The book is about the tension that results from unrequited love, family dynamics, and a generation gap.

But here's the problem. The English phrase "like water for chocolate" doesn't conjure up any particular image among English speakers. The heroine of the story is a cook, so people who read the book in English sometimes think that the "chocolate" in the title may refer to that. Other English speakers think that "water" instead of "chocolate" may be an image of poverty. But nothing clear comes to mind.

In Spanish, by contrast, "like water for chocolate" is a common expression based on the Spanish culinary tradition maintaining that hot chocolate is best prepared with water that is almost but not quite boiling. Therefore, "water for [making hot] chocolate" is water that is about to boil. "At the boiling point," we might say in English. The Spanish phrase has nothing to do with poverty and, actually, little to do with food.

So while "like water for chocolate" gets all of the words right in English, in the end it completely misses the point. Ms. Esquivel's title foreshadows the internal tensions of her characters. The English translation foreshadows nothing.

Similarly, Douglas Hofstadter points out (in *Metamagical Themas*) that Woodward and Bernstein's famous English-language book (and then film) *All the President's Men* has a clever title. The story is about the fall of President Nixon and the inability of the president's aides to help. The title calls to mind the well-known children's rhyme:

"All the king's horses and all the king's men/couldn't put Humpty together again." Like the king's men who couldn't help Humpty Dumpty, the president's men couldn't help Nixon. Once again, the title of the book foreshadows the content.

But the French version of the film is called *Les hommes du president*—literally, "the men of the president." Not only isn't that part of a nursery rhyme, it barely has anything to do with the book. Even disregarding the lack of the word "all" in the French, did the translators at least get it almost right? No.

The core of the issue is what it means to translate. We saw in the last chapter that it's hard just to figure out what the words and phrases in a foreign language mean. Many people, perhaps because of that difficulty, stop with the meaning of the words. In so doing, they miss the point of translation.

For example, "obtain" means the same thing as "get," but "How do you obtain from here to the airport?" is not English. "Sincerely" means "with sincerity," but only the first one is used to sign a business letter.

In the previous chapter, we saw that *blau* in German sometimes means "blue," but sometimes it has nothing to do with blue. "Blue" in English, similarly, sometimes has nothing to do with the color blue; rather, it connotes sorrow. But even though *blau* in German and "blue" in English have metaphoric meanings, they are not the same metaphoric meaning.

Jonathan Safran Foer's popular book (and then movie) *Everything Is Illuminated* features a native Russian speaker trying to express himself in English. The hero tells the reader that his clumsy brother is "always promenading into things," rather than "walking into things." Similarly, he has a dog: "If you're wondering what my bitch's name is . . . ," he says. Both of these demonstrate common translation mistakes. Foer humorously uses pretend translation mistakes to give the impression of a Russian writing English.

Unfortunately, we see these sorts of things—and much wo se—in mainstream Bible translations. So people who read the Bible in English frequently end up missing the whole point of the original Hebrew.

As a demonstration of how difficult translation is, we might consider two lines from the Joseph narrative in Genesis 40. Joseph is Jacob's favorite son, but Joseph's brothers can't stand him. They sell him to the Ishmaelites (their cousins!), who, in turn, sell him to a powerful man named Potiphar.

After Potiphar—who has misunderstood a situation between his wife and their new Hebrew slave—throws Joseph into jail, Joseph attempts to interpret the dreams of Pharaoh's butler and baker, who, like Joseph, find themselves locked up. (Probably "butler," "baker," and even "jail" aren't quite the right words, but they're close enough for now.) Joseph first turns to the butler's dream about a triple-branched vine whose blossoms produce grapes for wine. He has good news for the butler (Genesis 40:13): "Yet within three days shall Pharaoh lift up thine head" (KJV).

What does "lift up [your] head" mean? The rest of the line makes it a little clearer: ". . . and restore thee unto thy place." Apparently, "lift up your head" was a positive thing in Hebrew, while in English it doesn't make much sense at all. Even though we have similar English expressions, like "hold your head up" or "hold your head high," people can generally hold only their own heads high, not other people's.

The Hebrew phrase is used elsewhere, as, for example, in Jeremiah 52:31, where Evilmerodach (that's the guy's name) "lifted up the head" of King Jehoiachin and "brought him forth out of prison" (KJV). In Psalm 24:7, the Psalmist commands the very gates of the Temple to "lift up your heads." In Judges 8:28, Midian is "subdued . . . so that they lifted up their heads no more" (KJV). Job laments (in Job 10:15) that even if he is in the right, he will not "lift up [his] head."

So it looks as if to "lift up one's head" in Hebrew, like the Spanish and German examples we just saw, should not be translated word for word, lest the idiom lose its meaning. In English we do not use "lift up his head" to mean "take him out of jail"—in fact, we don't use that exact phrase for anything. (Heads are not the only body parts that are "lifted up" in Hebrew. Eyes are, too, leading to the perfectly ridiculous translation, "lifted up his eyes." The Hebrew idiom means "look around," while the English suggests torture or perhaps plastic surgery.)

Recognizing the idiomatic nature of the Hebrew, the New Living Translation translates Genesis 40:13 as "Pharaoh will take you out of prison" instead of the KJV's "Pharoah will lift up thine head." Similarly, the popular JPS translation offers, "Pharaoh will pardon you." At first glance, it looks like these two modern translations are better.

But the issue is trickier than that, because in Genesis 40:19, Joseph uses almost the same expression for the doomed baker. Joseph starts off with the same four Hebrew words that mean "Pharaoh will lift up thine head." (Surprisingly, though, the KJV uses "thy" here, not "thine"—the two English words meant essentially the same thing, but generally when two identical words are used in Hebrew, identical words should be used in their English translation.) In a beautiful linguistic play that distinguishes 40:19 from 40:13, Joseph adds the single Hebrew word *mei'alecha*—that is, "from upon you." Pharaoh will pardon the butler but will behead the baker!

We can almost imagine Joseph drawing out the words. Having already promised the butler, "Pharaoh will lift up your head [and save you]," Joseph turns to the baker and promises, "Pharoah will lift up your head . . ."

". . . off your body by hanging you."

But the NLT and JPS, having done so well with the idiomatic Hebrew, miss the entire wordplay here and translate Genesis 40:19 as "Pharaoh will cut off your head and impale your body on a pole" and "Pharaoh will lift off your head and impale you upon a pole," respectively. They got the meaning right but missed the wordplay.

The KJV, by contrast, translates Genesis 40:19 as "Pharaoh [shall] lift up thy head from off thee, and shall hang thee on a tree." Except for the minor mistake of changing "thine" into "thy," the KJV gets the play on words right—but at the expense of the meaning

What we need is an English phrase that means "save you" but that, with an additional word, can mean "hang you." Do we have such an option in English?

What if Joseph said, in English: "Pharaoh thinks you [the butler] have a head on your shoulders and he'll bring you back to the court. . . . Pharaoh thinks you [the baker] should have your head taken off your shoulders and he'll hang you from a tree. . . ." It has a play on words, and it even has the word "head," but it doesn't mean the same thing. Which is better? Capturing the meaning and missing the point, or capturing the point and missing the meaning?

As another option, what if Joseph said: "Pharaoh will befriend you. . . . Pharaoh will behead you. . . ." Or do we need to keep heads involved at all? Maybe, "Pharaoh will have you brought to the palace. . . . Pharaoh will have you brought to the palace gallows . . "?

As yet another option, what about, "Pharaoh wants you to hang around the palace," which seems to work for both the butler and the baker?

We have many options to choose from. We still don't have a final answer, but we've come closer to the tone and meaning of the original. More generally, though, we need an approach to translation that will help us put this, and many other issues, into a clearer framework.

FOREIGN LANGUAGES

The computer scientist Alan J. Perlis is reported to have quipped, "Learning French is trivial: the word for 'horse' is *cheval*, and everything else follows in the same way." He was joking, of course, but he put his finger on the two important parts of translation.

What do we mean when we say that the French word for "horse" is *cheval*? And how does everything else follow?

The Horse

We'll start with the first question. What does it mean to say that the English word "horse" and the French word *cheval* are the same?

Anyone who speaks French and English, or anyone who has access to a French/English dictionary, "knows" that "horse" and *cheval* mean the same thing. But precisely because this "fact" is so widely known, few people stop to ask what exactly we mean by it.

The tendency is to think that the two are interchangeable, but of course they are not completely interchangeable. For one thing, "horse" rhymes with "of course," while *cheval* does not rhyme with the French translation *bien sûr.* (Nor does *cheval* rhyme with the English "of course.") Obviously, in some contexts rhyming may not matter, but, equally obviously, it may be crucially important in other contexts.

For that matter, and this is a little more subtle, the two are not interchangeable precisely because they are in different languages. There is something about speaking English that goes beyond the English words, and, equally, something about French that transcends the French. This is why Leo Tolstoy wrote the opening of his Russian classic, *War and Peace,* not in Russian but mostly in French. The opening line—the very first words of the book—is in French, not Russian: *Eh bien, mon prince* ("Well, my prince"). Douglas Hofstadter therefore wonders how best to translate *War and Peace* into French. Should the opening passage stay in French? Or does that destroy the effect? If not French, perhaps English? What about translating the book into English?

Just the fact that we have to wonder whether keeping the French in French is the best way to translate French into French shows how tricky translation can be.

There's a third, even more subtle way in which "horse" and *cheval* are different. By and large, "horse" refers to a horse in America or some other English-speaking country, while *cheval* refers to a horse in France or some other French-speaking country. It's not that that's what the words necessarily mean, but certainly that's how they tend to be used. With "horse" and *cheval* we probably don't care, but what about with, say, "tree" in English and the obvious translation *eitz* in Modern Hebrew?

In the Northeast of the United States, for example, a "tree" almost always means a deciduous tree or a certain kind of pine tree. Unqualified, the word almost never means "palm tree." English speakers who plant a maple tree are likely to say, "We planted a tree," whereas if they plant a palm tree, they are likely to say, "We planted a palm tree." They qualify "tree" in this second case precisely because it is not the usual kind of tree.

By contrast, in modern Israel, palm trees are plentiful and common. Maple trees are not. And the pine trees are of a different variety than those in the United States. An Israeli who plants a palm tree may very well say, "I'm planting an *eitz*."

What is the better translation of the Hebrew? "I'm planting a tree" or "I'm planting a pine tree"? One better matches the Hebrew. The other makes it clear what's going on.

Consider another example. The Modern Hebrew word for "blue" is *kachol*. We've already seen how complicated color words can be when they are used metaphorically, but for now we can focus just on the color "blue" itself, because an interesting pattern emerges.

In English, the primary colors are "red," "green," and "blue." (Technically, these are the "additive primary colors," because when added one to another they produce white; shine a red, green, and blue spotlight on something and it's the same as shining white light. If colored filters or inks are used instead of lights, a combination of secondary colors are needed to filter all of the white light into black. These colors are cyan, magenta, and yellow, or, approximately, blue, red, and yellow. This is why painters know that the primary colors are red, blue, and yellow [RBY], while scientists know that they are red, green, and blue [RGB].) As it happens, the human eye decodes colors according to the RGB scheme, which is probably why red, green, and blue are usually the most basic color words. Languages do not have words for more exotic colors if they do not have those three.

In English, of course, "green" can refer to a variety of shades of green, including "dark green" and "light green." The same is true for blue. We have "dark blue" and "light blue." But "red" is different in English. While we have "dark red," there is no "light red," because instead we say "pink." In other words, we use four color names (green, blue, red, and pink) to describe the primary colors in English.

In Hebrew, however, there are not four but five words. Like in English, there is "green" (*yarok*), which comes in "light" and "dark" varieties. And like in English, there is "red" (*adom*), which comes in "dark" but not "light," because there's a separate word (*varod*) for what would otherwise be "light red." But, unlike in English, there's also a separate word for "light blue": *t'chelet*. So while there is a phrase "dark blue" in Hebrew, there is no phrase "light blue." Furthermore, this means that the Hebrew word for "blue," *kachol*, excludes "light blue," just as "red" (in English and Hebrew) excludes "pink."

Here's the question: What's the best English translation for *kachol*? Is it "blue"? That's not quite right, because "blue" includes light blue, while *kachol* does not. What about "blue but not light blue"? That's more accurate, but it seems like something else has gone wrong. Surely so short a word shouldn't have such a long translation. Or should it?

The way the color words work has broader ramifications. Consider four children's blocks. One is pink. One is red. And two are different shades of blue. In English, "Which two are the same color?" has an answer. The blue block and the light-blue block are both blue. But in Hebrew, the question doesn't have an answer. The *kachol* block is as different from the *t'chelet* block as the red one is from the pink.

In terms of translation, how could one possibly translate the English "Give me the two blue blocks" into Hebrew? No sentence that starts "Give me the two . . ." seems reasonable. "Give me the two blocks that are either *kachol* or *t'chelet*"? Clearly not.

And what happens if "two" is a central part of the content of the sentence? A poem might include something like, "and two blue blocks, one light, one dark. . . ." How does *that* get translated into Hebrew?

These are issues that arise even when the colors are used literally. As we have seen, the problems get compounded when we take into account the metaphoric meanings of words—in this case, colors. A (slightly) deeper poem might include, ". . . and two blue blocks to match my two blue moods. . . ." How would that get translated?

Everything Follows

The reason Perlis's statement is so jarring is that, as anyone who has ever tried to learn a foreign language knows, "everything else" does not "follow in the same way." In addition to vocabulary (which, even from the glimpse we just saw, can be very complicated), there's grammar.

More specifically, in addition to vocabulary, each language has its own **syntax**, its own **morphology**, its own **phonology**, its own **orthography**, and more.

Syntax is the way words are put together—that is, "word order." The first three words of the Bible—*breshit, bara,* and *elohim*—mean, roughly, "in the beginning" (that's the first word), "created" (the second word), and "God" (third). We'll come back to "in the beginning" later. For now, we note that the Hebrew reads ". . . created God . . ." even though God was the one who did the creating. (A thirteenth-century Jewish work that would become a cornerstone of the Jewish mystical movement known as Kabbalah offers a fanciful wordplay on this line, reinterpreting it as "something created God," not the other way around.)

In English, subjects—by and large the doers of actions—must usually appear before verbs. That's why we say "God created . . ." in English, not "created God. . . ." Biblical Hebrew works differently, preferring verb-subject ("created," the verb, followed by "God," the subject, or *bara elohim* in Hebrew), but allowing subject-verb as well. This is a matter of syntax. The syntax of Hebrew is different from the syntax of English.

(There are actually a few times when English not only allows but actually requires the subject to come after the verb. One such instance is after the word "nor." For example: "Abraham wasn't all good nor was he completely evil." Normally in English, subjects like "Abraham" come before verbs like "was," but after "nor" the order is reversed. That's also a matter of syntax.)

Morphology is how words get put together. So, what syntax is to phrases, morphology is to words. English morphology is fairly simple compared with that of other languages. In English, we add "-s" at the end of a word to mark a plural noun ("dog" becomes "dogs") and also a singular verb ("walk" becomes "walks"). We have other suffixes, like "-ly," "-ness," etc., and some prefixes, such as "re-."

Hebrew morphology is considerably more complex. The single word *vichuneka* has five parts and means "and he will favor you." (The reader needn't worry about the details, but for the curious: The first part is the prefix *v-*, which means "and." The second part is *y-*, which marks the future tense. The third part is the root Ch.N in combination with matters that are even more complex yet; together they express the verb "favor." The fourth part is something called an "infix"—that is, a word part that sits not before or after but in the middle of a word; the infix is *-n-*, whose meaning we do not know for sure, though some scholars think it emphasizes something. The fifth part is the suffix *-ka*, which means "you." A rule of Hebrew morphology changes the three letters *V-Y-Ch* . . . at the beginning of the word into *VIYCh*. . . . Another rule deletes the *-Y-* because it comes after a vowel and before a consonant.)

As a simpler example of Hebrew morphology, we might consider the first word of the Bible, *breshit*, which has two parts: the prefix *b-* ("in") and the word *reshit* ("beginning").

Phonology is the sounds of a language. In English, the "s" sounds different at the end of "dogs" than it does at the end of "cats." (In "dogs," the "s" sounds like a "z.") That's a matter of phonology.

Finally, "orthography" is a fancy word for "spelling."

When we're translating Hebrew into English, we usually pay less attention to orthography and phonology than to other aspects, because orthography and phonology tend to contribute less to the meaning than morphology and syntax. For example, we don't usually care what the Hebrew word *breshit* sounds like when we translate the word into English, and we don't care how it is spelled. We want to know what it means (a difficult task, as we saw in the last chapter), and we want to know how it contributes to the meaning of the sentence.

As we will see next, however, meaning is not the only part of translation, so sometimes the phonology will be important after all. And every so often we might even care about orthography.

TRANSLATION

On one hand, it's important to isolate the various aspects that comprise a language. We have no way to understand Hebrew, for example, if we don't understand its syntax.

On the other hand, fixating on any one part of a foreign language is one of the biggest traps in translation. In general, it's a mistake to mimic the syntax or morphology of a foreign language, just as it's a mistake to mimic the sounds.

In the book of Numbers, for example, King Balak asks the pagan soothsayer Balaam to curse the people of Israel. Balaam responds with three poetic blessings, the third of which begins with the Hebrew word *ma*. That word means "what." The next Hebrew word is *tovu*, and it means "were good." The rest of the line means "your tents, Jacob." The KJV translates, "How goodly are your tents, O Jacob . . ." The wrong translation is the literal "What good were your tents . . . ?" The translator has to know that the Hebrew word *ma* ("what") sometimes functions the same way "how" does in English, just as the translator has to know that the past tense in Hebrew poetry sometimes has the force of the present tense in English.

Unfortunately, translators are frequently tempted to mimic as much as possible. Usually, they can't blindly mimic the sounds. For example, in translating the Hebrew word *bara* ("created"), translators can't use the English word "bara" because there is no such word. So they don't mimic the sounds.

Sometimes it's just as hard to mimic the syntax. The part of Genesis 1:1 that reads *bara elohim* cannot become "created God" in English (". . . created God the sky and the earth"), because it doesn't make any sense. So even novice translators know they have to rearrange the words.

But even advanced translators blindly put "in the beginning," the translation of *breshit*, right at the beginning of the English translation, because that's where it occurs in the Hebrew. (We'll look at *breshit* a bit more later.)

The reasoning here is faulty (and usually subconscious). Just because English happens to allow both "in the beginning God created . . ." and "God created . . . in the beginning . . ." doesn't mean that the two word orders, even though they are identical, mean the same thing in the different languages. In other words, even though both word orders are possible, the syntaxes of the two languages are still different.

By comparison, we can look at the Modern Hebrew word *dog*. It's an animal in Hebrew. But it's not a dog. As we saw briefly in Chapter 2, it's a fish. No one is too deeply surprised by this coincidence. Hebrew and English have different vocabularies, and, surely, such happenstance similarities are to be expected. Similarly, again from Chapter 2, we know that the Hebrew word *kontzert* means "classical music concert." We expect things like that.

(Still, it's sometimes confusing. As we saw in Chapter 1, we get the phrase "jubilee year" only because the Hebrew *yovel* in its Latinized form, *iobileus*, sounds like the Latin *iubileus*, which means "jubilation." That mistake, though it involves longer words, is essentially no different than assuming that the Hebrew *dog* means "dog.")

In addition to coincidences like the Hebrew and English words for "concert" meaning almost the same things, we also expect happenstance similarities in other areas of language—in syntax, for example. In English, adjectives generally precede the nouns they modify. A block that is blue is a "blue block," not a "block blue." Hebrew works the other way around. The famous red heifer from Numbers 19:2 is, in Hebrew, "heifer red"—that is *para aduma*. *Para* means "heifer" (or, better, "cow"; a heifer is generally a cow that has not yet given birth, and there's no reason to think that the Hebrew word is similarly limited), and *aduma* means "red."

Translators all know that the literal "cow red" should become "red cow" in English, but they know it for the wrong reason. They know it because English doesn't allow the possibility of "cow red." There are a handful of situations in which English *does* allow the adjective to come after the noun. For example, "Chris is an expert in all things Greek." While it's not entirely easy to know how that sentence is different from "Chris is an expert in all Greek things," the two English sentences are different. And only one of them is the right translation of the equivalent sentence in Hebrew.

Unfortunately, most translators blindly jump at the chance to make the English superficially the same as the Hebrew, so they would choose "things Greek" for comparable Hebrew whenever they could, never stopping to realize that doing so is the same as blindly translating *dog* in Hebrew as "dog."

In other words, just because English has something that looks like the original Hebrew doesn't mean that superficially identical English works the same way as the Hebrew. Frequently it does not, as with *dog* that doesn't mean "dog," in spite of the similarity.

Another example, this time from Modern Hebrew and modern Russian, will further demonstrate the point. (It's convenient to use modern languages because it's easier to see if we are right about the exact nuances of the words. We can just ask people who speak the languages.)

Both Hebrew and Russian offer more flexibility in terms of word order than English does. For example, the simple English sentence,

"David saw Sarah yesterday," has only one grammatical permutation in English: "Yesterday David saw Sarah." By contrast, in both Hebrew and Russian, the words can be scrambled, so the equivalent of "Yesterday saw David Sarah" is grammatical in both languages. (The verb forms and other clues make it clear that David saw Sarah, but even without these clues the sentences would be grammatical, though they would also be confusing.)

Furthermore, Hebrew and Russian both have spoken and written dialects, and, as in English, the written language differs from the spoken one. The writing in *The New York Times* is different from the speech of the people who write the articles. The same is true in Russian. And the same is true in Hebrew.

One difference between the written and spoken dialects of Russian is that the spoken dialect allows for more word-order scrambling than the written dialect. Newspapers in Moscow frequently follow what we English speakers think of as "normal" word order. By contrast, casual Russian speech allows considerably more variation. So in most circumstances a newspaper would be unlikely to print the equivalent of "Yesterday saw David Sarah" (*vchera videl david saru*) to mean "Yesterday David saw Sarah," but it's a perfectly common way for Russians to speak. In other words, the word order in the Russian "Yesterday saw David Sarah" is a sign of colloquial, everyday speech. (The Russian word-order facts as a whole are actually much more complicated than what we see here.)

Modern Hebrew also has different sets of word-order possibilities in spoken and written dialects. However, in Hebrew, it's the *formal*, written dialect that allows for more variation. So the Hebrew equivalent of "Yesterday saw David Sarah" (*etmol ra'ah david et sarah*) is, in fact, the most reasonable way to write the sentence in a newspaper, while it's a fairly odd way to speak.

Here's the question: How should the Russian "Yesterday saw David Sarah" (*vchera videl david saru*) be translated into Hebrew? Should the translation simply copy the words, giving us *etmol ra'ah*

TABLE 1. TRANSLATION

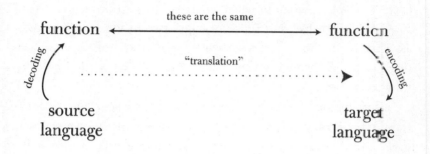

david et sarah? No. For that would be to take an informal, colloquial phrase and turn it into a formal one. Rather, the informal Russian deserves informal Hebrew. And in this case, the informal Hebrew has a different word order. (This distinction really refers to something called register, which we address in more detail later.)

The details are complex, but the point is not. Hebrew and Russian have different rules of syntax, so a syntactic construction in Russian doesn't mean the same thing that it does in Hebrew. This is exactly like the same set of sounds meaning one thing in Hebrew and meaning something else in Russian.

Obviously, the same principle applies to translating any language into any other, including ancient Hebrew into modern English. It is a mistake to simply mirror Hebrew in English.

Rather, the goal is to understand not just the vocabulary but also the grammar of the source language (Hebrew, in our case), and then try to do the same thing in the target language (English). The diagram in Table 1 depicts this process graphically.

A trivial example makes the chart clear. Hebrew has a word *dag*. We first decode its function, using the techniques in Chapter 2. We learn that the word is used to refer to swimmy things. Then we ask ourselves what performs the same function in English. And the answer is the word "fish."

Earlier, when we looked at the Hebrew *ma tovu* . . . , we contrasted the meaning of *ma* ("what") with its function ("how") to give us the correct "how good are your tents!"

Our Modern Hebrew/Russian example works the same way. We ask what the function is of a particular word order in Russian, learn that it's used for colloquial speech, and then ask how we do the same thing in Hebrew.

Blind mimicry involves skipping the most important steps of translation. Rarely, either because of luck or because languages often have common grammatical elements, the blind mimicry works well. That's one extreme on a spectrum of translation. At the other extreme, sometimes the blind mimicry works so poorly that even untrained translators realize they have to fix the situation. But most cases fall in the middle. The mimicry is just wrong enough that the translation misses something, but not wrong enough that untrained translators realize that the process has gone awry.

No one learning Hebrew is tempted to think that *bara* means "bara," because "bara" isn't an English word. That's a case of mimicry working really badly, at one extreme. At the other extreme, people who think that *amerika* means "America" are right. But it's the broad middle region that causes trouble. Most people learning Modern Hebrew wrongly think that *kontzert* means "concert," because that translation is close enough to seem reasonable.

And things get worse when it comes to grammar. Because there's a better chance that a grammatical construction in one language will at least make sense in another, there's a better chance of coming up with a translation that seems right but is actually wrong.

In addition to these sorts of issues about correctly understanding vocabulary and syntax, etc., there's a second, even less appreciated aspect to translation. Sometimes what one language does with syntax is accomplished not with syntax but with another part of another language. The same goes for morphology and vocabulary.

We've already seen one example of this. Hebrew has a word (vocabulary) to indicate direct quotation: *leimor*. As we saw on page 37, that word is usually blindly translated into "saying," even though in English we don't use a separate word to indicate direct quotation. We use punctuation. (In colloquial speech, we also sometimes use vocabulary, but in a very different way. We have a verb that means, "said, and I quote. . . ." The verb is "goes." It's slang, but when people use it, they use it only for direct quotation. Of the two sentences, "Chris said, 'Hello'" and "Chris said he was doing fine," only in the first can "said" become "goes": "[So I see Chris and] Chris goes, 'Hello. . . .'")

Another example comes from questions, which in English are formed through syntax—specifically, by putting a verb before the subject. So the question form of "Moses parted the Red Sea" is "Did Moses part the Red Sea?" The verb "did" gets put before the subject "Moses," and "parted" becomes "part" so that together with "did" it can form "did part." In Hebrew, by contrast, questions are formed through vocabulary. There's a prefix, *ha-*, that introduces a question. It goes at the beginning of a sentence.

When God asks Cain what happened to his brother, Cain's answer is, "Am I my brother's keeper?" In English, we change the order of the words in "I am my brother's keeper" to make it a question. Or, to think of it another way, the different word order marks the sentence as a question. Syntax is what differentiates a question from a statement in English. In Hebrew, the difference between "I am my brother's keeper" (*shomer achi anochi*) and "Am I my brother's keeper?" (*hashomer achi anochi*) has nothing to do with word order. Rather, the prefixed word *ha-* indicates that the sentence is a question. Where English uses syntax, Hebrew uses morphology.

This is but one example of the sort of cross-language mismatch that is typical of translation. So when we use Table 1, we have to remember that sometimes the function of one part of Hebrew is expressed through another part of English.

One particular way of merely mimicking Hebrew grammar rather than translating it is especially common. Translators have commonly but wrongly assumed that parts of speech have to be preserved in translation, so verbs stay verbs, nouns stay nouns, etc. But there's no reason to think that this is so.

We can demonstrate this important fact just by looking at English, because frequently in English, as in all languages, we see various ways of expressing the same thing or almost the same thing, but the different ways involve different parts of speech. For example, "Chris is the boss," "Chris is in charge," and "Chris runs the company" all mean almost the same thing, but the first sentence uses a noun ("the boss"), the second a prepositional phrase ("in charge"), and the third a verb ("runs"). Certainly there are subtle differences among these three sentences, but the differences do not stem from the differences in parts of speech.

Modern French further demonstrates the point. In English, a verb like "swim" can be modified by the phrase "across the river" to create what seems like a simple English sentence: "Chris swam across the river." But a quirk of French grammar prevents the combination of "swim" (*nager*) and "across the river" (*à travers la rivière*). The only way to express the same simple idea in French is to use the verb "cross," so the French sentence is, "Chris crossed the river by swimming" *(Chris a traversé la rivière à la nage).* In other words, the English verb ("swim") and the French prepositional phrase ("by swimming") function identically. The English prepositional phrase ("across the river") matches the French verb and object ("crossed the river"). It would simply be a mistake to translate the basic French sentence as "Chris crossed the river by swimming." But this is exactly the sort of mistake that plagues most Bible translations.

All of this confusion is what led the translators of the KJV to italicize words that, in their (wrong) opinion, were added in the English even though they were not in the Hebrew. In Genesis 1:4, one example out of literally thousands, the KJV reads, "And God saw the light, that *it was* good." The point of the italics is to make it clear that the Hebrew doesn't have words for "it" and "was," that the words of the Hebrew literally mean (in this order): "Saw God *et* the-light that-good." (The Hebrew *et* marks "the light" as an object of the verb "saw." The word *et* in Hebrew is generally used before definite nouns when they are objects of verbs. Definite nouns that are not names get the word "the" in English. "The light" is definite, so as an object it gets *et* in Hebrew. The indefinite object "light" would not.

In addition to the unfortunate fact that the KJV's authors are wildly inconsistent regarding the "missing" italicized words, they missed the point of translation in this regard. Different languages use different words to convey the same thing, and, except for people who are trying to learn Hebrew, the details of Hebrew grammar should be hidden from the English reader, not italicized. (This is why in this book we generally do not mimic the italicization of words when we quote the KJV.)

In this regard, we can consider two examples. Genesis 1:3 reads, in Hebrew, "Said God will-be light and-was light."

Linguists know that there are two kinds of languages. One kind, like English, almost always requires a subject. When the subject is the one doing the verb, as in "God said," every language includes a subject. But the question arises of what happens when no one or nothing in particular is the one doing the verb. The answer is that, in languages such as English that require a subject, a **pleonastic** subject serves as the subject of the sentence. In English, the pleonastic subject is usually the word "it" or "there."

The clearest example in English is "It is raining." The "it" is not "raining." Rather, the pleonastic "it" is included in English only because English always requires a subject. Similarly, we see a pleonastic "there" in "There is no reason to panic."

French, which behaves like English, similarly requires a subject even when the subject isn't doing the verb. "It's raining" in French is *il pleut. Il*—a pleonastic subject here—means "it" (or "he"), and *pleut* means "rains."

Other languages do not require a subject. Spanish is such a language. Accordingly, the Spanish equivalent of "It's raining" or *il pleut* is the one word *llueve*—literally, "rains."

How should *llueve* be translated into English? Obviously, the only reasonable answer is "It's raining." Italicizing the "it's," or marking in some other way the difference between English and Spanish grammar, would do only that: mark a difference in grammar. It would not make the translation more accurate or in any other way better.

Hebrew is a language like Spanish. It does not require a subject. That's why "There will-be light" in Hebrew (*y'hi or*) doesn't have a word for "there" and literally ends up "will-be light." We will ignore two other aspects of Hebrew grammar—they explain why "there will be" can mean "let there be" and why "will be" is only one word—and focus on the missing "there." Its absence in Hebrew is purely a consequence of the details of Hebrew grammar. In fact, not having the word "there" in Hebrew is exactly the same as having the word "there" in English. They both have the same force. In other words, the correct translation of a pleonastic subject in English is no subject in Hebrew, and vice versa.

The KJV gets this right and, perhaps surprisingly in light of Genesis 1:4, does not italicize anything in Genesis 1:3, offering as a translation the fairly accurate "And God said, Let there be light: and there was light."

Unfortunately, in the very next line, the word "it" is italicized: "And God saw the light, that *it was* good. . . ." Like "there" in the previous line, there is nothing unusual about "it" (or "was," for that matter). There is nothing missing in the Hebrew. There is nothing extra in the English. And italicizing "it" leaves the English reader with the mistaken impression that the "it" is somehow less a part of the original than other words.

From the point of view of studying Hebrew grammar, there might be some merit to that claim. The italicized "it" might remind students of Hebrew that Hebrew doesn't require pleonastic subjects, whereas

English does. But from the point of view of translation, it's simply a mistake. It leaves the English reader not with a better understanding of the original but with a misunderstanding of the original.

Similar but more complicated aspects of Hebrew grammar explain why we don't see a word that means "was" in Hebrew. And, again, similar reasoning shows us that it's a mistake to italicize the word in English.

As another way of looking at the same issue, English orthography requires apostrophes in certain places. Even though nouns and pronouns generally behave the same way—pronouns like "her" substitute for nouns like "Miriam"—possessive nouns require an apostrophe and *S* ('s), while possessive pronouns require an *-es* with no apostrophe. That's why "Miriam's" means "belonging to Miriam," but if we use a pronoun, the only correct way to spell the word is "hers," not "her's." Similarly, "its" means "belonging to it," while "it's" means only "it is."

Should a translation of English into Hebrew reflect this bit of arcane English orthography? Of course not. The only question is what the words mean, not which words have an apostrophe. That's another application of Table 1. If we were to start putting apostrophes in Hebrew (which doesn't use them for the possessive), we would be making the mistake of skipping directly from the source language to the target language, rather than translating.

Italicizing "missing" words is the same kind of mistake.

Most translations don't italicize missing words, but they do put them in square brackets. That's why this issue is so important. It doesn't apply just to the KJV and its typeface choices. It applies to any translation that tries to distinguish two kinds of words—those that are "really" in the Hebrew and those that . . . what? Aren't really there?

We should be clear. There are at least three times square brackets are used in translations, only one of which is a mistake. Some translations, doing roughly the same thing as the KJV, bracket English words that do not literally appear in the Hebrew. That's the (widespread) mistake.

In addition, square brackets are sometimes used for addtional information that the English reader might need. For example, a translation of Genesis 6:14–15 might read, "Make an ark . . . 300 cubits [about 450 feet] in length. . . ." Most English readers don't know what a cubit is. The translation offers an explanation, but to make it clear that the explanation is precisely that—an explanation—and not part of the translation, the explanation is set off by square brackets.

The third usage, really a subcase of the second, involves quotations. Genesis 6:15 reads, "This is how you shall make it . . ." Make what? A citation of Genesis 6:15 might read either, "This is how you shall make it [the ark] . . ." or just "This is how you shall make [the ark]."

There's some question as to when these second and third kinds of square brackets should be used, but they do have a place. The first kind, parallel to the italics in the KJV, does not.

All of this follows naturally from Table 1. and from an understanding of what translation is (and is not).

Language is perhaps the most complicated human creation, and its parts serve to inform, entertain, arouse, rally, etc. Now that we know how important function is in translating the Bible, we should learn a little bit more about how language functions.

LEVELS

It will be helpful to consider five possible levels of translation, in order of increasing accuracy:

Sounds	What are the sounds of the original?
Words	What do the original words mean?
Phrases	What do the original phrases mean?
Concepts	What concepts are involved in the original?
Affect	What does the original do?

Frequently, English translations differ from one another because they focus on different levels of translation. (They also differ in other ways, including the accuracy of the translation.) In addition to providing insight into the task of translation, understanding the levels and knowing which published translations try to do what makes it easier to uncover the original text. The Appendix offers lots of information about the various published translations, so we won't repeat that here. Rather, we'll jump right into the levels.

To demonstrate, we'll look at Song of Songs 1:1, the Hebrew for which consists of four written words: *shir hashirim asher lishlomo*. How do we translate that into English?

Sounds

At the most basic level, one might want to translate the sounds of one language into another. We'll see why in a minute, but first let's see what translating sounds entails.

In keeping with our general notion of translating, translating sounds means figuring out the function of the sounds of one language, and then finding sounds in the new one that do the same thing. Linguists and cognitive scientists agree that, by and large, sounds don't have any inherent function, so usually there's nothing to translate.

Returning to our earlier example, the three sounds of the Hebrew *dog*—"d," "o," and "g"—don't mean anything by themselves. And the sounds together mean something only as a word, not as sounds. So a translation of *dog* as "fish" is translating the word, not the sounds, and rendering *dog* as "dog" isn't translating at all. It's mimicking.

On the other hand, when words rhyme, the sounds absolutely play a role beyond their contribution to the meaning of the words. "A stitch in time saves nine," for example, has a nice ring to it precisely because of the (near) rhyme. The saying has a more powerful impact than the otherwise more reasonable "A stitch in time saves ten." Normally we use either round numbers or symbolic numbers in sayings. "Nine" is neither. And the saying certainly has more impact than the bland "Doing things in time saves more work later."

Would a translation of this line into Hebrew have to almost rhyme? Could it rhyme perfectly? Does it not matter?

To make matters more complicated, it turns out that what counts as rhyming differs from language to language. In classical Hebrew poetry—long after the Bible, but still many hundreds of years old—two words rhyme only if their entire last syllables are identical. In English, "time" and "nine" (almost) rhyme. "Time" and "chime" do rhyme. That's because only the ends of two syllables have to be the same for two words to rhyme in English. In classical Hebrew poetry, "time" and "double-time" would rhyme, as would "muse" and "use" (from Shakespeare's Sonnet 78). But "time" and "chime" would not.

Most scholars agree that in antiquity poetry itself worked differently. (The evidence is unclear, largely because we don't know how ancient Hebrew sounded.) What if they are right and ancient Hebrew poetry consisted of clever word sounds but not rhyming? Should that typical-of-the-time nonrhyming Hebrew poetry be translated into typical-of-our-time poetry that does rhyme?

All of this brings us back to Song of Songs 1:1—in Hebrew, *shir hashirim asher lishlomo.* The KJV and NRSV both translate it as "The song of songs, which is Solomon's." The Hebrew line, though, contains significant sibilance ("s"-like sounds) and alliteration (repeating sounds). That creates a certain she-sells-seashells effect. If we are to translate the sounds, we have to find English that captures the same effect.

Words

Words are what people think of when they think of translation. Continuing with Song of Songs 1:1, a word-level translation takes each of the words and translates it. The first word, *shir*, means either "song" or "poem." The second word, *hashirim*, consists of the same word *shir* with the prefix *ha-* ("the") and the plural suffix *-im*. It means "the songs." The third word, *asher*, means "that" or "which." The last word, *lishlomo* consists of the prefix *l-* ("to") and the name *Shlomo*, "Solomon."

So "song the songs which to Solomon" is one word-level translation.

Another similar word-level translation adds in the English words that are "missing," in the sense we saw earlier, from the Hebrew.

Putting two words side by side is one way that Hebrew expresses possession or, more generally, "of." Cain's famous question, "Am I my brother's keeper," reads literally ". . . keeper my-brother. . . ." Because two adjacent words indicate possession in Hebrew, in English this becomes "keeper of my brother" or "my brother's keeper."

Additionally, when two such words are juxtaposed, the word "the" gets put on the second, not the first, word. So "song the-songs" is how Hebrew expresses "the song of songs." The word-by-word pattern gives us "of," and we have to move the word "the" to make it English.

So that gives us "the song of songs."

Accordingly, another word-level translation offers, "the song of songs which is to Solomon."

Phrases

But we're not done translating, because words join together to form phrases and express ideas. Again, Song of Songs demonstrates, because "to Solomon" might mean "Solomon's." If so, a phrase-level translation would be "Solomon's song of songs." (There are other possible meanings for "to Solomon," including "for Solomon.") What makes "Solomon's song of songs" a phrase-level translation is changing "to Solomon" into "Solomon's" and moving the word to the beginning of the sentence.

But, in fact, we still might not be done. The construction "*X* of *X*'s" that we see in "song of songs" seems to have been used widely in ancient Hebrew to express "best." It may have functioned like our English "song to beat all songs" or like the spoken English "*the* song" (as in, "that's not just *a* song; it's *the* song"). If so, the English "song of songs" misses the point completely, and—depending on the nuances of the expression in Hebrew—it should be "the best song," "the song to beat all songs," or even just "The Song."

A similar example from Modern Hebrew will be helpful. Languages generally have three levels, technically known as **degrees,** of adjectives. The first is simply descriptive, as in the English "good": "Indian food is good," for example. The second (**comparative**) compares two things, as in the English "better": "Indian food is better than Thai food." The third (**superlative**) compares one thing to more than one other, as in the English "best": "Indian food is the best food." (Readers who disagree with the judgments will hopefully still be able to follow the logic.)

In English, as it happens, we have two ways of expressing the comparative and the superlative. Sometimes we have special words, either "good/better/best" or more regular words like "dull/duller/dullest," and other times we use phrases that involve "more" and "most." So even though "dull" and "boring" mean the same thing in some contexts, parallel to "duller" and "dullest" we have not "boringer" and "boringest" but rather "more boring" and "most boring." (Readers interested in why should consult the Appendix for further reading.)

Modern Hebrew has words like "more" and "most," but it doesn't have the first pattern, in which words change to form the comparative and superlative degrees. More importantly, though, the words for "more" and "most" in Hebrew are often optional. One way of saying "Indian food is better than Thai food" in Hebrew is, literally, "Indian food is good than Thai food." Similarly, the same word "good" works for the superlative "Indian food is the good food there is." Other parts of Hebrew grammar that are too complicated to address here substitute for "more" and "most."

A word-level translation of a Modern Hebrew sentence might be "Indian food is the good food," while a phrase-level one might be "Indian food is the best food." Unfortunately, both translations are grammatical in English, and in most situations when the second one is true so is the first. Taken together, these facts conspire to make the wrong translation sound plausible. It's grammatical. It even seems to mean almost the right thing. It does sound a little odd, but people who don't speak Hebrew may think the Hebrew itself is odd. But the translation is wrong.

We see that pattern a lot with word-level translations of the Bible: They are almost right even though they sound a little odd. But they are wrong. That's why we need phrase-level translations like "Solomon's Song of Songs" to start off the book of Song of Songs.

Genesis 1:1 (*breshit bara elohim*) gives us a more difficult challenge. While the word-level translation is fairly straightforward, the phrase-level one is not.

As we saw earlier, the verb in Hebrew normally comes before the subject, as it does here. Putting something even before the verb in ancient Hebrew has the force of emphasizing it or contrasting it with something else, in a process known as contrastive emphasis. In English, we don't have the exact equivalent of the Hebrew pattern that puts something before a verb to emphasize it, but we have something pretty close. The phrase "it was X that . . ." is nearly equivalent. Accordingly, one fairly accurate phrase-level translation of the first line of the Bible begins, "It was in the beginning that God created . . ."

The point is that Genesis 1:1 answers the question "When?" not "What?" We know that from the order of the words in Hebrew. A phrase-level English translation should reflect that nuance.

Even though we don't have a perfect way of indicating this sort of contrastive emphasis in written English, we can do it in speaking, by changing our tone of voice.

For example, we might imagine a man on trial for robbing banks. He's already admitted to robbing First National. When the thief is on the stand, his lawyer asks him, "What bank did you rob in February." The man has two answers, a safe answer and a dangerous one. The safe answer is simply, "I robbed First National in February," or, with neutral intonation, "In February I robbed First National." The thief is simply answering the question. However, in a more dangerous answer, the thief emphasizes the phrase "in February": *"In February* I robbed First National." The most reasonable way to understand this in English is that the man robbed another bank in another month. At the very least, emphasizing "in February" raises the possibility of other months, with which "in February" contrasts.

(This is why airlinese sounds the way it does. Flight attendants tend to emphasize exactly the words that normal speakers do not. For example: "We *have* arrived at the Atlanta airport. . . ." Most speakers naturally emphasize "arrived" in that sentence. But the emphasis on "arrived" naturally raises other possibilities in the minds of those who hear the sentence. "Crashed," for example, is one possibility the airlines would rather passengers not think about. By emphasizing "have," the flight attendants only raise the possibility of "have not [arrived]," which, by comparison, isn't so bad.)

By way of another example, we return to our observation that parts of speech need not be preserved in translation. We've already seen that the pattern noun-noun in Hebrew can represent possession, or, more generally, "of," as in "song the-songs," which means "the song of songs." The same Hebrew construction has another, related meaning, by which the second noun describes the first. In other words, the second noun acts roughly as an adjective.

It may not seem like these two meanings are related, but they are. This is why English has a similar construction using "of" in which the second noun describes the first. "Bricks of gold" are almost exactly the same as "gold bricks," though in English the construction is limited to certain words and kinds of description—"bricks of heaviness" doesn't work, for example.

Hebrew allows this construction more broadly. And when it does—as with the more basic meaning—the second word gets prefixes and suffixes that we might expect to see on the first one. So just as Hebrew grammar requires "song the-songs" to mean "the song of songs," so too "his song of songs" would become "song songs-his in Hebrew."

Psalm 47:8 (*malach elohim al goyim, elohim yashav al kisei kodsho*), numbered 47:9 in Jewish tradition, demonstrates why this is important. The second half of the verse reads, literally (a word-level translation), "God sits on throne his holiness." The KJV pretty much stops there, adding only enough words to make the sentence sound grammatical: "God sits on the throne of his holiness." But that's wrong.

It's wrong because it's not the holiness that's "his" but, rather, the throne. And it's wrong for another reason. The KJV translation doesn't reflect the fact that the noun-noun pattern in Hebrew here has adjectival force. The phrase-level translation is, "God sits on his holy throne." (The question of "throne" versus "chair" brings us back to Chapter 2 and the beginning of this chapter. The Hebrew word that we see here, *kisei*, can probably mean either one. Because the first half of the verse reads "God reigns," setting up an image of royalty, we assume that even if the Hebrew word is more general, here it means "throne.")

Once again, the word-level translation gets things roughly right but ultimately still wrong. The phrase-level translation helps. But, as with words, phrases go only so far. Just as words combine to create phrases, the phrases combine to create concepts, as we see next.

Concepts

Eugène Ionesco remarked that "the French for 'London' is *Paris*." His point was roughly that "Paris" plays the same role in the lives of French speakers in France that "London" does for English speakers in England. If so, should "London" be the English translation of *Paris*? The answer, of course, is no, but only because Ionesco's remark was an exaggeration (though he had a very real point to make).

English speakers know what "London" is and what "Paris" is, and they know that the two are not the same. But another example is trickier. There were no candles in antiquity, not until the melting wax that forms modern candles was invented. Instead, people used oil lamps for small sources of light.

So how are we to translate the Hebrew word *ner*? It appears to be an oil lamp or a lantern. The word-level translation suggests that if *ner* means "oil lamp," then the only possible translation is "oil lamp." But here's the problem. When the original text uses *ner*, the point is something readily at hand, a common object used by default to light up dark spaces (among other purposes). That's why, in Zephaniah 1:12, translations for *ner* are "candle," "lamp," or "lantern": ". . . I will search Jerusalem with candles" (KJV), "I will search Jerusalem with lamps" (NRSV), or "I will search with lanterns in Jerusalem's darkest corners" (NLT).

At a word level all of these translations are wrong. A "lamp" in English is almost always an electric lamp, not an oil lamp. (A decorator who is supposed to "just get any lamp that fits the decor" is not supposed to return with an oil lamp.) Modern lanterns are not of the same technology as ancient ones. And they didn't have candles in antiquity. But on a concept level, all three translations are better than "oil lamp."

Another example from modernity comes from the different dining habits in America and Argentina. In America, "dinnertime" is generally between 5:00 P.M. and 8:00 P.M. A late dinner might be 9:00 P.M. In Argentina, 9:00 P.M. is an early dinner, and families regularly bring their school-aged children to restaurants at 10:00 P.M. on school nights. How would we translate the Argentine Spanish equivalent of "He wandered around the city at dinnertime" into American English?

Is "dinnertime" the right translation? At a word level, yes. What else could it be? But at a concept level, the answer might be no. It depends on the point of the sentence. If the point is that it's summer but it's been dark for a while because it's dinnertime, then "dinnertime" doesn't work in English. If the point is that it's time to eat dinner, then maybe it does.

The Biblical story of Esther takes place in Shushan "the *bira*," from which Ahasuerus reigned over 127 *m'dina*s. The KJV renders *bira* as "palace," even though it uses the same English word for the Hebrew *bitan*. Other translations offer "citadel" or "fortress," even though, clearly, Shushan is a city.

One might think that, like "New York" and "New York City," perhaps Shushan refers both to the palace and to the city in which the palace is located, and that the word *bira* serves to make it clear that it's the palace, not the city. But we read in Esther 9:12 that the king laments to his wife Esther: "The Jews have slain and destroyed five hundred men in Shushan the *bira*, and the ten sons of Haman; what have they done in the rest of the king's *m'dinas*?" (KJV). So we know not only that Shushan the *bira* is a city but also that the *m'dinas* are the same sort of thing as Shushan.

The point was that Shushan was the seat of power, a *m'dina* from which the king ruled over other *m'dinas*. We almost have a word for that in English: "capital." Even though capital cities didn't exist yet, so *bira* couldn't have literally meant "capital," the translation "capital" gives the American reader a good idea of what Shushan was.

We'll have much more to say about concepts in Chapter 5, where we look at the very important Biblical concepts of "king" and "shepherd." But as a final example for now, and as a bridge to affect-level translations, we ask how "kilometers" should be translated into English. Almost everyone agrees that the translator should convert metric units into something the American reader will understand. So a Modern Hebrew sentence that reads "The speed limit in Israel is 120 kilometers per hour" should be translated into miles per hour: "The speed limit in Israel is 75 miles per hour."

But it's not as simple as that.

Affect

"The store is about 6.2137 miles away."

Is that a reasonable modern English translation of the Modern Hebrew sentence that literally means "The store is about ten kilometers away"?

The issue is twofold.

As we just saw, American readers usually don't know what kilometers are, which is to say they know that kilometers are a measure of distance, but they don't have a sense of how much distance a kilometer represents. Almost every translation of modern English into Modern Hebrew, in which the situation is even more pronounced, converts miles into kilometers. Usually, translations from Modern Hebrew into English convert kilometers into miles.

It turns out that one kilometer is about 3,281 feet, or roughly 6/10 of a mile. Ten kilometers is 6.213712 miles. The word- and concept-level translations therefore suggest, "The store is about 6.2137 miles away." The problem is that the phrase "about 6.2137 miles" is absurd. The figure 6.2137 is not "about" anything, but rather "exactly" something.

As a second possibility, we might suggest, "The store is about six miles away," rounding 6.2137 down to six. But ten is a nice round number, while six is not. Maybe "The store is about five miles away" is better.

As a third possibility, we have to wonder if the hypothetical store is just "far away." Perhaps the person describing the distance to the store is a child who doesn't drive and just likes the round number ten. If so, would the translation be, "The store is about ten miles away"? The phrase "thousands of years" has little to do with "one thousand." For that matter, "one hundred fortnights" is different from "four years" or (more accurately) "3.83 years."

The fundamental issue is that accuracy isn't the only criterion of successful translation, because language does more than convey information.

We can make the store situation just a little more contrived and demonstrate this fundamental fact even more convincingly with the following hypothetical Hebrew sentence: "Ten people went to ten stores at least ten kilometers away." Surely the point is "ten . . . ten . . . ten," and a translation shouldn't destroy the pattern.

Let us consider yet another possibility. What if the "cleverness" of having used "ten kilometers" doesn't come from within the sentence but rather from the culture? For example, suppose we have an American English story about a patriot who, in a demonstration of his love for his country, walks 1,776 miles by foot. How should that be translated into Modern Hebrew? Americans reading the story immediately recognize the figure "1776." Should the Hebrew translation have a number that, like the English, is immediately recognizable?

We run into this exact problem with numbers in the Bible, which generally refer back to the Babylonian system of base-60 mathematics. The Babylonians couldn't multiply large numbers—something like 671 times 419 was considered a math problem of immense difficulty, as was, even, 67 times 41. (Readers who don't understand why might remember that zero hadn't been invented yet and might try their hand at multiplication using a pencil, paper, and Roman numerals: XLI times LXVII, for example, or even DCLXXI times CDXIX. Good luck.)

But the Babylonians could multiply small integers. Accordingly, in addition to multiples of ten, "round numbers" in antiquity were products of small numbers. Two times three, three times four, etc. That's why there were originally six days in a workweek (two times three), twelve hours in a day and twelve hours in a night (three times four), sixty seconds in a minute and sixty minutes in an hour (three times four times five), and so forth.

How then should the description of Noah's ark in Genesis 6:15 be translated? The Hebrew tells us that the dimensions are "300 *ama*s long by 50 *ama*s wide by 30 *ama*s high." The KJV version, not surprisingly, keeps the numbers and translates *ama* as "cubit." By that translation, however, a matter-of-fact statement about the ark has become esoteric. (The English "cubit" comes from the Latin word *cubitus,* "elbow," and one cubit is the length from the king's elbow to the end of his middle finger. So "cubit"—that is, "elbow"—was just like "foot.")

The U.S. version of the New International Version converts the figures into feet: "The ark is to be 450 feet long, 75 feet wide, and 45 feet high." That's much more useful for an American reader, but what about the figures? Did they have some particular significance that they no longer do?

We have the same problem when talking about years. Genesis 5:8 tells us that Seth lived to be 912 years old. Notice the "12" at the end. That was a round number in antiquity. Whether Seth was really that age or not, readers of ancient Hebrew would see such a number as a round number, while we do not. Genesis 14:4 talks about "twelve years" of service. Should the translation make it "ten"?

An even clearer case for translating round numbers (according to antiquity) into round numbers (according to modernity) comes from Genesis 17:20. There the second part of Ishmael's blessing consists of two parallel parts: "twelve princes shall he beget, and I will make him a great nation." Clearly, having "twelve princes" is poetically akin to becoming a great nation. Any ancient reader of Hebrew—regardless of their view of the literal truth of the story itself—would know the "twelve" here isn't meant to be taken literally. Twelve was a round number, similar to the "thousand" in "I've told you a thousand times."

When we translate Modern Hebrew into modern English, sometimes we have to make sure that the number "ten" in the original stays "ten" in the translation, because, in both languages and cultures, ten is a round number. But in ancient Hebrew, "twelve" was also a round number, with perhaps more significance than "ten." If we follow the same principle, we might be forced to translate "twelve princes" as "ten princes."

This translation is where most people stop feeling comfortable. After all, the text clearly says twelve, doesn't it? Actually, it obviously does not. The text clearly says *shneim-asar*. What we do with that ancient Hebrew is up to us.

We started this chapter with the quite clear observation that "out of sight [out of mind]" doesn't mean "blind," even though, literally, "out of sight" sounds like it ought to mean "blind." Everyone agrees that taking an expression like "out of sight, out of mind" and turning it into a statement about the blind and the stupid is a mistake. There is no justification for it. But that fact is clear only because we fully appreciate the significance of the English, being English speakers ourselves.

An understanding of ancient Israelite culture makes it equally obvious that "twelve"—that is, *shneim-asar*—was a round number. Translating a round number into a non-round number is a mistake, particularly if, as here, the whole point was to choose a round number.

Fortunately, we have a third option in English. Rather than "twelve" we can translate *shneim-asar* as "dozen." Even though "twelve" and "dozen" both refer to the same amount of something (unless they are bagels, in which case a "dozen" is probably a "baker's dozen" and therefore "thirteen"), a "dozen" is a round number in a way that "twelve" is not.

In fact, the distinction in English between "twelve" and "dozen" demonstrates how a number can carry with it assumptions of exactitude or of approximation. Compare the two sentences, "I have a dozen reasons not to go out with you" and "I have twelve reasons not to go out with you." English-speaking Americans know that, in the first case, "dozen" is not meant literally. In fact, the statement is almost the same as "I have lots of reasons not to go out with you," and it leaves open the quite reasonable possibility that the speaker hasn't even given thought to the actual reasons. In the second case, "twelve" suggests that the speaker has actually made a list of reasons, and they happen to number exactly twelve.

Surprisingly, though, in other contexts "dozen" is precise. "Tell the waiter to set a dozen chairs" means exactly twelve chairs.

So at first glance, "twelve" and "dozen" mean the same thing. But upon closer examination, we find that they are used in different ways, and that very subtle clues let English speakers know what the words mean in context.

And this is an example of the underlying point of affect-level translation. Words do more than simply convey data.

In the case of Genesis 17:20, it turns out that we are lucky. We can translate the verse as ". . . a dozen princes . . . ," capturing the meaning of the text and the sense of the text. Even more than the particular solution, though, it's the nature of the problem and the issues involved that are important.

Poetry

The opening line of Song of Songs presents a challenge. We have already seen sound-, word-, phrase-, and concept-level translations.

Now we take into account the affect of the line, most importantly its alliterative and therefore poetic impact. As Mark Twain would say, it sounds well.

Each of the four words that form the title of Song of Songs has the sound "sh" in it: *SHir haSHirim aSHer liSHlomo*. We don't know for sure how the ancient words sounded, and, in particular, we don't know what the vowel sounds were. (Our current approximation comes from work done roughly one thousand years ago in Tiberias by a group of people called the Masoretes. It was the Masoretes that recorded the largely vocalic diacritic marks that supplement the mostly consonantal text of the Hebrew Bible. But the Masoretes lived well over a millennium after Song of Songs was written, and nearly that long after Hebrew had ceased to be a spoken language. So we expect that the Hebrew of the Bible sounded at least a little different than the way we currently understand it.)

This is important because it seems like the line has a certain poetic cadence in addition to the alliteration. In fact, with a minor emendation, the line demonstrates a catalectic form of dactylic tetrameter.

"Dactylic" means having a strong beat followed by two weak beats, as in the English word "poetry": PO-e-try. "Tetrameter" means having four sets to a line. Dactylic tetrameter, therefore, is four dactyls to a line: DUH-duh-duh, DUH-duh-duh, DUH-duh-duh, DUH-duh-duh. And "catalectic," from the Greek for "left off," refers to leaving off the weak beats at the end of a poetic line, in our case: DUH-duh-duh, DUH-duh-duh, DUH-duh-duh, DUH. (The reader may wish to memorize the phrase "catalectic dactylic tetrameter," as it may prove useful in resolving unpleasant situations at cocktail parties. Drop the observation, "That sounds like catalectic dactylic tetrameter," and an annoying interlocutor will almost certainly find someone else to bother.)

The Hebrew might have been read: *SHIR ha-shi-RI-im a-SHER li-shlo-MO*, with capital letters representing strong beats, either through emphasis (as is common in modern poetry) or length (as may have been common in antiquity). Or perhaps we have understood the pronunciation exactly, which would make the meter an even more complex tetrameter.

Whatever the case, Song of Songs seems, appropriately enough, to start with alliterative metrical poetry. In other words, like all poetry, the point is not just to convey information but to sound well. The function of the words, in this case, is to form poetry.

So we need to find a way of doing the same thing in English. Returning once again to Table 1, we have found the function of the Hebrew, and now we need to find English that achieves the same function.

But what counts as "the same function" here isn't clear. Does the English poetry need to be the same kind of poetry as the original Hebrew? Do we need catalectic dactylic tetrameter? Would another kind of tetrameter be good enough? Another dactylic form? Is the catalectic ending important?

Or is any poetry good enough? To judge by Greek and Roman works—Homer's lyric epic poems, for example—dactylic poetry was common in the ancient world, but the most widespread form was dactylic hexameter, that is, six dactylic units to a line, not four. If Song of Songs begins with an unusual amount of a familiar kind of foot, perhaps so too should our translation. Iambic pentameter (five beats of weak-STRONG, like Shakespeare's "this A-bove ALL to THINE own SELF be TRUE") is common in English. Perhaps, therefore, Song of Songs in English should begin with iambic tetrameter or even iambic trimeter, so that it, like the Hebrew opening, will be shorter than the common form of poetry.

Rhyming may have been rare in ancient Hebrew poetry (but it's hard to know for sure, because we don't know how the Hebrew sounded). It's common now. Should we translate nonrhyming ancient poetry as nonrhyming modern poetry? Or should we translate common-style ancient poetry as common-style modern poetry (in which case, even if the poetry didn't rhyme in antiquity, it still should now)?

And what about the alliteration? How important is it to capture that?

Remember the KJV translation of Song of Songs 1:1: "The song of songs, which is Solomon's." We've seen many problems with that translation, and now we add another. It's not poetic. In particular, the word "which" breaks things up. The New International Version suggests "Solomon's Song of Songs," which captures more of the alliterative feel of the original Hebrew. The New Living Translation, correctly realizing that "song of songs" is a superlative in Hebrew but not in English, translates: "This is Solomon's song of songs, more wonderful than any other." It got the phrases but missed the poetry, and therefore the affect, entirely.

What about "the Song of Songs Sung by Solomon"? That captures the alliteration and, probably like the original, it has four beats, making it a tetrameter of some sort, nearly an iambic tetrameter. It means nearly the same thing. By substituting "sung" for the KJV "which is," we augment the poetry and alliterative affect. But we also lose a bit of the meaning. The original Hebrew is vague about the connection between the Song of Songs and Solomon himself. All we know from the text is that the Song is Solomon's. We don't know if he wrote it, liked it, sung it, commissioned it, compiled it, or something else. (Tradition, however, ascribes the authorship of the Song to Solomon.)

What about "the Supreme Song Sung by Solomon"? That translation fixes the mistake of rendering "song of songs" too literally, adhering to the words but missing the meaning of the phrase.

Even though the solution may be elusive, the point is clear by now: The opening line of Song of Songs is poetic. The translation should be, too.

More Poetry

Rhyming and meter don't seem to have been widespread in Biblical poetry. Rather, as we saw on page 39, poetry in the Bible seems often to have been built around parallel lines; "saying the same thing twice," we might call it.

By way of example we can return to Balaam and Balak from Numbers 24:5. We saw the first half of Balaam's third blessing earlier. Here it is again, along with the second half: "How fair are your tents, O Jacob, your encampments, O Israel!" (Numbers 24:5, NRSV). Translations vary widely in the way they render "fair" and "encampments," but regardless of the nuances of those two words, the verse demonstrates the most common form of Biblical poetry.

The line is poetic because of the parallel structure between "tents" and "encampments" and between "Jacob" and "Israel."

We see the same form in Isaiah 1:2: "Hear, O heavens, and listen, O earth." Here the poetic effect comes from a pair of near synonyms in parallel ("hear"/"listen") coupled with a pair of opposites ("heaven"/"earth").

This form of poetry is in fact so common that scholars are careful to distinguish two varieties of it: simple parallel structure, in which two ideas are repeated in the same order, and **chiasmus** (pronounced kye-AZ-mus), in which the order is reversed. (The term comes from the Greek letter *chi*, which looks like our English letter *X*. The crossing arms of the *X* represent the crossed structure of the poetry.)

Numbers 24:5 and Isaiah 1:2, which we just saw, demonstrate straight parallel structure. We see chiasmus in Psalm 1:1, literally: "Happy is the one who does not walk according to the advice of the wicked, nor on the path of sinners stand." "Stand" is like "walk," and "advice of the wicked" is like "path of sinners." Unlike straight parallel structure, in which the two parallel parts appear in the same order both times, in chiasmus, as we have here, the order is reversed. Symbolically, parallel structure is "AB/AB," while chiasmus is "AB/BA."

Psalm 2:1 also begins with chiasmus, literally: "Why assemble nations, and peoples plot in vain." Because, as we have seen, Hebrew allows for more word-order variation than English, the phrase "why assemble nations" means "why do the nations assemble." In the Hebrew, the word order "assemble nations/peoples plot" is chiasmus. "Assemble" is like "plot," and "nations" is like "peoples." Unfortunately, "why assemble nations" doesn't mean what we need it to in English, which is why the KJV translation destroys the chiasmus, translating instead, "Why do the heathen rage, and the people imagine a vain thing?"

Psalm 2:2 follows up with more chiasmus, also difficult to translate grammatically in English. From the KJV we have, "The kings of the earth set themselves, and the rulers take counsel together," but the Hebrew reads "set themselves . . . kings/rulers . . . take counsel."

Following up on two lines of chiasmus, Psalm 2:3 offers straight parallelism: "Let us break their bands asunder, and cast their cords away from us." So Psalm 2 uses chiasmus for what "they" do and straight parallelism for what "we" do. The whole thing is poetic, and different reference points get different kinds of common poetry.

These are just a few of the numerous examples of chiasmic and straight parallel structure in the Bible.

Chiasmus and parallel structure are rare in English poetry. We do find it sometimes in Shakespeare (as in Othello 3.3: ". . . who dotes, yet doubts; suspects, yet strongly loves"; "dotes" is like "strongly loves" and "doubts" is like "suspects"), but certainly the poetry of Shakespeare comes more from rhythm, rhyme, and lyric beauty. By contrast, much of the poetry of the Bible comes from parallelism and chiasmus.

We should be careful to distinguish chiasmus from antimetabole, in which the exact same words are repeated in inverse order. We see antimetabole in the English "I want what I have and I have what I want." A chiasmic version of that might be, "I want what I have and I possess what I desire." Occasionally we find antimetabole in the Bible, but it's not as common as chiasmus. Genesis 9:6 demonstrates: "Whoever shed the blood of man, by man shall his blood be shed." The order "shed . . . blood . . . man/man . . . blood . . . shed" is antimetabole. (And let's add "antimetabole" to "catalectic dactylic tetrameter" as we build our list of cocktail-party words.)

More than the order of the words, though, in the Bible it's the choice of synonyms, near synonyms, or other words that creates the poetic affect. How is "hear" like "listen" in Isaiah 1:2? How is "heaven" like "earth"? In Numbers 24:5, how are "tents" like "encampments"? ("Tents" and "encampments" are probably only approximately right. Translating the words is difficult for roughly the same reason that translating "tree," earlier, was difficult. People used to live in "tents" and "encampments," but they don't any more. "Houses" and "developments" might be closer to the right modern idea, but those words are wrong for other reasons.) How are "swords" like "spears" and "plowshares" like "pruninghooks" in Isaiah's famous prediction about the end of war (Isaiah 2:4): "And he shall judge among the nations and shall rebuke many people: and they shall beat their swords into plowshares, and their spears into pruninghooks: nation shall not lift up sword against nation, neither shall they learn war any more." How is "lifting up swords" the same as even merely "learning war"?

We have a dilemma. If poetry in the Bible generally involves parallel structure, and if poetry in modernity generally involves meter and rhyme, should the parallel structure be translated as rhyming poetry in English? That is, is the function of the parallel structure in Hebrew the same as the function of, say, rhyming in English?

The problem is compounded by the fact that frequently the Hebrew poetry specifically uses near synonyms, putting two poetic words in parallel. But sometimes we don't have two poetic words to translate the Hebrew. In addition, translators have frequently, and wrongly focused on the literal meaning of each of the words, rather than on the effect that they create together. What results in English is a combination of two words, one or both of which is odd and sounds out of context, while the Hebrew had two words that combine to create poetry.

We don't have much parallelism or chiasmus in English, but we do have word doublets, so we can get an idea of how the Hebrew would have sounded. For example, "no rhyme or reason" is catchy because of the alliteration. The line comes from Shakespeare's *Comedy of Errors*: "Was there ever any man thus beaten out of season/When in the why and the wherefore is neither rhyme nor reason?"

Compare that original Shakespearian line to what seems like a paraphrase: "Was there ever any man thus beaten out of season/When in the why and the wherefore is neither poetical validity nor rational coherence?" While that ridiculous paraphrase means the same thing as the original, it misses the whole point, namely that Shakespeare's version sounds well. But most Bible translations are as bad as that paraphrase.

Shakespeare's *As You Like It* uses the same expression in an even more clever context. Rosalind asks Orlando, "But are you so much in love as your rhymes speak?" Orlando's answer is a pun of sorts: "Neither rhyme nor reason can express how much." His answer cannot be accurately "translated" as "nothing can express how much," because the whole point is the dual use of the word "rhyme"—once literally, once in an expression.

When we translate poetic or clever Hebrew into mundane English, focusing on the minutiae of each word rather than on the effect, we similarly destroy the effect of the Hebrew.

For example, Psalm 2:5 in the KJV reads, "Then shall he speak unto them in his wrath, and vex them in his sore displeasure." The biggest problem is "sore displeasure." The Hebrew chiasmus has two words that refer to speaking and two words that refer to anger. We might prefer in English something like "speak"/"chastise" and "anger"/"ire": "He will speak to them in anger and in ire chastise them." It's not a very good translation, but it's still better than ". . . sore displeasure." At least "anger"/"ire" form a nice pair. One reason it's not a good translation is the oddity of chiasmus in English. This sample translation sounds stranger than "He will speak to them in anger and chastise them in ire." So our translation sounds odd while the original Hebrew does not.

Going back to Psalm 2:1–2, we might prefer something like, "What purpose have gathering nations and peoples grumbling?" or "What purpose have gathering nations and grumbling peoples?" Again, "gathering"/"grumbling" creates a nice pair in English to match the nice pair in Hebrew. And again, it's still not very good, but it's much better than "Why do the heathen rage, and the people imagine a vain thing?" which has no hint of the poetry or chiasmic parallelism of the original Hebrew.

A full treatment of the poetry of the Bible, and possible poetic renderings of it in English, is a book unto itself, and space considerations force us to stop our discussion here. The nature of the issues is clear, even if the details and solutions are not.

It turns out that the lessons we learned about poetry apply to all parts of the Bible, even the prose. That's because prose, like poetry, always has a certain style to it. We classify poetic styles according to "meter," "rhyme," "alliteration," "imagery," etc. Prose has imagery, too, and it can even have meter, rhyme, etc. There's such a thing as poetic prose and, therefore, nonpoetic prose.

A good translation conveys the style of the original, so it's important to understand one of the biggest ways language can differ and still say the same thing, a topic we turn to next.

Register

The difference between "I don't care for that food you're eating" and "Yuck!" is called **register**. More generally, "register" includes such things as familiarity, politeness, humor, sarcasm, and even poetry. So the difference between "yes, sir" and "you betcha" is likewise a matter of register. Curse words are commonplace in some registers and rare in others. As we saw earlier, newspapers can have their own register, as can other narrow contexts.

We also saw that Hebrew word order in newspapers is more flexible than it is in spoken Hebrew, and that Russian works the other way around. A more systematic way of looking at the situation is this: Both Hebrew and Russian have a newspaper register, and they both have a colloquial spoken register. By chance, one difference between the two

registers in each language is the degree of possible word-order variation, and, again by chance, different registers in each language allow
greater variation.

We also saw that in airlinese, also a register, different words are
emphasized than in other English registers. With airlinese, we also
found a reason behind the difference, but usually we are not so fortunate.

A few more examples of register from English will be helpful.

In formal settings, the past tense can be used for the present tense.
At the end of a meal, a tuxedoed waiter in a fancy restaurant might ask
a diner, "Did you want some more coffee, ma'am?" The wrong answer
is, "I did, but now it's too late." In restaurantese and, more generally,
in very formal registers, the past tense substitutes for the present
tense.

In slightly less formal registers, the conditional is used instead of
the present: "Would you like some coffee?" Again, the wrong answer
is, "If what? Would I like it if what?"

Other registers offer other ways of asking the same question: "Do
you want some coffee?" "Want some coffee?" "Coffee?" Or, between a
husband and wife, perhaps just a barely intelligible pre-morning-
caffeine grunt.

As a final example, we might consider sports. In certain situations
sportscasters use the future tense instead of the past. For example,
take the often-cited cliché of a baseball grudge match that comes
down to the bottom of the ninth inning with the team at bat down one
run: There are two outs, the bases are loaded, and the batter has two
strikes against him. It all comes down to one pitcher against one batter.
The sportscaster watches the pitcher throw a strike and then yells into
his microphone, "And that'll be stike three!"

"That will be"? Why not "that *was*"? It's a difference of register.

Different languages have different registers. Most languages have
different styles for casual and polite speech. Some have odd things like
special language for sports or music or whatnot.

In addition, the particular ways that register is expressed differ from language to language. Many languages, among them French and Spanish and German, have formal and informal pronouns for "you," with verb forms to match. Some have short words that indicate register. And others, as we have seen, have different word orders in different registers.

We know the drill by now. A good translation preserves register—the function of the language—and not necessarily the parts of the language that indicate the register. Funny things should stay funny in translation. Formality should stay formal. And, as we just saw, poetry should stay poetic.

Most translations do a fairly good job of noticing when the original Hebrew is poetic (even if their success in rendering the poetry is limited). Unfortunately, most translations do a terrible job in preserving other register distinctions.

Instead, they choose a register and force the entire text into that register. Proponents of the KJV frequently like it because it all sounds archaic (even though the Hebrew wasn't). Partially in response the New Living Translation was created. In the NLT, everything is chatty. In the NRSV and JPS translations, everything is (supposed to be) colloquial.

But the Bible contains a great many registers. The story-laden prose of Genesis is different than the legalistic prose of Leviticus or the narrative prose of Kings. And even within Genesis, the Joseph story is graced with particularly vivid writing.

Reading most Bible translations is like reading *The New York Times*, Shakespeare, and Beatles lyrics but destroying the differences among the three. When Shakespeare sounds like the daily news, something is wrong. When everything in the Bible sounds identical, the same thing is wrong.

And we know exactly what is wrong. We go back to Table 1 and remind ourselves that the point of translation is not to mimic the original but, rather, to translate it. Getting the words right and failing to

preserve register is no different than getting the sounds right and getting the words wrong. They are both mistakes.

An Example

Before we move on, a quick example is in order. Here's a passage from
Numbers 31, as it appears in the KJV:

"And the LORD spake unto Moses, saying, Avenge the children of
Israel of the Midianites: afterward shalt thou be gathered unto thy
people. And Moses spake unto the people, saying, Arm some of yourselves unto the war, and let them go against the Midianites, and
avenge the LORD of Midian. Of every tribe a thousand, throughout
all the tribes of Israel, shall ye send to the war. So there were delivered
out of the thousands of Israel, a thousand of every tribe, twelve thousand armed for war. And Moses sent them to the war, a thousand of
every tribe, them and Phinehas the son of Eleazar the priest, to the
war, with the holy instruments, and the trumpets to blow in his hand."

Here's the same passage in the usually easier-to-read NRSV:

"The LORD spoke to Moses, saying, 'Avenge the Israelites on the
Midianites; afterward you shall be gathered to your people.' So Moses
said to the people, 'Arm some of your number for the war, so that they
may go against Midian, to execute the LORD's vengeance on Midian.
You shall send a thousand from each of the tribes of Israel to the war.'
So out of the thousands of Israel, a thousand from each tribe were conscripted, twelve thousand armed for battle. Moses sent them to the
war, a thousand from each tribe, along with Phinehas son of Eleazar
the priest, with the vessels of the sanctuary and the trumpets for
sounding the alarm in his hand."

And this is what the passage should be:

"Adonai said to Moses, 'Avenge the people of Israel on the Midianites; then you will die.' And Moses said to the nation, 'Choose men and
form an army, and let them avenge God on Midian. Send one unit from
each and every tribe to the army.' So one unit from each tribe was
furnished from among Israel's units (twelve units of soldiers in all) and

Moses sent them (all twelve units) to war, them and Pinchas Son of Eleazar, the army priest, armed with holy instruments and loud trumpets."

By focusing too closely on the words, both the KJV and the NRSV miss the point of the passage, which is to describe the start of a war and to show how Moses changes God's command. (God tells Moses, "Avenge the people of Israel," while Moses tells the people, "Avenge God on Midian.") The text is not supposed to be flowery, obscure, archaic, or otherwise dense. It is supposed to convey a message, a message that is hidden by most translations.

TRANSLATION, AGAIN

In light of all this, we return to the question of what a good translation should be. And the answer is that in addition to being accurate, the ideal translation will work at every level—from sounds, through words, and up to concepts and effect. But because this is seldom possible, the translator must choose which levels should be given priority. Most people are of the mistaken opinion that the words should always be given priority, that as long as the words are translated correctly, everything else falls into place.

But this is not usually true. In fact, there are very few times when the words themselves are the most important part of a text, just as there are very few times when the sounds are the most important. While it's hard to understand the text as a whole without knowing what the words mean, just knowing the meaning of the words, as we have seen, is not nearly enough to understand the text.

More generally, a "literal" translation is almost always just a "bad" or "wrong" translation, inasmuch as it fails to give a reader of the translation an accurate understanding or appreciation of the original.

We have now seen how to use context to figure out what the ancient Hebrew words mean and what to look for when we render those words in English. Now it's time to turn to some more concrete and important examples. In Part II, we'll apply our knowledge to some of the most commonly quoted parts of the Bible, including Jesus' most important commandment, Psalm 23, the Ten Commandments, and finally Isaiah's prophecy of a "virgin birth."

We'll see that bad translations have radically misrepresented even these central themes.

❖PART TWO❖

Moving Forward

4

HEART AND SOUL:
WHAT MAKES US HUMAN

‹‹—››

וְאָהַבְתָּ אֵת יְהוָה אֱלֹהֶיךָ בְּכָל־לְבָבְךָ וּבְכָל־נַפְשְׁךָ וּבְכָל־מְאֹדֶךָ

And thou shalt love the LORD thy God with all thine heart, and with all

thy soul, and with all thy might.

καὶ ἀγαπήσεις κύριον τὸν θεόν σου ἐξ ὅλης τῆς καρδίας σου καὶ ἐξ ὅλης τῆς

ψυχῆς σου καὶ ἐξ ὅλης τῆς δυνάμεώς σου

The most important commandment, according to Jesus in Matthew 22:37, Mark 12:30, and Luke 10:27, is to "love the Lord your God with all your heart, all your soul, and all your mind" (NAB and, essentially, NRSV).

Jesus himself (using Greek) is quoting Deuteronomy 6:5 (which is in Hebrew), and that line is central to both Jews and Christians. Deuteronomy 6:5 is part of the text that Jews traditionally affix to their doorways, and, as we just saw, Jesus calls this the most important commandment.

The combination "heart and soul," or some variation of it, appears nearly forty times in the Bible, further emphasizing how important these two ideas were in antiquity. But here's the problem. The Hebrew words for "heart" and "soul," the words in Deuteronomy 6:5 that Jesus quotes, are *levav* and *nefesh*, respectively. And they are severely mistranslated. In fact, the translations miss the point entirely.

We will use the techniques of Chapter 2 to figure out what the Hebrew words really mean, and then the techniques of Chapter 3 to find a suitable translation that captures what the ancient text really tried to teach us. That is to say, we'll start by looking at the context in which the Hebrew words *levav* and *nefesh* were used. Then we'll look at the role they play—alone and together—and see if we have a way of doing the same thing in English. Along the way, we'll learn about how the authors of the Bible saw the human condition, and, perhaps surprisingly, we'll find that the original concepts mirror conversations and discussions that seem more at home in our third millennium A.D. than in the first millennium B.C., when they were first penned. Finally, we'll see how what we learn can be applied to other quotes.

"HEART"

We'll start with the Hebrew word *levav*, commonly mistranslated as "heart." Our task is twofold. We want to figure out how *levav* was used in ancient Hebrew (as in Chapter 2), and then figure out if we can do the same thing in English (Chapter 3).

To avoid prejudicing the issue, we'll use the original Hebrew *levav* in our discussions of the word, asking "What does *levav* mean?" in some particular place, rather than "Does the word 'heart' capture what *levav* means?" This way, we won't have to get bogged down in the various ways that "heart" is used in English—even though the topic will come up—and more importantly, this way we can try not to be blinded by the mistakes of previous translators.

Just to get started, we might look at Song of Songs 4:9, where the noun *levav* is used as a verb. Of course, we have no reason to think that verbs must mean the same thing as the nouns they are related to, but in this case it sets the stage nicely. We read, "You have *levav*ed me . . . my bride." (We'll deal with the missing text, most commonly mistranslated as "my sister," in Chapter 6.) What follows are images of beauty and romance: "beautiful," "better than wine," "love," references to lips and tongues, and so forth. There can be little doubt, in this context, that *levav*ed has something to do with love and romance.

As it happens, the English word "heart" is also associated with romance, at least sometimes. The common translation (KJV, NRSV, NAB, etc.) of "ravished my heart" takes advantage of this happy pairing between English and Hebrew. But we shouldn't jump the gun and try to find a translation yet. Our goal now is simply to figure out what *levav* means. And, at any rate, this verbal example is really just to get us started. Based on Song of Songs, it appears that *levav* has something to do with romantic love, but we don't know nearly enough yet.

So we look at more examples. Leviticus 19:17 is a great place to continue. We read, "Do not hate . . . in your *levav*." We know better than to ask, "What word represents *levav* here?" and instead ask, "What role does *levav* play?" Unlike some of the examples we'll see in just a moment, Leviticus is relatively clear here. The *levav* is where hatred lies. This meshes well with what we saw in Songs of Songs, where the *levav* was the locus of love.

We see a pattern developing. What love and hatred have in common is that they are both emotions. The *levav* seems to represent emotion.

But rather than jumping to Song of Songs, we could have started at the beginning of the Bible and worked forward. Had we done this, we would have first encountered Genesis 20:5, where it's not so clear what *levav* represents. In Genesis 20, Abraham misrepresents the nature of his relationship to his wife, Sarah, passing her off as his sister. Thinking Sarah is therefore available, King Abimelech nearly takes her for himself. Later, when he learns the truth, he pleads that he acted with a "*levav* of purity" or, perhaps, a "*levav* of integrity." We don't know for sure what this expression means—and, for now, we don't care, but we do care what kinds of things the *levav* can represent.

So we note that *levav* here has something to do with Abimelech's intention or his understanding, but probably not his emotions. Either he misunderstood the situation regarding Sarah, or, more likely, he had good/pure/righteous/etc. intentions. Either way, the fact is represented in Hebrew by the state of his *levav*.

So Genesis 20:5 isn't definitive, but it is our first warning sign that "heart" is the wrong translation for *levav*. While in English the heart might represent emotions, it doesn't extend to intentions. By contrast, it seems that *levav* does.

In Exodus we read about Pharaoh and his servants, who vacillate between wanting and not wanting to let the Hebrew slaves leave Egypt. In Exodus 14:5, after letting the slaves leave and after hearing that they have indeed left, Pharaoh and his servants find their *levav* changed. They no longer want to let the slaves go.

Again, as chance would have it, we have two convenient ways in English to represent what happens to Pharaoh and his servants in Egypt. Either "they changed their mind" or "they had a change of heart." In spite of the different words in English, both of these expressions mean the same thing, and both are ambiguous. Did Pharaoh feel differently? Or did he think differently? We don't know the answer from this context.

Deuteronomy 19:6 is more helpful. In the laws concerning manslaughter, murder, human retribution, and cities of refuge, our attention is turned to someone whose loved one has been killed. "While his *levav* is hot," we read, he might overtake and slay the original killer. Once again, it looks like *levav* represents emotion. We know that "hot" across the various languages of the world tends to represent the same sorts of things ("hot under the collar" in English, for example). "Hot emotion" is exactly what we might expect from someone whose family member has just been killed. So *levav* can represent love, anger, intention, and something from Genesis 20:5 that we haven't nailed down yet.

Deuteronomy 20 addresses the issue of who can and cannot go off to fight in war. After the interesting opt-out clause exempting from duty the owners of vineyards who have not yet harvested the grapes, the owners of houses who have not yet lived in them, and any fiancés who have not yet married, we find another category of people who are not sent off to war: people who are "weak of *levav*" or, perhaps, "soft of *levav*." These weak-*levav*ed people should be sent home, lest they "melt the *levav*" of their fellow soldiers. Almost certainly, the point is that cowards shouldn't go off to fight, lest they convince the other soldiers similarly to be afraid. Accounts of warfare in the book of Joshua (2:11, 5:1, 7:5, etc.) buttress the notion that a melting *levav* conveys fear of losing a battle. So we add "fear" (and probably "courage") to what *levav* represents.

Beginning in Deuteronomy 27, we find a litany of curses and blessings, punishment and reward, for behavior after Moses dies. Deuteronomy 30:1 tells the Israelites what to do in the future when the curses and blessings come about. They are to "return" to their *levav*. The idiom is confusing, because, just as the meaning of *levav* is complicated, so too is "return." The KJV translates "call them [the blessings and curses] to mind" here, suggesting "remember." We don't know the nuances, so we don't know if the KJV got it exactly right here, but it looks like memory, too, may lie in the Hebrew *levav*.

Deuteronomy 30:14 adds yet another aspect to our understanding of *levav*. Regarding God's teaching, the particularly poetic Chapter 30 in Deuteronomy promises something not beyond the seas, nor ensconced in heaven, but rather very near. "It is in your mouth and in your *levav*. You can do it." Ignoring the bit about the mouth for now, we ask what "in your heart" has to do with "doing it." Various possibilities present themselves, but the most likely is that "in your *levav*" means "you understand it."

If we approach the issue of *levav* with the (wrong) preconception that *levav* must mean "heart," it might be hard to appreciate Deuteronomy 30:14. Indeed, the KJV, even though it translates *levav* as "mind" in Deuteronomy 27, gives us "it is in your mouth and in your heart." But in this context, "in your heart" doesn't mean anything in English. And certainly it has nothing to do with being able to do anything. (People who read the Bible frequently, though, sometimes encounter nonsensical phrases like this often enough that the phrases start to sound like coherent English.)

Rather than wrongly assuming that *levav* means "heart," and then wrongly assuming that *levav* in Hebrew therefore represents the same constellation of concepts that "heart" does in English, we should now ask if we find support elsewhere for *levav* having something to do with understanding. We've already seen one place where it might (Genesis 20:5), and now (in Deuteronomy 30:14) we see another. Are there more?

In fact, there are many others. Ezekiel 38 is about Gog and Magog. Gog (a person) is the ruler of Magog (a place) and, according to the text, a threat to Israel. Ezekiel relates that the Lord commands him to prophesy against Gog of Magog. In verse 38:10, Ezekiel makes the connection between thoughts and the *levav* when he warns Gog that "things will arise in your *levav* and you will think evil thoughts." Similarly, Zechariah's plea to treat people nicely (Zechariah 7:10) includes: "Do not think evil . . . in your *levav*." The Chronicler in I Chronicles 29:18 reports that David begs God to uphold the "thoughts of the *levav* of" God's people. Ezra (Ezra 7:10) prepares his *levav* for study. Job (Job 9:4), in his moving response to Bildad, argues that God is "wise of *levav*." And Isaiah 6:10 is especially clear: ". . . lest they see with their eyes, hear with their ears, and understand with their *levav*." So, too, is Isaiah 10:7: "His *levav* does not think this way."

This expanded view also helps us understand a fairly common expression in the Bible: "to say in the heart." For example, Deuteronomy 7:17 deals with what happens if the people "say in their *levav*s" that other nations are too powerful. If the *levav* represents thoughts and not just emotions, the expression is clear: "To say in the heart" means "to think." The KJV missed that in Deuteronomy 7:17, but other translations tend toward "say to yourselves" instead of "say in your heart," at least getting the right general idea. We see the same expression, with the same basic meaning of "think," elsewhere as well.

So, clearly, the *levav* involves thoughts, understanding, and, in general, cogitation. In English we use the "mind," "head," and "brain" to represent that sort of thing: "a sharp mind," "a feeble mind," "comes to mind," "use your head," "brainy," etc. In ancient Hebrew, thinking took place in the *levav*.

As it happens, we have an expression "thinking with your heart" in English. It would be easy to make the inappropriate leap from he Hebrew phrase in which a *levav* thinks to the seemingly similar English one. But the English phrase has a particular meaning. "Thinking" with the heart isn't really thinking at all. It's responding with emotion to the exclusion of rationality. A schoolgirl in love, for example, who "thinks with her heart," is specifically not thinking rationally. She is reacting emotionally.

We have seen nothing in our Hebrew examples to suggest that the *levav* excludes rationality, and, in fact, these most recent examples suggest the opposite. The *levav* in Hebrew, unlike the "heart" in English, can specifically be the site of rational thinking and understanding.

But ancient Hebrew also used the *levav* for emotions, as we saw in Leviticus 19:17, Deuteronomy 19:6, and potentially Song of Songs. Other examples support this side of *levav*: Proverbs 6:25 connects romantic beauty and the *levav*. Isaiah 7:2—in the same sort of prose that used *levav* for thinking and understanding—notes David's profound sorrow at hearing that Ephraim has joined Syria in attacking Jerusalem. David suffers in his *levav*. Isaiah 21:4 connects the *levav* with fear or panic, as does Jeremiah 32:40.

So our final list of concepts associated with *levav* is this: love, hatred, fear, courage, intention, understanding, and thinking.

We noted above that modern American culture seems to separate rationality from emotion, putting one in the mind and one in the heart. The word *levav* shows us that the ancients saw the two as connected. Both emotion and rational thought were in the same place—namely, the *levav*.

The word "heart" is a terrible translation to convey this combination of concepts, because that English word specifically excludes half of what the ancient Hebrew word meant. But precisely because we tend to distance emotion from rational thought, we don't have a good modern English word to represent them both. "Psyche" might work—or, at least, be closer—but it is clearly the wrong register. The *levav* was a common part of how the ancients viewed their lives, while the same cannot be said for "psyche."

Furthermore, based on external evidence like how the Hebrew word was translated into other languages, it seems that the *levav*, in addition to everything else, was also an anatomical organ—or, at least, some physical part of the body. The point of *levav* was to pinpoint where thinking and emoting takes place in our bodies. Just as modern English puts the thoughts in the brain and the emotions in the heart, Hebrew put both in the *levav*. (In this regard, the Hebrews' culture was similar to the Greeks'. Aristotle thought that the heart was used to think and that the brain's purpose was merely to cool off the body. He was close. The brain does cool the body, but it does much more than that.)

In the end, we don't have a good English word for *levav*, at least not when *levav* is used by itself. But as chance would have it, English gives us a fine phrase to capture the combination of *levav* and *nefesh*. So we turn to that Hebrew word next.

"SOUL"

We first find the word *nefesh* in Genesis. As an example of how it's used, we consider Genesis 1:30: "[I have given green plants for food] to every beast of the earth, and to every bird of the sky, and to everything that creeps on the earth, and to everything that has the *nefesh* of life" (NRSV). It looks like every living being has a "*nefesh* of life," though the Hebrew grammar leaves open another possibility, too. Every living being may have a "living *nefesh*."

Unfortunately, many people already (wrongly) "know" that *nefesh* means "soul," so they jump to the conclusion that in Genesis 1:30 God puts a soul in every living being. It's a lovely thought. But there's no support for it in the text. Based on just Genesis 1:30, *nefesh* could mean "cell" or "blood" or "eye" or any of the other myriad things that walking, flying, and creeping creatures share.

Or it could mean "life force" or "destiny" or some other ethereal quality. Genesis 1:30 is so vague that it tells us little beyond the fact that *nefesh* seems to have something to do with life. And even that could be wrong—again, just based on Genesis 1:30—if the Hebrew means "living *nefesh*," because in that case there might be two kinds of *nefesh*, a living one and a nonliving one.

Fortunately, the situation will become much clearer, but Genesis 1:30 is an important reminder that we should not use a preconception of what a word could mean to prejudice our investigation of what a word really means. We want to look to each example for evidence of what the word *nefesh* means, not for confirmation of a wrong preconception of what we want it to mean.

Genesis 2:7 gives us a little more information. God breathes the breath of life into Adam, and Adam becomes a "living *nefesh*." Again, it seems that *nefesh* has something to do with life, because Adam didn't become a living *nefesh* until life was breathed into him. But we still don't know if "living *nefesh*" is poetically redundant or if there can be a "dead *nefesh*."

Genesis 2:19 uses the same phrase, "living *nefesh*," to mean the animals, buttressing the idea that *nefesh* has something to do with life—but we still have precious little information. So far—if animals have a soul—"soul" is one possible meaning for *nefesh*, but we have not seen anything specifically to point in that direction, and we have lots of other reasonable options.

Genesis 9:4 connects "flesh," "blood," and the *nefesh*, but, unfortunately, the Hebrew grammar is confusing. The KJV translates, "But flesh with the *nefesh* thereof, which is the blood thereof, shall ye not eat." (Ironically, because the Hebrew grammar is confusing, the confusing English grammar of the KJV is appropriate here.) The KJV translation implies that the *nefesh* is the blood. That's one possibility, another being that *nefesh* is connected to "flesh," and the "blood" represents the combination.

Genesis 9:15 continues in the vein we just saw, using "living *nefesh*" for any live animal, including humans.

English has a deficiency that Hebrew may not have had. In English, it's hard to group animals and people together while still not denying that people are animals. Most of us in the modern world consider people part of the animal kingdom but are yet somewhat uncomfortable specifically calling people "animals," except to stress some particular animalistic behavior. Statements such as "People have a lot in common with animals" coexist with "People are a kind of animal, too." Carl Sagan's observation from Chapter 2 (page 16) about women and pain in childbirth is difficult even to express in English, because phrases like "women, more than any other female animal . . ." grate at the ear of the modern English speaker. Perhaps "living *nefesh*" was a way around this, a way specifically to include people and animals in one neat category. It would be a convenient thing for a language to have, but this interpretation of "living *nefesh*" is little more than speculation. And regardless, we don't want to get bogged down by one phrase that happens to contain *nefesh*.

Genesis 14 relates the battle of the four kings against the five, an ongoing altercation that takes place near Sodom and Gomorrah over the course of two decades. Abram (Abraham's name until God changes it in Genesis 17:5) gets involved after his nephew Lot, who had settled in Sodom, is captured. And after Abram successfully rescues Lot, capturing other people and things taken from Sodom along the way, the king of Sodom offers a deal to Abram. In Genesis 14:21, the king says, "Give me the *nefesh*es, and you take the property." (Abram rejects the offer, not wanting to give the king of Sodom the bragging rights as the one who "made Abram rich.") The word *nefesh* here almost certainly refers to "person." We must ask, though, if this is what the word means or if we have a case of metonymy here. (Remember that "metonymy" means using a word for something related to the word, like "hands" for "people who have hands.") If *nefesh* meant "life" (as the KJV thinks it does in Genesis 9:4), it could easily have morphed metonymically into "something that has life," specifically a person.

In fact, we see the same progression in English. We've already seen the phrase "not a soul was left in the room." Similarly, in some parts of the country the English phrase "bless his (or her) soul" is a way of referring to a person. Death reports from accidents at sea report how many "souls were lost," again referring to people, not just their souls.

Genesis 46:18 shows us this same potentially metonymic use: "These are the children of Zilpah, whom Laban gave to his daughter Leah; and these she bore to Jacob—sixteen *nefesh*es." Zilpah didn't give birth to amorphous life forces or to "lives," but rather simply to people.

And presumably these people to whom she gave birth were babies at the time. But that doesn't mean that *nefesh* specifically means "baby." Rather, we have a demonstration here of another potential way we can misunderstand ancient Hebrew. A word doesn't always convey everything that the reader has to know. Some things come from context, background, other parts of the text, etc.

So here, *nefesh* means "person" of any age, and, from context, we determine that these are baby people. It's an obvious point about the word *nefesh*, but an important general principle. We have to be careful to distinguish between what a word means and what we can gather from context. To consider one more silly example, certainly the word *nefesh* here doesn't mean "children born to anyone named Zilpah." In the case of person/child/child-born-to-Zilpah this obvious fact is clear. Context can supplement the meaning of the words. Another example might come from the English statement "Billy has a pet at home." The pet might be a dog. But even if everyone knows that Billy's pet is a dog, "pet" still includes cats and fish and whatnot.

Because of the widespread desire to find deeper meaning in the Bible, people sometimes want to put deeper inherent meaning into the individual words of the Bible. For example, some people want Genesis

46:18 ("these are the children of Zilpah . . . sixteen *nefesh*es") to allude to the potential of a new human being. Or they want Adam, in Genesis 2:7 (where Adam becomes a "living *nefesh*"), to become more than just alive. They want him to embody humankind. These can all be true (or not) regardless of what the actual words mean, but until we know what the words mean we will be misreading or misinterpreting the Bible rather than reading or interpreting it.

Still, perhaps *nefesh* refers to one aspect or another of human life. Just as *levav* tends to represent thoughts and emotions, perhaps *nefesh* does indicate human potential, or God-givenness, or other lofty matters. We have seen nothing to suggest anything more specific, but neither have we seen anything to rule it out. So we keep going.

Discussing the regulations for Passover, Exodus 12:16 reinforces the idea that *nefesh* means "person": "[on Passover] only what will be eaten by each *nefesh* shall be prepared. . . ." Here, *nefesh* again refers to a person, but it specifically refers to the aspect of a person that does the eating.

Leviticus highlights the *nefesh*'s relationship to eating. Leviticus 7:18, for example, is essentially a guide to how long meat can be kept before it goes bad. It warns against eating the meat of a sacrifice after the second day, cautioning that the "*nefesh* that eats of it" will be guilty of an offense against the Lord. Leviticus 7:27 cautions anyone who "eats any blood" (drinks, I guess we would say in English), again using the word *nefesh*: "Any *nefesh* that eats any blood" will be cut off. . . .

This connection between eating and the *nefesh*—or, at least, the compatibility between *nefesh* and eating—is our second clue that "soul" is a terrible translation for *nefesh*. (The first came from Genesis, where *nefesh* seems to have something to do with the blood and the flesh.) English speakers will disagree about what, exactly, is meant by "soul." For some, it's the intangible core of a person. For others, it's the essence that lives on after death. Some people don't believe in a soul.

Yet no one uses "soul" specifically for the part of being alive that involves eating.

Leviticus 17:11 is even more of a problem. It offers a reason why eating blood is forbidden: "The *nefesh* of flesh is in the blood." The whole line reads: "For the *nefesh* of the flesh is in the blood: and I have given it to you upon the altar to make an atonement for your *nefesh*es: for it is the blood that maketh an atonement for the *nefesh*" (KJV). Surprisingly, the KJV translates *nefesh* as "life" the first time but "soul" the next two. The problem faced by the King James's translators is that the soul, as the word is and was used in English, isn't in the blood.

What we have here, though, is classical magic—that is, using a thing to affect that very thing, like dressing up as a daemon to repel daemons or, as they did in ancient Egypt, using a pig's eye to cure eye disease. In the case of Leviticus, the idea was that blood could affect blood. More specifically, blood could affect the *nefesh*, a process "explained" by the fact that the *nefesh* is in the blood. We are left wondering, though, what part of human existence might lie in the blood.

Certainly "soul" is the wrong answer. The human soul—whatever it is—does not lie in the blood. Just looking at the first part of Leviticus 17:11—the *nefesh* is in the blood—we find lots of options for *nefesh*: hemoglobin, for example, or dissolved oxygen, or even pressurized hydraulic flow. But, obviously, none of those concepts works with the second half of the line or, more generally, with what we have already seen. And at any rate, the authors of the Bible seemed to be unaware of our modern medical taxonomy.

To summarize, then, at this point we know that *nefesh* has something to do with life, can be used to mean "person," can specifically refer to the aspect of being alive that involves eating, and is in the blood. Certainly we have no English word for that.

Leviticus 24 gives us more clues about *nefesh*. In Leviticus 24:17, we read that anyone who mortally wounds the *nefesh* of a person will be put to death. The next verse adds animals, declaring that anyone who wounds the *nefesh* of an animal will pay for it, by paying a *nefesh* for a *nefesh*.

These laws have nothing to do with souls—at least, not directly. We do not wish to rule out the possibility that the reason behind the laws has (or doesn't have) something to do with the immortality of the soul and the inherent value of life. But the passages are very clear. Leviticus 24:17 is about killing a person, and Leviticus 24:18 is about killing an animal. The KJV, recognizing the difficulty of using "soul" to convey these simple ideas, translates "a *nefesh* for a *nefesh*" as "beast for beast." But in so doing, they have paraphrased, not translated. (The KJV uses "beast" where I have used "animal." Neither translation is entirely accurate, because the Bible divides animals into different categories than we do, using different words for domesticable and undomesticable wild animals. "Animal" is too broad, while "beast" has the wong connotation.)

Numbers answers the question that arose in Genesis about whether "living *nefesh*" is redundant, because Numbers 6:6 forbids Nazirites from approaching a corpse. But the phrase for corpse there is "*nefesh* of the dead." So, it seems, both the living and the dead have a *nefesh*. Once again, "soul" is a terrible translation, and no major publication uses it for *nefesh* here. Instead, we generally find "dead body" or "corpse." Our question now is not what Numbers 6:6 means, though. We know what it means. We want to understand how the words combine to create that meaning.

It's like a complicated riddle: What do living animals and people have? And it has something to do with the flesh. And it's in the blood. And it sometimes means "person." And it sometimes means "animal." And it has something to do with eating. And it means "corpse." (And let us not forget the part that raised the issue in the first place: You use it to love God.) Fortunately, we'll find a clear answer soon.

Psalm 63 adds another piece of the puzzle. Hebrew poetry, as we saw on page 39 and then more extensively in Chapter 3, often relies on synonyms or near synonyms ("saying the same thing twice"), the poetry of a passage coming from the particular words the author chooses to put in parallel. We can use this to help us know when two words significantly overlap. Psalm 63:1 (". . . my *nefesh* thirsts for You, my *basar* longs for You . . ."), numbered 63:2 by Jews, puts *nefesh* in parallel with *basar*. The second word means "flesh" or "meat," so we have a clue that *nefesh* has something significant in common with flesh. Yet again, we see that "soul" is a terrible translation, but, surprisingly, the KJV and the NRSV both chose to use it to translate Psalm 63:1.

We see similar evidence in Ezekiel 4:14, where Ezekiel assures God that his *nefesh* has not been polluted by eating the wrong things. In isolation, this verse in Ezekiel doesn't tell us much—we don't know for sure what part of the body or mind or soul or whatever was affected by food. But the most natural interpretation is that eating the wrong things is bad for the body.

I Kings 17:22 gives us another crucial bit of evidence. Elijah, while fleeing King Ahab, finds himself in the house of a widow whose son was so sick that before long "there was no breath left in him" (NRSV)—that is, he died. (The word for "breath" here is the Hebrew *n'shama*. Some translations use "breath" for the Hebrew *nefesh*, so we have to be careful. We do not want to define a word using the word itself or, worse, using a bad translation of the word itself. But even though in some English translations it looks like we're using "breath" to define "breath," we are actually just using *n'shama* to define *nefesh*.)

Elijah revives the dead boy by laying him down (I Kings 17:19) and stretching himself over the boy (I Kings 17:21), after which the *nefesh* "of the child came into him again, and he revived" (KJV). What we have in I Kings 17 is almost certainly an ancient case of mouth-to-mouth resuscitation.

Elijah's disciple, Elisha, seems to have learned the procedure from his mentor. In II Kings 4:8, Elisha happens upon an old childless Shunammite woman (that is, a woman from a place called Shunem). Elisha prophesies to the woman that she will conceive. She does, and bears a son. By II Kings 4:31, the son is lying dead on his bed. But, fortunately,

Elisha is around again. Elisha "lay upon the child, and put his mouth upon his mouth . . . and the child sneezed seven times, and the child opened his eyes" (KJV).

Mouth-to-mouth resuscitation would have been a perfectly reasonable thing for the ancients to try. They surely knew that living people had breath and that dead people did not. Particularly before the advent of modern science, which showed us that people inhale oxygen and exhale carbon dioxide, it would have been preeminently sensible to try to put breath into someone who had none of his or her own. (Even though respiration uses up oxygen, so people exhale less oxygen than they inhale, they still exhale enough oxygen to give life. That's why mouth-to-mouth works. But Elisha would have had no way of knowing about this potential problem or its resolution.) Elijah, it seems, was skilled in the technique, and he taught it to Elisha.

For our current purposes, we are particularly interested in the last phrase of I Kings 17:21 (about Elijah and the widow's son), in which "the *nefesh* of the child came into him again." The most natural interpretation of *nefesh* here is "breath." After all, the boy had no breath, Elijah blew into his mouth, and then the boy had a *nefesh* again.

If so, here's what we know so far: The *nefesh* has something to do with life. All life forms have some connection to a *nefesh*. (Maybe they are one; maybe they have one. The Hebrew grammar is imprecise here.) At least potentially, *nefesh*es come in two varieties, living and dead. The word *nefesh* is so connected with life that it is used metonymically to mean (human) "person" or (human or animal) "body." These are all broad connections with life.

But we also have more specific information. From Genesis 9:4 we know that *nefesh* is somehow connected to the flesh and to the blood. From Leviticus 17:11 we know that *nefesh* is directly connected to the blood. And from the books of Kings we now know that *nefesh* is directly connected to the breath.

What "flesh," "blood," and "breath" have in common is that all three are tangible aspects of life. One can hold flesh, touch blood, and feel breath. Flesh and blood are always visible, and in cold weather, so too is breath. The loss of any one of these physical things causes death. The ancients knew that a wound to the flesh could be fatal. Blood loss could be fatal. And what they perceived as loss of breath could be fatal. (Now we tend to see things the other way around, conceiving of the loss of breath as a symptom, not a cause. But in fact, the ancient view is equally accurate. People do live on for at least a few moments after they stop breathing. That's why mouth-to-mouth works. The ancients also must have known about drowning.)

The word *nefesh*, then, seems to have referred specifically to everything about life that could be touched. In the Bible, the three most central touchable parts of life were flesh, blood, and breath. (In modernity, too, those three seem like reasonable choices for the parts of life that can be touched.) The physical body is an extension of "flesh." Human life is only a bit more of an extension. (In English, we have a phrase, "flesh and blood." It plays on the same themes.) What dead people still have, even when their life force has left them, is a body. That explains Numbers 6:6, where "*nefesh* of a dead person" was used for "corpse." And it explains why the *nefesh* is the part of the human condition connected with eating. Eating is a physical act, and the *nefesh* reflects physical existence.

We now see that "soul" is a particularly disastrous translation of *nefesh*.

The English word "soul" means different things to different people. For some, it is the essence of life—generally, though not always— human life. For others, it has more to do with life after death. (The French scholar Ernest Renan, one of the leaders of the post-Kantian French school of critical philosophy, is reported to have pleaded, "O God, if there is a God, save my soul, if I have a soul.") But however it's used, "soul" in English always emphasizes the untouchable, ethereal, amorphous aspects of life. The *nefesh* is just the opposite.

But before we find a more accurate translation, we look at *nefesh* and *levav* as they are used together.

"HEART" AND "SOUL"

We have seen that *levav* represented thoughts, emotions, fears, etc. When we compare *levav* to *nefesh*, we find another, more accurate, and succinct way to express *levav*. While *nefesh* was everything about life that could be touched, *levav* was its counterpart, representing everything about life that *could not* be touched.

In other words, the Biblical view was that our lives have two parts: our physical side (*nefesh*) and our harder-to-define, impossible-to-see nonphysical side (*levav*).

We don't have anything like that in English for human life, but we can understand the concept by looking at two words from the realm of computer science: "hardware," which, like *nefesh*, is touchable; and "software," which, like *levav*, cannot be touched. (Or, as the saying goes, the software is the part of the computer you can't kick.)

The *nefesh* was like the hardware of humanity and the *levav* like the software.

It should not surprise us, then, that *levav* and *nefesh* were used together to form an expression. And it is precisely that expression that appears in what Jesus calls the most important commandment. We are supposed to love God with everything about us that makes us human. Unlike the usual English translation, which limits the commandment to our "heart," excluding our thoughts, the Biblical commandment includes emotions and thoughts and more. And again unlike the usual English translation, the Biblical commandment specifically addresses our corporal, physical existence.

Even though we don't have specific words in English for the tangible versus intangible aspects of life, we are lucky that we have an expression in English to combine both: "mind and body."

The past few decades have seen increasing interest among Western doctors and researchers into the "mind-body" connection. Even though the word "mind" is usually limited to rational thought, not emotion, and even though the word "body" does not normally refer to the breath, in the phrase "mind-body" both terms are broader and more inclusive. The point of the mind-body connection is precisely that our physical well-being is intimately connected with our non-physical well-being. Sorrow or anxiety can cause physical illness. Good news can help an ailing patient. When researchers proclaim a "connection between the mind and the body," they are referring to the *levav* and the *nefesh*. They are also reaffirming something the authors of the Bible knew three thousand years ago.

Furthermore, like "mind-body" in English, the combination of *levav* and *nefesh* in Hebrew formed a common expression in the Bible, and we see it not just in Deuteronomy 6:5. Deuteronomy 4:29, for example, promises that "you will find [God] if you search after him with all your *levav* and *nefesh*" (NRSV). Joshua 22:2 commands, "Serve [God] with all your *levav* and with all your *nefesh*."

I Samuel 2:35 equates a "faithful priest" with someone who will "do what is in my [God's] *levav* and my [again, God's] *nefesh*." The reference to God's *levav* and *nefesh* is further evidence that the combination is not meant to be taken literally. In I Kings 2:4, David instructs Solomon about God's promise that "if your [David's] children walk before me in truth with all their *levav* and with all their *nefesh*," then the line of David will never end. And so forth.

Accordingly, we can translate Deuteronomy 6:5—and therefore also Matthew 22:37, Mark 12:30, and Luke 10:27—as "love the Lord your God with all your mind and body. . . ." The mind-body connection is new to the Western world, but it was a key part of how the Bible understood the human condition, and it formed the basis of this central commandment.

We have now investigated the two words *levav* and *nefesh*, along the way learning about how the Biblical authors viewed life. To understand Matthew 22 (and Mark 12, Luke 10, and Deuteronomy 6:5), we need to fill in two more puzzle pieces.

The first is the verb in Jesus' commandment. The Hebrew is *ahav*, normally translated as "love." It is indeed similar to the English concept of love, but like in English it has many meanings and depends on context. Loving ice cream is different than loving a spouse, which is different than loving a child, which in turn is different than loving one's country. The English phrase "love . . . with your heart/soul" necessarily stresses the emotive part of "love," because of the connection between love and the heart in English. Our new translation, "love . . . with your mind-body," leaves open broader possibilities.

The second loose end is the last word of the phrase (*m'od* in Hebrew). And it is more troublesome. The KJV translates it as "might," and most other translations agree. But unlike *levav* and *nefesh*, which frequently appear together, we find the addition of *m'od* only in Deuteronomy 6:5 (which Jesus cites) and in II Kings 23:25, where it is probably a paraphrase of Deuteronomy 6:5. And while *m'od* is a noun in those two places, elsewhere it has adjectival or adverbial force. It usually means "very," as in God's famous observation at the end of the sixth day that everything was "very good." It's as though the phrase in Deuteronomy reads, ". . . all your mind and body and very."

With so little context to help us understand *m'od* in Deuteronomy 6:5, we are forced to guess what it might mean. Two logical possibilities present themselves, and it's hard to choose between them. The word *m'od* may summarize *levav* and *nefesh*. Or it might augment them. In the first case, the verse would mean: "love . . . with all your mind and body," that is, "all your *m'od*." Or it might mean ". . . with all your mind and body" and, in addition, "all your *m'od*." The KJV takes the second position.

A Greek translation from the third century B.C. called the Septuagint (which we discuss in more detail on page 212) translates *m'od* here as *dunamis*, a word otherwise used to mean "strength." This is where we get the common translation, "(heart and soul and) might." But even the Gospels didn't agree on how exactly to finish the quote. Furthermore, *m'od* doesn't usually seem to mean "might," and usually *dunamis* is used for other Hebrew words. Still, if the notion is "power to change the world"—as suggested by some theologians—then this would make a fitting ending for the commandment.

While Matthew, Mark, and Luke agree on the quotation up to *levav* and *nefesh*, their continuations differ, suggesting that we are not the first generation to wonder what to make of the third word, *m'od*.

Though the dilemma is linguistically frustrating, it is perhaps appropriate that only two thirds of the commandment is clear. We have to figure out the remaining third for ourselves.

More generally, in addition to understanding Jesus' commandment, we gain considerable insight into what it means to be human. We exist in the physical world. We exist in the nonphysical world. And there's something else, maybe our power to effect change, that we don't quite understand.

5

KINGS AND SHEPHERDS:
WHO WE ARE

◄◄··►►

יְהוָה רֹעִי

The LORD is my shepherd

κύριος ποιμαίνει με

YOU ARE MY SUNSHINE

Few images from the Bible are more well known than the poetic opening of Psalm 23: "The Lord is my shepherd." Equally, few images are more widely . The problem is that shepherds, once common, are now rare.

We likewise find a problem with kings. The word "king" appears thousands of times in the Bible, usually in reference to human kings, sometimes refer to God. However, while we still have kings now—in Morocco and Sweden, for example, and potentially in England—the role of kings has changed.

In the last chapter, we saw the power of using a word symbolically. The Hebrew *levav* literally meant "heart," but it did not represent the same constellation of concepts as the English "heart." That's why "heart" is a terrible translation for *levav*. In the case of "shepherd" and "king," we see a slightly different problem.

The reader may remember from Chapter 2 that there are at least two ways to use a word nonliterally.

The first is general figurative usage, in which a speaker or writer spontaneously expands the meaning of a word. This is how the "stationary" of "stationary booths" came to mean what it does now. This is also what happens when a waiter says that "the corned-beef sandwich needs more milk." And it's what happens when someone says that the "president is the CEO of the country."

The second way usually begins with the first, and it's when a word acquires a second definition. This is what we see with "stationary" and "stationery" in modern English. Neither word has anything to do with the other. It's what we see in "There's more than one way to skin a cat." And it's what we saw in the last chapter, with *levav*. The word *levav* has two meanings, "heart" (the organ) and "everything intangible about life."

By comparison, we have a word in English, "pastor." Originally that word, too, meant "shepherd." The early expansion of the word was of the first variety. A spiritual leader was considered a shepherd over people, guiding people and tending to their needs the way a shepherd does for sheep. Over time, the word moved from the first category to the second. A "pastor" is now almost always a member of the clergy.

For that matter, we could go back even further, when shepherd—from the words "sheep" and "herd"—was a herder of sheep. The word progressed in meaning from "herder of sheep" to "herder of sheep and/or sheeplike animals," such as goats, perhaps, or even cows.

Chapter 4 was concerned with one example of what goes wrong when we don't recognize the second way the meaning of words can expand: There, translators failed to take into account the meanings that the words *levav* and *nefesh* had acquired. In this chapter, we return to the first way—that is general figurative usage. The Hebrew word in Psalm 23, *ro'i*, does literally mean "my shepherd." Unlike *levav*, it doesn't have a second meaning. But the impact of the word is not the same as the English "shepherd."

By way of example, we might consider Shakespeare's *Romeo and Juliet*: "But soft, what light through yonder window breaks? It is the east, and Juliet is the sun." Like the Hebrew word for "shepherd," the English word "sun" has only one meaning that we care about. Obviously, Juliet is not literally the sun. Rather, she is like the sun in some way that is both poetic and clear to people who know English.

The sun has a variety of qualities. For example, it's too hot to support life. Its rays damage human tissue. It causes sunburns and skin cancer. It is the most massive object most humans will ever see. And so forth. Yet certainly Shakespeare does not mean that Juliet is dangerous, damages people, or is the fattest woman Romeo will ever see.

Rather, the poetry builds on a whole system of metaphors in English. Light is good. Darkness is evil. The sun represents the best qualities of light and the absence of the worst qualities of darkness. The famous song "You Are My Sunshine" works the same way, and it makes sense only through the same set of images.

It's not difficult to imagine a society in which the "sun" is a symbol not of beauty but rather of destructive power. In fact, we see just this imagery in Psalm 121, where God is a "shadow" (usually translated "shade" or "protection") so that the "sun will not kill you." (In different contexts, the sun in the Bible is also a symbol of eternity.)

So "Juliet is the sun" really means that Juliet is like the sun only in the ways that our society uses the metaphor of "sun."

Similarly, "the Lord is my shepherd" means that the Lord is like my shepherd in certain ways, this time determined not by our culture but by the culture of the Bible. Our task is to figure out what those ways are, and then figure out if we have a way of expressing them in English. As we look into "shepherd," we will also look at other words used to describe God.

SHEPHERDS

Before we get started we need a bit of Hebrew grammar to help us understand the words here. The Hebrew word for "shepherd" is *ro'eh*. In Hebrew, the suffix *-i* means "my," and when the suffix attaches to a word that ends in a vowel sound, that sound frequently drops out. So "my shepherd" in Hebrew is the one word *ro'i*. The vowel sound at the end of *ro'eh* (*-eh*) drops out when the suffix *-i* is added to the word. In Psalm 23 we find the word *ro'i*.

Shepherds in the Bible

Shepherds used to be commonplace. Every community had livestock that lived in herds—primarily sheep and goats—and therefore had someone in charge of the herds. That person was the *ro'eh*.

Our first warning sign that something has gone wrong in the translation is that a common, familiar word like *ro'eh* has been translated as a rare, unfamiliar one. While *"ro'eh"* was common in Hebrew, "shepherd" is uncommon in English. We know that this is always a mistake. We also know that sometimes this sort of mismatch results in only a slightly wrong translation, but sometimes it misses the mark completely. Here we have the latter.

To understand why the mistake is so serious, we have to look at how *ro'eh* is used elsewhere in the Bible.

Exodus 2:16–20 is a good place to start. The priest of Midian had seven daughters who were tasked with drawing water and filling troughs so that their father's flock could drink. But they had a problem in the form of shepherds who would come and drive them away from their work. Moses rescues the daughters from the shepherds, helps provide water for the flock, and saves the daughters so much time that they return early to their father, who wonders how it is possible for his daughters to come home so quickly. Their father is so impressed with the man who helped them that he has Moses brought before him and, as a token of appreciation, offers Moses his daughter Zipporah.

Using a daughter as a thank-you gift violates American social customs, but perhaps even more jarring is the image of the shepherds. They are fierce troublemakers. Moses demonstrates his courage by standing up not to a king, not to an armed warrior, but to a shepherd. The daughters even use the language: "[Moses] *saved us* from the shepherds." Why would shepherds be so fearsome?

Next we look at Jeremiah 25:35, one of three verses in a row that have shepherds in them. In 25:35, one effect of God's wrath is that "the shepherds shall have no way to flee." (The Hebrew is considerably more poetic.) Conquering the shepherds is a sign of God's power. This can only be because, as in Exodus 2, the shepherds themselves were mighty. The image in Jeremiah here is not one of God stepping on ants but rather of overpowering a mighty adversary. And this is confirmed in the second half of the verse—". . . nor will the mightiest of the flock be able to escape"—where "the mightiest of the flock" is in parallel with "shepherds." (The KJV translates "mighty" as "principal" here.) As we learned in Chapter 3, this is a good indication that shepherds were considered mighty.

In Jeremiah 49:19, the prophet Jeremiah quotes God, and we again see that shepherds are mighty: "Like a lion coming up from the thickets of the Jordan against a perennial pasture, I will suddenly chase Edom away from it [the Jordan]; and I will appoint over it [again, the Jordan] whomever I choose. For who is like me? Who can summon me? Who is the shepherd who can stand before me?" (NRSV). The verse sets the stage with the image of a lion, among the most powerful of animals. God is more powerful even than the lion. The second half of the verse is even more telling, describing in three ways how God is more powerful than a lion: "Who is like Me?" "Who will challenge Me?" And third, "Who is the shepherd who can stand up to Me?" So one of the ways of being mightier than a lion is being able to stand up to a shepherd. (The same language is repeated in Jeremiah 50:44.) In other words, God is stronger than a lion, and the proof is that even shepherds can't match God's strength.

Jeremiah 51:23, again describing God's power, also uses three images: "I will shatter shepherds and flocks, shatter farmers and oxen, shatter captains and rulers." The English doesn't do justice to the Hebrew, because the Hebrew is particularly poetic, and because a full understanding of the words "captains" and "rulers" is intertwined with the details of the various leadership positions in ancient societies. Still, the overall image is clear. Shepherds are powerful enough that shattering them is a sign of might.

Ezekiel 37:24 builds on what we just saw. There, David is destined to be "king" and "shepherd": "My servant David shall be king over them; and they shall all have one shepherd" (NRSV). It doesn't look quite like a parallelism—"David" is not parallel with "all [of them]"—so we shouldn't jump the gun and assume that "shepherd" is like "king," but certainly the two are compatible.

Amos has a particularly gruesome and graphic image. In Amos 3:12, the prophet describes the eventual salvation of the Israelites with a comparison: "As a shepherd rescues two legs and a bit of ear from the mouth of a lion, that is how Israel will be saved. . . ." So shepherds, apparently, challenged lions, successfully retrieving food from the lions' mouths!

So far we've seen two aspects of shepherds. They are mighty, and they are regal. We see both images reinforced in Micah 5:5, which addresses a potential invasion by Assyrians: "If the Assyrians come into our land and tread upon our soil, we will raise against them seven shepherds and eight . . . rulers" (NRSV). Here we clearly have parallel structure. "Seven" is not the same as "eight," but it is almost the same. Perhaps, in this metaphor, rulers are just a bit higher than shepherds (just as eight is a bit higher than seven), but more likely they are essentially the same here. And in Nahum 3:18 ("Your shepherds are asleep, O king of Assyria; your nobles slumber" [NSRV]), we once again see shepherds compared to nobility.

Song of Songs makes another element of shepherds clear: The shepherd in the Bible was a romantic figure. One of the most often-cited verses from Song of Songs is 2:16, *dodi li va'ani lo*, "My lover is mine and I am his. . . ." (Translations commonly soften the language, turning it into the less overtly sexual "my beloved," a topic we address in the next chapter.) The line ends with two Hebrew words that describe "my lover," and they are *haro'eh bashoshanim*, "who is a shepherd among flowers."

The flowers are probably lilies of some sort, but their exact genus isn't the point. They are a romantic image, like "roses" in English. And, more importantly, *ro'eh* is equally romantic. Song of Songs 2:16 is mirrored in 6:3: "I am my lover's, and he is mine," again with the addendum, "[he] who is a shepherd among flowers." The same image of "shepherd among flowers" becomes even more overt in Song of Songs 4:5, where the hero extols the heroine with the words, "Your two breasts are like two fawns . . . that are shepherds among flowers."

The word for "shepherds" here—*ro'eh*, as before—is usually translated as the verb "feed," so that the fawns are "feeding among flowers." That translation matches the Greek Septuagint, though the Greek there is frequently unreliable. (Some additional information about the Septuagint appears on page 212.) The translators of the Septuagint may have tried to avoid translating, ". . . like fawns that are shepherds." They may have instead tried to figure out what fawns were most likely to be doing among the flowers. In so doing, though, the Greek translators, and the English ones after them, missed the general point that poetry frequently mixes images that don't usually appear together. And they missed the specific point that the Hebrew word *ro'eh* is a romantic image, not merely an occupation.

Finally, when the heroine of Songs of Songs wants to find her lover, she pleads, "Tell me, you whom I love so dearly, where you shepherd [your flocks]." It's hardly a mainstream romantic image now, but it was then.

So far, a reasonably clear, if perhaps surprising, picture emerges. The picture has four parts. First: Shepherds were fierce and noble.

They were like kings and other royalty. They were powerful. Crushing a shepherd was a sign of great strength, and shepherds were used to stave off invasion. Second: The job of a shepherd was to provide sustenance, care, and defense. Third: Shepherds were romantic. And finally: Shepherds were common.

Shepherds in America

None of those things is true about shepherds today. Ignoring for the moment the nearly total lack of shepherds in modern countries, we find that shepherds are considered meek, humble, powerless, and, perhaps the most prevalent image in America, not a part of mainstream society. Though some farmers are essentially shepherds, at least in part, we use the word "farmer" to mean someone who has a job working with animals, perhaps caring for them. We use "shepherd" primarily figuratively or in jest. (Try to get a job or a bank loan by listing "shepherd" as your current occupation and see what happens.)

In short, the only thing that the English "shepherd" and the Hebrew *ro'eh* have in common is that the job descriptions overlap. Even here, though, they aren't identical. The job of modern shepherds in the modern world—again, to the extent that there are any—is to make sure the flocks stay in the right place and get food. In antiquity, the shepherd had to protect the flock from wild animals, too. In I Samuel 17:34–35, David brags to King Samuel about his prowess as a shepherd (already something that hardly resonates with modern Americans), claiming that he was in charge of the sheep. When a lion or bear came and snatched a sheep, he claimed that he would run after the wild animal, kill it, and rescue the poor sheep.

So even if we are talking about the actual job, "shepherd" might not be the right word for *ro'eh*. If we are talking about anything metaphoric, it is certainly wrong.

Do we have anything similar to a *ro'eh* in America? Nothing is a perfect match, but a variety of options point in the right direction.

"Marine" is partly the right image. Marines, at least stereotypically—and that's what we're talking about here—are strong, and their job is defense. It would be a symbol of great power if someone, or a deity, could cause marines to flee, as we saw regarding shepherds in Jeremiah 25. Similarly, as in Micah 5, a country might use marines in defense against an invader. On the other hand, marines' main mode of operation is military in nature, while the same is not true of the *ro'eh*. Not only is the *ro'eh* not a military figure, but, unlike the marine, the *ro'eh*'s main job doesn't involve conflict at all. So we reject "marine" but still try to remember that *ro'eh* shares with "marine" the qualities of bravery and might.

"Fireman" is another wrong but close option. Like the duties of the *ro'eh* (and marine) firefighting calls for physical prowess and bravery, and, like the *ro'eh* and unlike the marine, people see firemen in the normal course of life, not just in combat. And again like the *ro'eh* and unlike marines, firemen have a job that does not involve conflict, seldom involves violence, and includes significant civilian responsibilities. Still, firemen are also not like royalty. While everyone appreciates them after they have saved people from a building, they are not generally exalted the way the *ro'eh* was. So we reject "fireman," too.

What about "lawyer"? At first glance, it seems to miss the mark completely. Lawyers, after all, are not known for being particularly strong. On the other hand, violence in America has almost completely been replaced by lawsuits. What once would have resulted in physical violence now usually ends up in court. Even retribution for the rare bit of overt violence is handed over to the lawyers. People preparing to fight one another amass lawyers these days. And, if pay scale is any indication, lawyers seem to be more valued by society than marines or firefighters. Being a lawyer is even a reasonable stepping-stone to the presidency. Is that like being royalty?

In a different direction, what about "lumberjack"? Lumberjacks are typically strong, have a job that doesn't involve violence (at least not toward people or animals), and, like the *ro'eh*, even work outdoors. What about "cowboy"? Or "pilot"?

In yet a third direction, perhaps "doctor" or "nurse" is the right idea. After all, their job, like that of the *ro'eh* and unlike marines, is primarily one of caretaking. Or, sticking to the theme of animals, maybe "veterinarian" is better. What about "zookeeper"? Or, for that matter, what about "farmer"? While these all have a little merit, they fall short in terms of the physical attributes that a *ro'eh* seems to have embodied.

None of these options is right, but every one is better than "shepherd," which, as we have seen, is completely wrong. And the various wrong options—particularly marine, fireman, and lumberjack—show at least one side of *ro'eh* that most people never consider because the role of shepherds has changed so much.

In addition, we have so far had no luck coming up with anything in modern society that has the regal flavor of *ro'eh*, a topic we turn to next. Because the *ro'eh* is like a king, we have to better understand what "king" meant in the Bible. Only then can we return to *ro'eh* and understand Psalm 23.

KINGS

Unlike shepherds, there are still kings in mainstream Western society. His Majesty the King of Sweden personally hands out Nobel Prizes, for example. England had a king until recently, and might again someday; for now it has a queen, who is at least in principle the same as the king. Morocco has a king. So does Spain.

The Bible, too, speaks of kings, *melech*s in Hebrew. And they are no small matter. Two books of the Bible (probably originally one big book) are called "Kings," and considerable attention is given to ascension to the throne, continuity, and so forth.

So at first, based on tradition and near consensus, it looks like the English word for *melech* is "king."

But a closer look reveals that the issue is more complicated.

Kings in the Bible

The most obvious quality of the ancient *melech* was his unsurpassed power. The king was the most powerful figure in a certain region.

We first come across kings in Genesis 14, where we find a variety of them waging war. So one function of the king was warfare. And we learn something else. It's not clear if the events in Genesis 14 are meant to be historical or not—the fact that Sodom has a king whose name means "with evil" and Gomorrah has a king whose name means "with wickedness" suggests an allegorical bent to the narrative—but either way we learn that Sodom and Gomorrah each have a king. But Sodom and Gomorrah are cities. Jericho, too, had its own king. So did many other cities.

Nowadays, only countries have kings. (In fantasy, "realms" have kings," a topic we'll turn to in a moment.) We should not be surprised, of course, that kings were not in charge of countries in the Bible, for until recently there were no countries as we understand them. But here we have our first major problem. Most people nowadays understand that kings wielded absolute power over a certain region, but they radically misunderstand the nature of the region over which the kings ruled.

Some people compare ancient kings to the modern American president (and though the comparison misses a lot, it also has a lot to recommend it). But in some cases, a more accurate comparison would be to a mayor. This is our first obstacle to understanding what kings are—and the first reason not to use the English "king" for the Hebrew *melech*. Everyone believes that kings are more powerful than mayors, but they might be wrong.

The Egyptian Pharaoh is called "king" in the Bible. (Frequently it seems that a "king" is what he is, and "Pharaoh" is his name.) Certainly Egypt was larger than a city, and there were cities under control of the Pharaoh. Similarly, King Ahasuerus—who according to the Book of Esther reigned over Persia, and who is frequently equated with the Persian ruler Artaxerxes—ruled a region that extended beyond just Persia to some 127 regions. Jerusalem never had a king, but Judah and Israel did. Not every city had a king, and some kings ruled more than one city. So the situation is complex. We don't need to understand the details to realize the mismatch between *melech* and "king."

Another fact is easy to miss because we tend to pay it so little attention. Stories in the Bible frequently begin, "It was in the days of King So-and-so." Just for example, the book of Isaiah begins, "The vision of Isaiah the son of Amoz, which he saw concerning Judah and Jerusalem in the days of Uzziah, Jotham, Ahaz, and Hezekiah, kings of Judah." The book of Ezekiel begins similarly. After a vague reference in Ezekiel 1:1 to the "thirtieth year"—of what we don't know—Ezekiel's first oracle is dated in 1:2: "In the fifth day of the month, which was the fifth year of king Jehoiachin's captivity" (KJV).

The reigns of kings were used to reckon years.

For more exact references, the number of years after an event regarding the king was used. For example, I Kings 6:1 notes that Solomon began building the temple in the "fourth year of Solomon's reign." Or II Kings 3:1: "In the eighteenth year of King Jehoshaphat of Judah, Jehoram son of Ahab became king over Israel . . ." (NRSV). Or Ezra 6:15: "And this house was finished . . . in the sixth year of the reign of King Darius. . . ." Or even Esther 1:3: "In the third year of [King Ahasuerus's] reign, he gave a banquet for all his officials and ministers." (It is reasonable to ask why the king waited until his third year to throw what seems like an inauguration party.)

For this system of counting years to have worked, the reign of a king had to have been widely known and of great importance. Yet how many English readers of this book can name the current king of Sweden or Morocco or Spain, let alone previous monarchs? Most readers will know the name of the Queen of England, but probably not the year she ascended to the throne. (If you're curious, it was on February 6, 1952, putting the publication of this book almost seventy years to the day from the rule of Queen Elizabeth II of Britain.)

On the other hand, most Americans know who was president during important events. (Some are trivially easy: The Kennedy assassination took place while Kennedy was president.) People who remember the attack on Pearl Harbor usually also know that Franklin Roosevelt was president at the time. The 9/11 attacks took place under the second President Bush. And so forth.

This is one reason we might want to consider translating *melech* as "president," at least in America. To the extent that people in America always know who is president and, in general, use presidents to reckon years, the equivalent of *melech* in at least one regard is "president."

As we just saw, some *melech*s were in charge of great swaths of land—empires, even—while others ruled over areas no larger than a city. For the last group, perhaps "mayor" is the right translation? Taking all of these together, what about "elected official"? One obvious objection is that kings weren't elected. Do we care? Is (non)electedness an important part of *melech*ness?

To look at it another way, even though the president of America is in charge of a large country, some very small countries have presidents, too. Micronesia ("The Federated States of Micronesia") has a president who, like the American president, is both the chief of state and the head of government. But Micronesia has just over a hundred thousand citizens. And some presidents aren't elected at all. The widely mocked president of Turkmenistan was what most people would call a dictator. Maybe "president" is right after all, so long as we don't let the president of America define the role.

Or maybe we're looking at the issue too narrowly. What about "CEO" for *melech*? Many CEOs wield more power than presidents, and like *melech*s, CEOs aren't elected. And again like *melech*s, some CEOs are vastly more powerful than others.

But all of these miss another element of *melech*s. One role of the *melech* in the Bible was to provide justice and ensure the safety of the people. We see this from I Samuel 8:20, when the people of Israel demand a king for themselves. They want a king so that they will be like the rest of the nations, having a king "to judge" them and "to fight [their] battles."

We learn more about what makes a good *melech* by looking at the description of King David in I Samuel 16:18. David is a musician, a man of war, wise, handsome, and God is with him. The list contains another phrase, *gibor chayil*, which fits into the same constellation of ideas, but which is hard to translate accurately: The word *gibor* is associated with valor, might, and military prowess. The word *chayil* is similarly used for physical might and, sometimes, specifically for "soldier" or "warrior." But the word also has connotations of worthiness, propriety, and, more generally, worth, as in Proverbs 12:4. There the phrase *eshet chayil*, a "woman of *chayil*"—often translated a "woman of valor" or a "virtuous woman"—begins a poem celebrating the merits of women or, perhaps, a specific woman.

Jewish husbands traditionally recite this poem to their wives on Friday night over dinner as they welcome the Sabbath together, so among traditionally observant Jews the phrase *eshet chayil* is among the best known of the Bible. Modern Hebrew has preserved only the military aspect of *chayil*, and in Israel the word now means simply "soldier." This narrowing of the meaning of *chayil* created a phrase in Modern Hebrew that most naturally refers to a mighty woman, so when the television series *Wonder Woman* aired in Israel, the translators called the program *eshet chayil*. Unfortunately, thousands of ultrareligious Jews, recognizing the phrase from their Sabbath ritual, tuned in, only to find a woman in her underwear.

Inasmuch as David is regarded as the king par excellence, we learn from the list of qualities in I Samuel 16:18—and from the narrative that follows, in which the various kinglike traits of David's are demonstrated—what a king ought to be. Some of this confirms what we have already seen. The king is supposed to command the army and provide physical security, so being a "man of war" is helpful. The king is supposed to ensure justice, so being wise is good.

These two qualities—military ingenuity and wisdom—match what people in America have generally wanted in a president, though the trend is changing. Whereas the military used to be a path to the presidency, because people wanted a "man of war," increasingly a degree in law or business is required of presidents.

But the match is only partial. Presidents are not expected to be musicians. Though many of them have been, their musical skills are not seen as part of the job of president, while just the opposite was true for David. First on the list of job skills was his ability to play music. The king was supposed to be artistic.

Two more qualities of the Biblical king separate the role from almost anything we have in modern culture.

The final element on the list in I Samuel 16:18 is that God is with David. The king was supposed to have a connection to God beyond that of ordinary people. Obviously, we don't have space here for a full discussion of the role of God in the Bible, but we can note generally that kings were supposed to have a closer relationship to God than other people. Kings were a special kind of human.

Numbers 23:21 reinforces this connection between godliness and king-worthiness. In the second half of the verse, when Balaam blesses the people of Israel a second time, he proclaims: "The Lord their God is with them, and the sound of a king is among them." (Our translation here ignores some details, like the Hebrew *tru'ah*, "sound," which is in fact probably a specific kind of sound associated with war.) These two parallel lines follow another set of parallel lines in the first part of the verse: "He has not beheld misfortune in Jacob; nor has he seen trouble in Israel" (NRSV). There, two words for "saw," two words for "evil," and two words for "Israel" set the stage for a classical Hebrew poetic parallelism. It is in this context that Numbers 23:21 demonstrates that a connection to God was part and parcel of being a king.

Other kings, too, have God with them—for example, King Hezekiah in II Kings 18:7. (On the other hand, this privileged status was not reserved for kings. Moses has God with him. Bezalel, the Biblical artist par excellence, similarly has a connection with God that others do not.)

So the *melech* was supposed to be a different sort of person than other people. He was supposed to be not just royalty but also inherently royal. This is one of the biggest differences between the roles of president (at least in the United States) and king. Kings, even today, come from "the royal family." They are treated differently than "ordinary people" precisely because they are not ordinary.

We don't have anything like that in modern America, but some roles come closer than "president." "Superstar" is an example. Actors, rappers, sports figures, and some others have an aura of "otherness" to them, and they are treated as somewhat of a different class than ordinary people. One way to see the difference between superstars and presidents is to look at the people who are second best, or third, or even tenth. The person who loses the presidential election is just an ordinary person. It takes the actual office of the president to confer the distinction of presidentiality. But even the person who loses a musical competition, or almost gets an Emmy, etc., can still be a star. We expect more of stars than we do of other people, and they are held to a higher standard. We scrutinize their behavior. Many people even strive to emulate them. It is in these ways that superstars are more like royalty than anyone else in the United States.

Kings Today

Other countries, of course, have actual royalty. We might reasonably ask if the Queen of England, for example, plays the same role in England that royalty played in the Bible. The answer is that even though British kings and queens are closer to Biblical kings than are American superstars, they are different enough that translating *melech* as "king," even in modern British English, is inaccurate. In addition, citizens of the British Empire are lulled into thinking that they know what's going on when they see the English word "king" for *melech*. At least in America we know that we don't have kings. In England, and in most other countries in which a king (or queen) reigns, they have no such warning flag. That's because the British monarch is essentially a powerless figurehead, whereas the *melech* of antiquity was just the opposite—the most powerful person in the area.

Medieval Kings

Beyond currently reigning foreign kings, in America we have at least two other reference points for "king"—and, unfortunately, neither of them helps us understand the Biblical *melech*.

Most Americans are at least passingly familiar with medieval European history, and the kings, castles, knights, etc., that in retrospect formed the glorious larger-than-life picture of life in Europe. "King Arthur" is a well-known figure. So are the "Knights of the Round Table." In many ways, in fact, we are still living in the aftermath of the culture of medieval Europe. Chivalry, for example, was an invention of that time, and to this day the custom of opening doors for women forms part of American culture.

This context also gives us a framework for (wrongly) imagining what a *melech* was. Kings in the Bible, it's easy for Americans to think, were probably like King Arthur. Leaving aside for the moment the fact that there was no King Arthur, the kings of medieval Europe were different from the *melech*s of the Bible: Medieval kings were judged by standards of chivalry—they jousted, lived in castles, fought in the name of Jesus Christ, and so forth. (Some popular notions about medieval kings are inaccurate, but they nonetheless contribute to how people understand the word "king.") These differences between famous figures like King Arthur and the Biblical kings lead those who read the word *king* in the Bible astray.

So trying to understand *melech*s by comparing them to medieval kings doesn't help. That's one false clue modern readers have.

Kings and Dragons

The second false clue is even worse. Most readers are familiar with mythic, fictitious kings from fables. These are the "rulers of the realm," and they inhabit fantasy worlds where they slay dragons and save women stuck in towers, escape from dungeons, and so forth. Most people have no trouble keeping in mind that stories like these are not real. But it is more difficult to know that the word "king" in these stories is different than the word "king" in Bible translations.

So in the end, modern American readers have three reference points for "king": currently reigning kings, who are powerless figureheads; medieval kings; and fictitious kings. Of the three, medieval kings come closest to the ancient *melech*, but only because "powerless figurehead" and "pretend" are so very far away from the ancient reality.

More About Biblical Kings

So we go back to I Samuel 16:18, which describes the king as "musician, man of war, wise, handsome, and with God." Certainly, this was at least somewhat of an exaggeration. And we know from descriptions of other kings in the Bible that kings frequently fell short of the ideal. But we see what a king was supposed to be. The king was supposed to provide for security against internal threats (by administering justice) and external threats (by maintaining an army). And the king was supposed to ensure prosperity. In this regard, the king was more like an ancient pharaoh (whom the Bible even calls "king") or like a Roman emperor than anyone we call "king" now.

The next line of I Samuel brings our discussion full circle. I Samuel 16:18, as we have seen, describes David's qualities and why he would make a good king. In 16:19 we learn that David is "with the sheep." That is, he is a shepherd.

This line further demonstrates the close connection between *ro'eh* and *melech*. They are both in charge of a group and, in particular, in charge of ensuring the safety of that group from within and from without. And they were both held in high esteem.

MY SHEPHERD

All of this brings us back to Psalm 23. We know that "The Lord is my shepherd" suggests all of the wrong images and none of the right ones.

The modern "shepherd" conveys a marginalized loner who spends more time with sheep than with people. The original model was a brave, strong, valiant, regal protector of the weak, providing safety and food and ensuring tranquillity.

One very tempting translation is: "The Lord is my knight in shining armor."

It's a cliché, but the reference of the cliché is almost exactly what we need. (Though the imagery in the cliché is of knights, which no longer exist, the cliché itself is commonly used for real things, so it doesn't suffer from the problems that we saw with "king.")

The "knight in shining armor" is someone who comes in to save the day, someone who can be trusted, someone who is invincible. And it's generally someone who has a certain romantic appeal, like David (who was handsome) and like the shepherds in Song of Songs.

"Knight in shining armor" is, unfortunately, completely the wrong register and also seems too fanciful, so we reject that translation, too.

Other words capture some of what a *ro'eh* was: "The Lord is my captain." "The Lord is my teacher." "The Lord is my parent." And so forth. In the end, though, nothing matches everything we need. We don't have anything like a *ro'eh* anymore. We don't have any job or position or role that includes the crucial aspects of a *ro'eh*: might, bravery, romance, and exalted social position.

Nor does moving away from nouns toward other parts of speech help. (Remember from Chapter 3 that we don't always need to translate nouns as nouns.) "The Lord is valiant." "The Lord is brave." "The Lord protects me." "The Lord guides me." Nothing conveys the package that was the *ro'eh*.

We shouldn't be surprised by how hard it is to find an English word for *ro'eh*. Consider going the other way. How might we say "brain surgeon" in ancient Hebrew? How would we translate the phrase "It's not brain surgery"? They had (almost) no surgery in ancient Israel, and they didn't know that the brain was where thinking took place. So certainly the literal "brain surgeon," even it were possible (there's no ancient Hebrew word for "surgeon"), would be completely wrong. "Brain doctor" would be no better. "Doctors" back then were people who usually failed. "Magician"? "Miracle worker"? No one in antiquity could amass the amount of knowledge and training that brain surgery requires. (We'll see in Chapter 8 that most ancient life spans were too short to allow for what we now consider a specialized medical education.)

The only way to convey "brain surgeon" would be to carefully spell out the relevant implications, perhaps with a background on the culture. That's what we've done with *ro'eh*, carefully looking at the qualities of the *ro'eh*. But nothing in modern American English comes close.

So any translation we come up with will be deficient. But "shepherd" is nowhere near the top of the list of reasonable choices. It's not just incomplete; it's massively inaccurate.

If we choose a more general word, we can at least avoid some of the mistaken impressions. "Hero" is a word that comes to mind. It's not as poetic as *ro'eh* was, because *ro'eh* is more specific than "hero." But it's also not as wrong as "shepherd" is, because shepherds, as we have seen, have only one relatively unimportant quality in common with *ro'eh*s: They both work with sheep.

If we use "hero," we can at least try to make sense of the rest of the Psalm.

The second half of the opening line reads, "I will lack nothing" or "I will not lack." It's hard to choose between them, because what we really want is something in the middle. We want something not quite as chatty as "I will lack nothing" but not so formal as "I will not lack." We arbitrarily pick "I will not lack," giving us: "The Lord is my hero and I will not lack." (Let's be clear, though. This isn't a very good translation. It's just the best we have.)

In other words, God will give me protection, guidance, security, and safety—like a *ro'eh*—so I'll have everything I need and I won't have to worry about anything. The nuance of "my *ro'eh*," not just any *ro'eh*, adds the refinement that even though we all have the same God, God's work will be tailored to me.

The second line starts with a "shepherding" verb, *hirbitz*. The common translation "makes me lie down" misses the point that *hirbitz* is most naturally associated with shepherding. In Song of Songs 1:7, *hirbitz* is in parallel with the verbal form of *ro'eh*, as if *hirbitz* meant "to shepherd." In Isaiah 13:20, the description of desolated land is that "*ro'eh*s won't *hirbitz* there." And Jeremiah's vision (in 33:12) of the restoration of desolate land is that "*ro'eh*s will *hirbitz* the flock." Ezekiel 34:15 puts the two words directly in parallel, "I [God] will shepherd my flock and I will *hirbitz* them."

Just as the point of the first line has nothing to do with sheep, the point of the second line has nothing to do with the verb related to sheep. Sheep are incidental. (This is like "He's no brain surgeon," which has nothing to do with surgery.) Coming after *ro'eh* as it does, *hirbitz* is exactly the verb we would expect. It adds nothing new. Rather, the new information is "in pastures," a concept that is refined in the second part of the line, which adds, "by tranquil water." So while the first line sets the stage of God as "my valiant protector," the second line explains what God will do: bring me to the tranquillity of a meadow, perhaps with a quiet bubbling brook. We can keep the metaphors of pastures and water—even though they are more closely related to *ro'eh* than to "hero"—using something like the KJV: "He lets me lie down in green pastures. He leads me beside still waters."

But even here we have a dilemma, because in the context of Psalm 23, a green pasture is a particularly poetic place. It's a place of serenity but also a potentially dangerous one. It is only the *ro'eh* that keeps it tranquil.

Brilliantly, the psalm then seamlessly abandons the sheep metaphor while still keeping the metaphor of the *ro'eh*—that is, the hero. By the fourth line—"Even though I walk through the darkest valley, I fear no evil . . ." (NRSV) or "Even when I walk through a dark valley, I fear no harm . . ." (NAB), both reasonable translations—we find truly human emotions such as fear and the potent symbol of darkness. The symbolism is even more powerful in the original Hebrew, where "darkest valley" is literally (as in the KJV) the "valley of death." Even better would be "the Valley of Death" or "Death Valley." Yet the end of the fourth line—". . . your rod and your staff comfort me"—maintains the image of the ro'eh.

At this point we realize the futility of translating the poem into English. By line four, we need a translation of ro'eh that covers everything we have seen—might, bravery, etc.—but that also works with a staff and a rod! This is why most translations are forced to stick with the terrible translation "shepherd."

But the psalm is not about shepherds. It is about supreme might, protection from safety, gallant heroism, and the nearness of God even in the face of seemingly insurmountable obstacles. The shepherd imagery is just the canvas upon which the poetry is painted.

In this regard, our investigations into ro'eh and melech show us something fundamental about looking at Bible translations. Biblical passages frequently have important parts and also less important parts that serve to bind the key points together. By way of comparison, we might once again imagine translating a modern English passage into ancient Hebrew. Something as simple as "I remember the first time I landed in a Communist country" is surely about Communism, culture clashes, etc. But to an ancient reader, all of that would be overshadowed by "landed." A human landed? A human was *flying*? It must be a miracle!

Just as it would be hard for an ancient reader to ignore the "landed" bit and focus on the Communism, in Psalm 23 it's hard for modern readers to ignore the shepherd bit and focus on the real point. More generally, when we read the Bible we have to be careful not to get caught up in the wrong details.

In the next chapter, we will see another glaring mistranslation that draws our attention away from a fundamental and timeless message.

6

MY SISTER, MY BRIDE:
HOW WE SEE EACH OTHER

◄-‹--›-►

לִבַּבְתִּנִי אֲחֹתִי כַלָּה

Thou hast ravished my heart, my sister, my spouse

ἐκαρδίωσας ἡμᾶς ἀδελφή μου νύμφη

We have already looked at the romantic and poetic imagery in Song of Songs enough to suspect that the incestuous translation "my sister, my bride" (NRSV and NAB) must be wrong. The KJV's "my sister, my spouse" is no better. Other translations, like "my treasure, my bride" or "my own, my bride" may be poetic, but they are inventions of the translators that do not reflect the original Hebrew. So what's going on?

The very first line of the book—which is actually numbered Song of Songs 1:2, because 1:1 is the title—begins, "Let him kiss me with the kisses of his mouth" (KJV). Ths makes it pretty clear what the book is about. Song of Songs deals with romantic, erotic love.

The love story has two main characters: an unnamed man and an unnamed woman. (Incidentally, we also learn from this fact that major characters in the Bible need not have names. This will be important later, as we try to understand Manoah's unnamed wife.) Because Hebrew has grammatical gender, it's usually pretty clear who is talking to whom, even when the context would otherwise be ambiguous. For example, the sentence "I slept, but my heart was awake" (Song of Songs

5:2; NRSV) could equally apply to a man or a woman in English, but in Hebrew the feminine verb for "slept" makes it clear that the woman is sleeping.

Even though the grammatical gender in Hebrew lets the reader know who is speaking, we usually find additional clues in the form of an epithet each character enjoys.

The man is frequently called *dodi*—that is, "my *dod*." (Remember from last chapter that the Hebrew suffix -*i* means "my.") Translations for *dodi* include "my beloved," "my love," and "my lover," though in some other situations the word almost certainly means "son-in-law." Here, based on context, "lover" is probably right. We won't spend more time analyzing *dodi*, though, because our focus is on the heroine of Song of Songs, and why she is called "my *achot, kalah*."

We will work in reverse order, starting with the easier *kalah*. Our first task is to get a sense of how words like *kalah* function in society.

BRIDES

The English word "bride" is interesting because of its surprisingly ambiguous relationship to marriage. A bride may be a woman who is about to be married, one in the process of becoming married, or one who has recently been married. "The bride" walks down the aisle, but even months after the ceremony someone might ask the husband how his "new bride" is doing.

"Wife," by contrast, refers only to a married woman. So what's the difference between a "wife" and a "bride"? How is it different for someone to ask "How's your wife?" compared with "How's your bride?"

For that matter, by most people's definition, a man marries his girlfriend. (That is, if a man gets married, it is to his girlfriend. It is not true that if he has a girlfriend he necessarily marries her.) Why is it a "bride" and not a "girlfriend" who walks down the aisle? Similarly, a man marries his fiancée, but, again, we don't talk about the fiancée attending the marriage ceremony. It's the bride. Why?

The answers have to do with the importance of marriage in our society and of its various functions. Marriage has legal, societal, and physical aspects, in addition to any religious and moral roles that might be involved.

Marriage is a legal contract between two people. The state is involved, and—at least in America and other Western countries—a representative of the state has to sanction a marriage. The state decides who can marry whom. The marriage has legal ramifications, among them certain rights and responsibilities for the husband and wife, like a change in tax status.

But marriage, unlike almost every legal matter, is also a social contract. Most people wear jewelry that lets other people know they are married, even though those other people are not involved in the marriage or in the legal contract. The U.S. Constitution does not give the president's spouse any particular role, but society has a title for the role: "first lady," and maybe someday "first man" (or "first husband"?). The title "Mrs." originally meant "wife of . . . ," so "Mrs. Smith" was the "wife of Mr. Smith," and her fuller name could be, for example, "Mrs. John Smith"—that is, "the wife of John Smith." The title is still in popular use in America, even though its meaning for most people has changed. (It now means "a married woman whose last name is . . .".) "Miss" is used for an unmarried woman, and the much newer "Ms." is used for both. This variety of titles reflects the social importance of marriage.

In addition to its legal and social aspects, marriage also represents a physical relationship between two people (prompting the Scottish novelist and playwright Ian Hay to quip that marriage is a ". . . public confession of a strictly private intention." Mr. Hay, born John Hay Beith, also sensed the difficulty of translation. In his play *Housemaster*, one character complains of another that "he can translate English into a Greek not spoken in Greece, and Greek into an English not spoken anywhere").

Even though the legal and social contracts of marriage could be completely separate, in the United States one ceremony usually marks them both. The state authorizes a socially and legally recognized figure—either a religious leader such as a priest or a representative of the state such as a judge—to oversee the legal process along with the social process. That leader is free to introduce religious content, too. The degree to which the physical contract is connected to the social and legal ones is frequently a matter of debate.

All of this is important because different words refer to different aspects of marriage.

In English, we have a word that refers to a woman in a state of being closely involved—either in the near future, the present, or the near past—in a wedding. That word is "bride." We also have a word that focuses not on the ceremony but on the result: "wife." In other words, "wife" is associated with being married, while "bride" is associated with *becoming* married. (For historical reasons, compounds with "bride" have other meanings, most notably "brideless," which generally doesn't mean a man who hasn't married recently but rather a man who hasn't married at all. For that matter, "bride" originally may have meant "daughter-in-law." But we know from Chapter 2 that what words mean and where they come from are two separate issues.)

Unlike "bride," which refers to a legal status, "girlfriend" emphasizes a woman's social and physical status, namely that she has a unique physical relationship with one other person (usually her "boyfriend"). In a quirk of English, the social word and the legal word combine after marriage into "wife." In other words, "being a wife" is a social statement and a legal statement. The social statement is remarkably close to what "girlfriend" means.

Or, at least, a "girlfriend" becomes a "wife" after marriage in the ideal. A husband can have a wife and a girlfriend. Even though that state of affairs is commonly frowned upon, it represents a fairly clear situation. A man has a legal-marriage relationship to one person and something like a social-marriage relationship to another.

Marriage is so important in modern America that we even have a legal term, "ex-wife"—and a related social term, "ex"—that applies equally to an ex-wife and to an ex-girlfriend. And because English is generally nongendered, it also refers to an ex-husband and an ex-boyfriend. (We don't have an English verb for the feeling one has for an ex, but Russian conveniently does: *razlubit'*—literally, to "unlove"—is how you feel for someone you used to love. It's like the English "falling out of love.")

In addition to the social and legal words, we have terms to express physical relationships, like "lover," which is compatible with almost any social and legal relationship. A wife, a bride, or a girlfriend—and also a friend, an acquaintance, or even a stranger—can be a lover.

We find another combination of physical, social, and legal aspects in the words "prostitute," "mistress," "concubine," "date," etc. And even these combinations have variations. A "hooker" and a "whore" both do roughly the same thing, but the second term is generally more insulting.

Even though these words refer to specific combinations of society, law, and physical intimacy, they also, like most words, have other connotations, and here is where we see the difference between "wife" and "spouse." Just as "hooker" and "whore" refer to the same person but convey different aspects of the relationships involved, "wife" and "spouse" are the same person, but they differ in what they emphasize. All wives are spouses, and all female spouses are wives. But "wife" has a different flavor than "spouse." And just as these words can have moral implications, they also can have legal, societal, and physical implications beyond what they actually mean. "Wife," though fundamentally expressing a legal status, also conveys societal information. Even more, "ex-wife," another legal category, entails a host of societal implications. We don't have a common word "ex-spouse," because divorce entails the termination of the "wife" part more than the "spouse" part.

Though we use these words, and others like them, all the time, we don't usually consciously consider the division into social, legal, and physical qualities of what men and women do together. But if we are to use these words to understand another culture, we must take all three into account.

All of this finally puts us in a position to evaluate the merits of the KJV translation "spouse" and the NRSV translation "bride," among other possible ways to convey the epithet *kalah* from Song of Songs. So let's look at that Hebrew word.

Just to get started, *kalah* sometimes means "daughter-in-law," as in Genesis 11:31: "Terah took his son Abram [who will later be renamed "Abraham"] and his grandson Lot, son of Haran, and his daughter-in-law [*kalah*] Sarai [who will later be renamed "Sarah"], his son Abram's wife . . ." (NRSV). Terah's family tree is clear in Genesis, and even if it were not, Genesis 11:31 is particularly unambiguous. Sarai is Terah's son's wife, and she is called Terah's *kalah*.

(Genesis 11:31 also provides yet another example of how etymology can lead us astray. The Greek word for *kalah* there is *numpha*, from which we get the English word "nymph"—that is, a "semidivine . . . beautiful maiden," according to the *Oxford English Dictionary*, though the word has other, more recent connotations, too. In spite of the etymology, Sarai is a daughter-in-law, not a nymph.)

The word *kalah* is also the female version of *chatan*. The pair almost certainly means something like "bride" and "groom," or "bride" and "bridegroom," depending on your dialect. But we don't know what aspect of "bride" and "groom" the words capture. Is it the legal status of marriage? The social contract? The physical relationship? The state of love between a man and a woman? The intention of having children? Or is it some combination?

The more common word for "wife" in Hebrew is simply *isha*, a word that also means "woman" in general. (The English word "wife," too, used to mean "woman"—in particular, one of humble background. This is where we get the expression "old wives' tale." It's a tale from uneducated women; it has nothing specifically to do with marriage.)

We see this same sort of situation with the English word "girl." It refers to children, to young women, and also, at least colloquially (in phrases like "my girl"), to girlfriends; sometimes it even more generally refers to older women. (We'll talk more about these and similar words in Chapter 8.) The English "girl," in other words, is any girl, but also one in a particular relationship. The Hebrew *isha* seems to work that way, too. It means any woman, but particularly a wife.

Hebrew also offers the somewhat rare word *pilegesh*, which is normally translated "concubine," or something like it. We know from Genesis 25 that in addition to his wives, Abraham has some *pilegesh*es, by whom he has additional children. But it looks like "concubine" is a misleading translation, because Abraham's *pilegesh*es are also his wives. In addition, Judges 19:1 makes it clear that a *pilegesh* is also an *isha*. Furthermore, polygamy was the norm in the Bible, and most men had more than one *isha*. It is tempting to say that most men had "more than one wife," but in America a wife is generally the one woman to whom someone is married, so for most people "more than one wife" is almost a contradiction. Instead, we tend to use words like "mistress," "lover," or even "girlfriend" for anyone except the "main wife."

What we see, in the end, is that the word *isha* is so broad that, in addition to its general meaning as "woman," it can refer to almost any relationship a woman might be in with a man: wife, certainly, but also girlfriend, concubine, and so forth.

The word *isha* can also refer to a category we don't have in America—at least, not officially: sex slave. Slaves and slavery were common in the Bible, though here too we have to be careful, because "slavery" in America most commonly means the horrific condition Africans endured on this continent, and because there are forms of organized forced labor that are considerably less oppressive. We call all of them "slavery," but the slavery of the Bible may not have been as terrible as the slavery on the shores of America. Whatever the case, slaves in antiquity did a variety of jobs—including, it would seem, providing sex.

Hebrew has a word for a female slave, *shifcha*, but even though the word frequently refers to a "sex slave," it really just means any slave who is female, whatever she might be assigned to do. Sarai, for example, has a *shifcha* named Hagar whom she gives to her husband, Abram, because she herself can't conceive (it's a particularly ill-conceived strategy to find happiness at home—but that's for another time). We read of this in Genesis 16:1. It's clear that she is simply offering her personal servant, not her personal sex slave, to her husband. Various translations use different words to convey very different apsects of this transaction. So depending on the translation Hagar is Sarai's handmaid, maid, maidservant, woman, or even slave-girl. The various words in English reflect various combinations of what the Hebrew meant and implied. Hagar was a woman, a servant, a maid, and a slave. We don't have a word for that combination, probably because we don't have such people in America.

But servitude was common enough in antiquity that Hebrew has not just *shifcha* but also *ama*, which also refers to a female servant. So at this point, in addition to the general *isha*, which refers to any woman, we have *pilegesh*, "concubine" or something like it; *shifcha*, female slave, perhaps in particular a sex slave; and *ama*, also a female slave, perhaps specifically not a sex slave. English doesn't have any of these words.

On the other hand, English does have words like "ex-husband," "ex-wife," "divorcée," and so on, perhaps because divorce is common in America. By contrast, no couple in the Bible ever gets divorced. (The concept does seem to be represented, but it's rare, and we find it only in the abstract. Four out of the five times the Bible refers to divorce at all, it is in the general phrase, "widowed and divorced [women]," as opposed to a particular person.)

Even though there is no divorce in the Bible, men take second wives. In America, if a man marries, divorces, continues to pay child support to his former wife, and marries a new wife, we call one woman "the ex" and the other "his wife." Perhaps the Bible called them both "his wife." Certainly, American men have legal and other obligations to their ex-wives. Men in the Bible had obligations to their "unloved" (or "disliked" or "hated") wife, as we see in Deuteronomy 21:15: "If a man has two wives, one of them loved and the other disliked, and if both the loved and the disliked have borne him sons, the firstborn being the son of the one who is disliked, then on the day when he wills his possessions to his sons, he is not permitted to treat the son of the loved as the firstborn in preference to the son of the disliked, who is the firstborn."

In short, the terms the Bible uses for relationships between a man and woman overlap only partially with what we now have in English, but we still need a word to translate *kalah* in Song of Songs. What should we call the heroine?

Our answer might depend on whether or not the man and woman in Song of Songs are married, engaged, or otherwise involved with each other. If they're married, "bride" and "spouse" seem like good options. If they are not, though, then certainly "spouse" is wrong. And if they don't plan on getting married immediately, then "bride" is wrong, too. Maybe they are just dating.

But, perhaps surprisingly to the modern reader, the Bible is silent on the issue of commitment here. They may be boyfriend and girlfriend, husband and wife, high-school sweethearts, or more generally "lovers." The focus of the book seems to be the physical and emotional relationship between the man and the woman, not their legal status or their involvement with any other potential lovers.

In light of this ambiguity in Song of Songs, we have a third translation option, beyond the common "bride" or "spouse." We might simply translate *kalah* as "lover," akin to *dodi*. On the one hand, "bride" is poetic in a very different way than "lover." Furthermore, *kalah* is reserved for women. We don't have gendered words for "lover" in English. (There's no word "lovress," like "actress" compared with "actor." We do have a word "mistress," but it usually means something else.)

So "lover" is not a perfect translation. It doesn't match the kind of poetry we seem to find in Song of Songs, and it will make it very hard to use different epithets for the man (*dod*, "lover") and the woman.

But because Song of Songs seems to have nothing intrinsically to do with marriage, in the end we cannot accept "bride" or "spouse" as a translation.

So "lover" it is for the second word, giving us "*achoti* (my) lover." We started with the observation that "my sister, my bride" cannot be the right translation. Clearly, "my sister, my lover" is no better. "Sister" is simply wrong.

To understand the real role of *achoti* ("my sister"), we have to recognize the fact that even beyond the words—girlfriend, wife, lover, etc., in English, or *isha, shifcha, kalah*, etc., in Hebrew—the relationship between a man and a woman is always complicated. We tend to speak in this country of "marriages of convenience," "marrying for money," "marrying for love," etc., using "husband" and "wife" for the participants in all of these very different situations. Even a man and woman who marry solely so that one partner can have health insurance are called "husband" and "wife." And all of that complication is just in the realm of "marriage." "Dating" is even more ambiguous.

In the Bible, too, the words convey only part of the story, with the added complication that in addition to the various sorts of marriages and involvements we find today, slavery was still common back then. A man and woman might have been involved in a marriage of convenience or an affair. Or the woman might have been the man's legal slave.

This is why *achoti* is so important.

SISTERS

There is little doubt that *achot* literally means "sister," so *achoti* literally means "my sister." We are fortunate that Genesis is replete with family trees, all spelled out in words. For example, from Genesis 24:29 we know that Laban is Rebekkah's brother. So in 25:20, when we read that Rebekkah was Laban's *achot*, we know what family relationship *achot* represents.

But across the world's languages, we commonly find that kinship terms such as "brother" and "sister" enjoy expanded meanings. In English, "brother" and "sister" are colloquial terms for friendship, or even inclusion in a social group. "Son" is used not just for progeny but also as a term that includes endearment and sometimes a note of condescension.

In addition to their usually vague expanded meanings, kinship terms often have specific meanings that were once related to the expanded meanings. "Brother," "sister," "father," and "mother" in English are kinship terms, to be sure. They also have expanded meanings. And even beyond that, they are religious terms. A "sister" is a nun, for example.

The reader will remember from the discussion on page 51 that words can be expanded in two ways. There we saw that, on the one hand, a word's meaning can be spontaneously expanded to mean something new, in which case the new meaning is usually vaguely related to the old meaning. Or a word can acquire a specific new meaning. Here we see both kinds of extension. When "brother" is used to mean "someone like a brother in some vague sense that I have not made clear," it's the first kind of extension. That's what we see when someone calls a friend "brother" (or "bro"). When "brother" is used specifically to mean "monk," we see the second kind of extension.

The distinction is important. If the meaning of *achot* in Song of Songs was used to mean "like a sister in some vague way," we might want to translate it as "sister." If, on the other hand, it was used for a specific relationship (like "sister" for "nun") that is not used in English, then "sister" is the wrong translation.

Returning for a moment to the general pattern of kinship terms acquiring specific meanings beyond familial relations, we note that in Modern Hebrew, *ach* means "brother" but also "(male) nurse," while *achot*, in addition to meaning "sister," means "(female) nurse." These are examples of specific extensions of the meaning of the Modern Hebrew words *ach* and *achot*. It would simply be a mistake to translate the Modern Hebrew *achot* meaning "nurse" as "sister" in English. Even though both in Modern Hebrew and in English the word *achot* has general extensions, the English and Hebrew words also have specific extensions, and they do not overlap entirely.

By contrast, if an Israeli calls a friend *ach* to indicate that they are closer than mere friends, "brother" may be the right translation. That's because, in this case, both the Modern Hebrew extension and the English one are of the first, more general variety.

This information about English and Modern Hebrew (and many other languages) doesn't directly tell us anything specific about ancient Hebrew, but it does encourage us to at least look for a nonliteral meaning for *achot*. So we will.

To help us understand *achot*, it will be useful to look as well at the related word *ach*, because it's clear that *ach* and *achot* are essentially the same word in the Bible—the first for males, the second for females.

For example, in Genesis 24:29, which introduces Rebekkah's family tree, the word for "brother" is *ach*. In that context, *ach* and *achot* are kinship terms, meaning exactly what their English counterparts do.

Hosea 2:3 puts *ach* and *achot* in parallel, as does Jeremiah's prophetic message to the sons of Josiah, which includes, "oh, *ach*" and, in parallel, "oh, *achot*." Both of these make the connection between *ach* and *achot* particularly transparent. Whatever *ach* means, *achot* is the female variety of the same thing.

Most translations render these lines as "ah, brother . . . ah, sister" or "alas, brother . . . alas, sister," but clearly these are not kinship terms here. Because "brother" and "sister" in English are, like the Hebrew, not strictly limited to kinship, the translation doesn't immediately seem so jarring. But we know by now that translating a metaphoric term in one language as a metaphoric one in another just because the two words share the same literal meaning is usually a mistake.

For now, we don't really care about exactly what Jeremiah or Hosea meant, so we won't probe the issue further. We do care that "brother" and "sister" seem to be essentially the same word, and that their meanings are not limited to kinship. (Jeremiah is a stronger case for expanding the meaning of *ach* and *achot* than Hosea, because we know from looking at the text more generally that Hosea uses kinship words poetically for their imagery. He may have been using "brother" and "sister" to represent kinship terms, and then using those kinship terms poetically, in the same way he uses marriage, for example, and divorce. We'll look at Hosea's imagery in the concluding chapter.)

So we know that *ach* and *achot* work basically the same way, and we know that their meanings are not limited to "brother" and "sister." This is, of course, good news for Song of Songs.

Our next task is to figure out what these two words represent. Fortunately, a clear answer will present itself.

To start, we note that both *ach* and *achot* are used in phrases that mean roughly "each other." II Kings 7:6 reads, ". . . a man said to his *ach*"—that is, "they said to each other." Ezekiel (Ezekiel 1:9) uses "a woman to her *achot*" to mean "each other" in the phrase "the wings [of the creatures that Ezekiel envisions] were touching each other." (Every noun in Hebrew is either grammatically masculine or grammatically feminine. Because body parts that come in pairs tend to be feminine in Hebrew, when *k'nafayim*, "wings," touch each other it's "a woman to her *achot*" and not "a man to his *ach*.") So there is something about *ach* and *achot* that means "another one just like this one." Of course, one aspect of siblinghood is being the same in some sense. The leap from kinship to the expression "each other" or "one another" is not huge, but it is nonetheless a leap—and a leap that we do not find in English. "People nowadays use e-mail to write to their brothers" in English cannot mean "people . . . write to each other." And, "The captain of the ship spoke to her sister" surely does not mean that the captains of two ships spoke to each other. But the Biblical Hebrew words *ach* and *achot* do function in those ways.

Beyond "another one like the first one," we find a more specific expanded meaning for *ach* and *achot*. Numbers 20:14 is an example. When Moses wants to pass through the land of Edom, he sends word to Edom's king with the introduction, "Thus says your *ach*, Israel . . ." (NRSV). So Israel is Edom's *ach*.

We first note that Moses does not say, "Thus says *Moses* your *ach*." Even though Moses is the one sending the message, he wants to represent the relationship between the people of Israel and, presumably, the people of Edom. It is one of *ach*ness.

In fact, this language between leaders was entirely typical of much of the ancient world. Rulers would commonly use "brother," son," and "father" to refer to one another. The terms represented power structure. Two kings on equal footing might call each other "brother." A powerful king addressed a minor one as "son," and the response was "father." In a surviving document from the fourteenth century B.C., the relatively minor Adad-nerar I wrote to a powerful Hittite king, calling the Hittite "my brother." The response was essentially, "Who do you think you are, my son? Why should I call *you* my brother . . . ?"

We should be careful not to draw conclusions about Hebrew from correspondence in other languages, but we find support for the same pattern in the text of Numbers 20. Moses' letter to Edom was from one leader to an equal leader. At least, that's how Moses wanted to portray the situation. In this light, Moses' request and Edom's response make perfect sense. Moses wants to pass through Edom's country, not venturing into fields or vineyards, not drinking water from any well. "The People of Israel will stay on the king's road" (Numbers 20:17). This would be a perfectly reasonable request from one equal leader to another. Edom refuses the request, though, in response to which (Numbers 20:21) "Israel turned away" from Edom. Moses offered friendship based on equality to the king of Edom, and Edom refused.

In II Kings 5:13, we similarly see "my father" used as a sign of respect. The prophet Elisha tells the Syrian general Naaman, who is suffering from disease, to wash in the waters of the Jordan river. Naaman refuses, preferring the waters of his native Damascus. But Naaman's servants try to convince him to follow the advice of Elisha. "My father," they begin, making it clear that they are speaking to a superior. They know they are walking a politically dicey path, and to ease the way they start with a term of deference.

In the next chapter, no less than the king of Israel calls Elisha "my father" (II Kings 6:21). Normally a king would not call a prophet "my father," but normally a king would not ask permission from a prophet before ordering an attack. That is just what happens there, though. "My father," the king asks Elisha, "shall I kill them?" Elisha has earned the respect of the king, and, accordingly, the king calls him "my father."

In Joshua 7:19, Joshua chastises Achan. From Joshua 7:1 we know that Achan's real father is a man named Carmi, not Joshua. Nonetheless, Joshua says, "My son, give glory to the LORD God of Israel and make confession to him" (NRSV). The mighty Joshua is speaking to the less powerful Achan, telling him what to do. He therefore addresses Achan as "my son."

So we see that "father," "brother," and "son" represent power in Biblical Hebrew. Because kinship terms are not typically used this way in English, "son," "father," and "brother" are the wrong translations. In English, these terms are used broadly and are not limited to kinship, so the translations don't jump off the page as wrong. But they are. Moses doesn't want to portray Israel and Edom as brothers; he wants to portray them as equals. To consider the difference, we might note that politicians do not refer to one another as "son," "brother," and "father."

It is harder to find direct proof that "mother," "sister," and "daughter" also represent power structures, because there are far fewer women than men in the Bible, and because the women are less likely than the men to be involved in ambiguous power relationships. But we already know that the female terms are used roughly the way the male terms are, because they appear in parallel.

We also know that there is one case in particular when the nature of a woman's power relationship would be crucial—and that is when she is with a man. Is she less powerful than the man, equal, or more powerful? All three possibilities are attested to in the Bible. Many readers are surprised that the Bible has the last category, in which a husband serves his wife. While the situation is rare, we do see it in Judges 13. Manoah is basically a bumbling fool (his name translates roughly as "lazy"), and his wife, though unnamed, runs the family and is the one who talks to God. At the other extreme, a woman might be a slave to her husband.

At the beginning of the chapter we saw that the Hebrew words *kalah* and *isha* are so general that they include all sorts of power relationships. An *isha* might be what we would now call a "wife," on equal footing with her husband. Or she might be a concubine or even a sex slave. Or, at the other and rarer end of the spectrum, she might run the family, as we see with Manoah and his anonymous but dominant wife. Similarly with *kalah*: A *kalah* might be a new bride, doted on by her adoring husband, or she might simply be a daughter-in-law, married off to cement a pact or even just for monetary gain.

It is in this context that *achoti kalah* becomes so important. We have translated *kalah* as "lover," recognizing that *kalah* does not convey any particular state of commitment or any particular hierarchy of power. Inasmuch as the hero and heroine of Song of Songs are *dodi* and *kalah*, the heroine might dominate the hero, or she might be his sex slave. We don't know.

But the addition of *achoti* makes the situation clear. The hero considers his lover to be "my *achot*"—that is, as we have seen, "my equal." She is not his slave. She need not be subservient. She is his equal partner in the relationship, at a time when subservience was considerably more widespread than it is now, and the potential servitude included not merely service but outright slavery.

Song of Songs is about equality between lovers, and the Hebrew phrase means "my lover who is my equal" as opposed to "my sex slave/ concubine/property/etc." In a world where women were frequently subservient, Song of Songs uses epithets that emphasize not only the physical aspects of the relationship between the unnamed man and the unnamed woman but the power structure between them as well.

They are equals.

So Song of Songs is about romantic, erotic love, but at the same time it centers around equality. The hero is simply "my (male) lover" and—lest there be any question about the nature of the relationship— the heroine is "my equal (female) lover." The common translation "my sister" completely fails to convey this crucial apsect of Song of Songs.

Finding an English translation that is better is easy ("my equal lover," for example), but finding one that is entirely accurate is more difficult. Certainly, "my sister, my spouse" and "my sister, my bride" are dreadfully wrong. In addition to the error of "bride" or "spouse," the word "sister" in English in this context does not convey the sense of equality that is central to Song of Songs.

"My partner, my lover," comes pretty close in some dialects. But for many speakers, "partner" now primarily means a "same-sex partner."

We also have another potential translation problem. The Hebrew is very clearly "my *achot*," but it is not "my *kalah*." Rather, it is "my *achot, kalah*." One interesting possibility is that the unnamed male lover in Song of Songs has many female lovers, but only one with whom he is engaged in a relationship of equality. More likely, the "my" modifies the entire phrase. If so, we might translate, "my equal, lover." But that sounds stilted in English and lacks the poetry of Song of Songs. Two variations, "my lover, my equal" and "my equal, my lover," seem slightly more poetic, and they are the best we can do. Because the Hebrew puts *achoti*, "my equal," even before "lover," we do the same in English: "my equal, my lover."

It is perhaps heartening to learn that conscious attention to the role of women in society is as old as the Bible itself, and that in its only full-length description of romantic love, the Bible hits the reader over the head with the centrality of equality in a loving relationship.

The right translation can remind modern readers of this all-important message.

7

WANTING, TAKING, AND KILLING:
HOW WE LIVE

≺‹··›≻

לֹא תִּרְצָח / לֹא תַחְמֹד

Thou shalt not kill / Thou shalt not covet

οὐ φονεύσεις / οὐκ ἐπιθυμήσεις

___

Perhaps more than any other part of the Bible, the Ten Commandments have shaped Western culture. They adorn houses of worship and appear in courts of law. Unlike most parts of the Bible, they have influenced secular laws. And it seems that their importance was recognized even in the days of the Bible, for they comprise the only extended passage to appear twice in the Five Books of Moses.

The good news is that most of the commandments have been translated accurately. The bad news is that two have not.

Before we look at what went wrong and what the commandments really mean, it makes sense to understand what the Ten Commandments are and why they are so important.

COUNTING TO TEN

Perhaps surprisingly, there is no universal agreement about which commandments are the Ten Commandments. Nor does everyone agree that all ten are actually commandments.

The nearly identical lists that appear in Exodus 20 and Deuteronomy 5 form the basis of the Ten Commandments. But people disagree about where the introduction to the commandments ends and where the first commandment begins.

Exodus 20:1 reads, "Then God spoke all these words:" (NRSV). Everyone agrees that that line is an introduction (though, surprisingly, many sources nonetheless cite Exodus 20:1 as the start of the Ten Commandments).

Counting to One

But then disagreement sets in. Exodus 20:2 reads, "I am the LORD your God, who brought you out of the land of Egypt, out of the house of slavery" (NRSV). Exodus 20:3 continues, "You shall have no other gods . . ." (The end of the line is particularly difficult to translate, so we're leaving it out for now. It probably means ". . . other than Me.")

Because 20:2 looks like a statement, not a commandment, most Protestants (but not most Lutherans) group 20:2 with the introduction in 20:1, and call Exodus 20:3 the first commandment. So for most Protestants, the first commandment is the entirety of Exodus 20:3: "You shall have no other gods. . . ."

Catholics (and most Lutherans), on the other hand, group 20:2 with 20:3 into one longer first commandment: "I am the Lord your God: you shall have no other gods. . . ." The Catholic first commandment, then, is an abridgement of Exodus 20:2 and all of 20:3.

On the third hand, Jews see two commandments, one in 20:2 and one in 20:3. For Jews, the first commandment is the entirety of 20:2 ("I am the Lord your God. . . .").

Two

Because Jews have completed the first commandment by the end of 20:2, Exodus 20:3 in its entirety forms the second commandment: "You shall have no other gods. . . ." The Jewish second commandment is thus the same as the Protestant first commandment and the second half of the Catholic first commandment.

Exodus 20:4 deals with what are commonly called "graven images." There's some question as to what exactly the Hebrew means—the issue has been the source of more than a little bloodshed, as when Calvin used his understanding of the line to condemn Catholicism—and we're not going to address the question here. The point of Exodus 20:4, though, is not to make them. Depending on whom you ask, the forbidden 'item" may be idols, pictures, pictures of people, carved images, etc.

For Protestants, that's the second commandment: "You shall not make . . . any graven images."

Jews and Catholics, though, group Exodus 20:3 with 20:2 as an instance of how not to have other gods. That is, one way not to have any other gods is not to create idols.

As we just saw, Jews have already used Exodus 20:3 for the second commandment. Catholics, however, jump ahead to Exodus 20:7 to find the second commandment: "Do not take the name of the Lord your God in vain."

Three Through Ten

Jews and Protestants agree that "Do not take the name of the Lord your God in vain" is one of the Ten Commandments, but, unlike Catholics, the Jews and Protestants have already counted to two by Exodus 20:7. So for both of those groups, Exodus 20:7 is the third commandment.

From here to the tenth commandment, the Jewish/Protestant numbering is ahead by one compared with the Catholic numbering. The Jewish/Protestant fourth commandment is about the Sabbath. For Catholics, that's the third commandment.

Similarly, the Jewish/Protestant fifth commandment is about honoring parents. For Catholics, that's the fourth commandment.

At this rate, the Catholics will run out of commandments, because the Jewish/Protestant tenth commandment, commonly translated as "do not covet . . ." is the Catholic ninth commandment. (We'll see below that it doesn't really have anything to do with coveting. It's a major mistranslation.) To get to ten, Catholics have two commandments about "coveting." The ninth commandment regards "your neighbor's wife," and the tenth, "your neighbor's goods." Table 2 summarizes the content of the commandments according to the three numbering systems.

The summaries in the table are purposely vague, for two reasons. Most importantly, we don't want to prejudice our translations before we take a closer look at what the commandments really mean. But also, as we have noted, there are in fact two sets of commandments. So far, we've seen the one in Exodus. Deuteronomy contains another set, starting with Deuteronomy 5:6.

The Ten Commandments in Deuteronomy are mostly the same as the ones in Exodus, but there are differences. For example, the fourth or third commandment in Exodus is specifically to "remember" the

TABLE 2. SUMMARY OF THE TEN COMMANDMENTS

	JEWISH	PROTESTANT	CATHOLIC
1	"I am the Lord"	Other gods	"I am the Lord"/other gods
2	Other gods	Graven images	Lord's name
3	Lord's name	Lord's name	Sabbath
4	Sabbath	Sabbath	Parents
5	Parents	Parents	Killing
6	Killing	Killing	Adultery
7	Adultery	Adultery	Stealing
8	Stealing	Stealing	Testifying
9	Testifying	Testifying	Neighbor's wife
10	Neighbor's wife/stuff	Neighbor's wife/stuff	Neighbor's stuff

Sabbath day, while in Deuteronomy the commandment is to ' keep" or "observe" it. (Because Moses says in Deuteronomy that the list there is the same as the one in Exodus, a Jewish tradition holds that God simultaneously uttered the words *zachor* ["remember"] and *shamor* ["keep"].)

Only the Catholic version contains ten actual commandments. The original Jewish list and the much-later Protestant list both contain at least one statement. Why?

Commandments

The original Hebrew word for the commandments, in Exodus itself, is *davar*.

Though we know better than to use etymology to figure out what a word means, it just so happens that the story behind *davar* is interesting in its own right. Originally, the word may have been an imitation of beelike buzzing. Indeed, the same root that gives us *davar*—that is, D.B.R—also gives us the Hebrew word *d'vorah*, "bee." Perhaps from that original meaning, we get the verb *diber*, "to speak," and the noun *davar*.

The noun *davar* means both that which is spoken (a "word") and also that which is spoken about (a "thing").

Exodus 20:1 tells us that God "spoke" (using the verb *diber*, from the root D.B.R) "all these words" (using the noun *davar*, also from the root D.B.R). So far, there is no specific mention of commandments. (The NAB nonetheless translates "commandments," perhaps in keeping with the goal of translating and also explaining where necessary.)

Exodus 34:28, Deuteronomy 4:13, and Deuteronomy 10:4 all refer to "ten *davars*" (*d'varim* in Hebrew) that Moses wrote upon the tablets. (The tablets number two, but there's no reason to think that they were arrayed in the now-familiar pattern of two columns with rounded tops, five commandments to a column. Equally likely is that all ten commandments were written twice, once on each tablet. Before the advent of carbon paper, pacts would be written in duplicate.)

The word *d'varim* in those three places cannot mean "words," because certainly there are more than ten words. But, in spite of the KJV translation "commandments," there is no reason to think that *d'varim* means "commandments." Much more likely is that it means "things." Just as in colloquial English we might say that God told us "ten things," so too the Bible refers to the ten things that were written on the tablets. (The Talmud, which dates from the second to sixth centuries A.D. and which forms much of the foundation of Judaism as it has been practiced for most of the past two thousand years, uses a similar word, *dibrot*, instead of *d'varim*. To this day, the Ten Commandments in Hebrew are called the "ten *dibrot*," not the "ten *d'varim*." But *dibrot* also doesn't mean "commandments.")

Although the Bible tells us that there are ten *d'varim*, it doesn't actually number them, so we have no way of knowing which numbering tradition more closely reflects the original intention. And because the original Hebrew doesn't mean "commandments," we don't know if all ten aspects of the "Ten Commandments" were commandments, preambles, or whatnot.

We do know that they are unique in the history of civilization.

DOS AND DON'TS

It's easy to miss a subtle but very important distinction that separates the Ten Commandments from other ancient and modern legal codes.

We can use the eighth or seventh commandment ("don't steal") to demonstrate, because the Hebrew is particularly clear, and, unlike some of the other commandments, translators have generally tried to convey the meaning of the Hebrew, rather than turning the translation into what they want it to mean.

It will be useful to compare the commandment against stealing to the laws in the United States that, at first glance, do the same thing. So we'll take a brief detour into American law.

Title 18 of the U.S. Codes ("18 USC") deals with crimes and criminal procedure. The first part of 18 USC deals with the crimes themselves. Chapter 103, in that part, is about robbery and burglary, and Section 2113, which happens to be in that chapter, is about bank robbery. (Just that one section contains about three times the number of words as the entire Ten Commandments, a fact that demonstrates the vast complexity of American law compared with anything in antiquity.)

The law in the United States known as 18 USC 2113, "Bank Robbery and Incidental Crimes," declares, among other things, that "Whoever takes . . . any property or money or any other thing of value not exceeding $1,000 belonging to . . . any bank . . . shall be fined under this title or imprisoned not more than one year, or both." In other words, the penalty for taking up to $1,000 from a bank is a fine, up to one year in jail, or both. Similarly, the penalty according to 18 USC 2113 for taking more than $1,000 is a fine and/or up to ten years in jail. This is what is commonly known as the federal law against bank robbing. When we say that it's illegal to rob a bank, we're referring to 18 USC 2113, which connects the crime with a specific punishment.

Other laws against taking things work a little bit differently. For example, in New York State, Article 155.25 of the NYS Penal Law declares that "A person is guilty of petit larceny when he steals property. Petit larceny is a class A misdemeanor." "Larceny" is what most people call "theft," and Article 155 is what most people call New York State's law against theft. (Later sections of Article 155 define "grand larceny" as taking more than $1,000, so petit larceny is generally considered to be taking less than $1,000.)

As it happens, New York State uses the word "theft" more generally than the way most laypeople do. The legal term includes not only larceny, but also robbery ("forcible stealing"), jostling (which nonlawyers generally call pickpocketing), fortune-telling (which has a near parallel in Leviticus 19:26), possession of stolen property, etc. All of these other laws work essentially the same way, stating the crime and category of that crime. For example, "A person is guilty of fortune telling when, for a fee or compensation . . . he claims . . . to tell fortunes. . . . Fortune telling is a class B misdemeanor."

Working in concert with these and many similar laws in New York State are laws regarding sentences of imprisonment. For example, Article 70.15 metes out punishment of up to one year for stealing less than $1,000. The way it does that is by stating, "A sentence of imprisonment for a class A misdemeanor . . . shall not exceed one year." According to Article 155, as we just saw, stealing up to $1,000 is a Class A misdemeanor. Taken together, Articles 70 and 155 create a punishment of up to one year for theft of up to $1,000.

Article 155.40 declares, "A person is guilty of grand larceny in the second degree when he steals property" worth more than $50,000, and "Grand larceny in the second degree is a class C felony." Article 70 matches with: "For a class C felony, the term . . . shall not exceed fifteen years."

So take up to $1,000 (and get caught and convicted) in New York State, and you go to jail for up to a year. Take more than $50,000, and you go to jail for up to fifteen years. Even though the laws of New York State, and most other criminal codes, list the crimes and punishments in separate places, the effect is the same. "Class C felony," for example, becomes an abbrevation for "up to fifteen years in jail." These laws work exactly the same way as 18 USC, which lists the punishment explicitly next to the definition of the crime, while the laws of New York State refer to the punishment indirectly. But either way, the point is to connect behavior with consequences.

It is in this context that we see the power of the Ten Commandments and why they are fundamentally different from the laws of modern countries. In the Ten Commandments, *there are no consequences.* There are no punishments listed for breaking the Ten Commandments. Unlike 18 USC, the Ten Commandments don't directly list any punishment for stealing, and unlike the New York State laws that we saw, the Ten Commandments don't indirectly list any punishment for stealing. (Technical words help distinguish the Ten Commandments from other laws. Laws that prescribe consequences are call "casuistic." Those that simply state right from wrong are called "apodictc" And we have two more words for cocktail parties.)

The Ten Commandments essentially state that some things are wrong, regardless of the punishment. The Ten Commandments are value judgments: Stealing is wrong. Other parts of the Bible (like Leviticus 5 for theft, Numbers 35 for murder, etc.) function more like American law, connecting behavior and consequences, but they do not refer back directly or indirectly to the Ten Commandments, and the Ten Commandments do not refer to them. Even if there were no punishments, claim the Ten Commandments, stealing would still be wrong.

A few examples will further demonstrate the difference.

Suppose a man wants money so much that he's willing to spend time in jail to get it. Perhaps he wants to buy a gift for someone he loves. Perhaps he thinks jail isn't so bad. Or maybe he thinks he will get away with it, and he's willing to take the chance. He might think he'll only get caught one time out of twenty, so he thinks he can probably walk away with $20,000 and only spend a year a jail, a bargain in his mind.

In New York State, he reads up on the law, learns that if he steals $1,000 he will not have to spend more than one year in jail, and for whatever reason, he decides it's worth it. Nothing in the entire body of the New York State and federal law says that he isn't entitled to make this calculation. Nowhere does it say that it's wrong, immoral, or otherwise undesirable. The law has punishments for behavior, but it doesn't take a stand on the nature of the behavior itself.

Some people attach moral judgments to legal states—looking down on felons, for example, or using the word derogatorily. But these moral judgments are not part of the law. They are part of society. Even the difference between felony and misdemeanor is just a technical distinction in the law. Qualitatively it is no different than other technical differences, like Class A versus Class B. While there is a general sense that felonies are worse than misdemeanors, there is also a general sense that Class A violations are worse than Class B violations. Some employers refuse to hire felons, and some states don't let them vote. But again, any moral judgments involved in these practical decisions do not come from the law.

By way of a second example, we might consider a situation that arose in Boston's Logan Airport in the 1980s. The fine for illegal parking at the airport was sometimes less than the price of legal parking. So people started leaving their cars illegally at the curb of their terminal of choice. They knew that the police would tow the car. They knew that they would have to pay a towing charge and a fine. But they also knew that the combined expense was less than legal parking fees would be, so they decided it was worth it. Massachusetts law made no judgment about their behavior, and most of these illegal parkers were proud of the inexpensive valet parking they had managed to find at the airport. (Massachusetts has since upped the fines for illegal parking and the charges for towing.)

Most modern people agree that illegal parking and theft are in different categories. They're both illegal, but only the second one is wrong in some larger sense. There is generally no moral implication, people think, to where they park. (Of course there are exceptions, like blocking a fire hydrant.) By contrast, they think, theft is a matter of morality. In fact, most people don't have much trouble categorizing other behaviors. Running a red light at night when there's no other traffic on the road may be illegal, but if it's not dangerous, they think, it's not immoral. It's like the parking at Logan. Killing a person for no reason is different. It's like stealing. It's immoral.

It is the Ten Commandments that makes the distinction overt. The Ten Commandments list the behavior that is wrong. Regardless of the punishment—or, for that matter, lack of punishment—people shouldn't steal. Even if they are willing to pay the fine, even if they are willing to spend the time in jail, even if they don't think they will get caught, they shouldn't take what belongs to someone else. In light of Leviticus 5, which details the punishment for theft, the Ten Commandments might seem superfluous. Why say "Don't steal" when another part of the Bible already has a punishment for stealing? The answer is that Leviticus 5 is a legal system, while the Ten Commandments are a moral framework. The point is that stealing is wrong. The severity of the offense has nothing to do with getting caught or punished.

So even though the Ten Commandments at first seem like modern laws, they are in fact completely different. They are different, in fact, from every other system of law.

The Ten Commandments are frequently compared to the Code of Hammurabi. Named after the ancient Babylonian ruler Hammurabi, the code dates from the first part of the second millennium B.C.—long before the Ten Commandments were written—and details the punishments that were in force for a great variety of crimes in ancient Babylonia. (Curiously, court records of the time don't reference the Code of Hammurabi in the way we would expect them to if they were really the law of the land. So the role of the code may not be exactly what it seems.)

Some scholars think that the Code of Hammurabi, coming as it does before the Ten Commandments, diminishes the importance of the Bible. In their minds, the Ten Commandments are merely a revision, sometimes not even a good one, of something that the Babylonians had long before. But like our modern American laws, the Code of Hammurabi merely prescribes consequences. It lacks the fundamental force of the Ten Commandments. (In technical jargon, all of the laws in the Code of Hammurabi are casuistic, not apodictic like the Ten Commandments.)

So when we study the Ten Commandments, we are studying perhaps the first and most lasting list of behavior that, regardless of other considerations, is wrong.

In this context it is particularly unfortunate that the commandments have been translated into English so poorly. The common mistranslations distort one of the foundations—perhaps the most important foundation—upon which humankind's sense of right and wrong is built.

SHALT

Before turning to what the verbs in the Ten Commandments mean, we need to look at the grammatical form of those verbs.

For example, the seventh/eighth commandment in Hebrew is *lo tignov*. The Hebrew *lo* expresses negation. The verb literally means "You will steal." So, literally, the phrase means "You will not steal." This is where we get the familiar KJV translation, "Thou shalt not steal." Remember from Chapter 1 that "thou shalt" was formal but ordinary English when the KJV was written.

The word *lo* appears thousands of times in the Bible, in contexts that range from descriptions of the present, predictions of the future, commandments, and more. It is very clearly a general word used for all sorts of negation, just like the English "not." Because "not" in English works (almost) exactly like *lo*, it's not hard for English speakers to understand that part of the phrasing of the Ten Commandments.

The future tense here, however, is misleading. We know from Chapter 3 that we should avoid the temptation to blindly translate grammatical forms, so the future tense in Hebrew may or may not correlate with the future tense in English. In this case, it does not.

In fact, the future tense in Hebrew is used for imperatives: commandments, but more generally commands, requests, etc. The "go" in the English "Go home" is an imperative, for example. Across the world's languages, we find that the imperative is closely related to the future, both in form (sometimes they are the same) and in meaning. That's because one key function of the future tense is to express what has not yet happened, and one key function of the imperative, likewise, is to express what has not yet happened.

This is why, in English, only the future tense can be conjoined (connected with "and") to the imperative. For example, if you're planning a party with a friend, you might tell the friend: "You get the drinks and I'll buy the food." The imperative "you get" is conjoined with the future "I'll buy." By contrast, the past tense doesn't work at all in the same situation: "You get the drinks and I bought the food."

So based on general linguistic principles, we have reason to believe that the future-tense form might simply be the Hebrew way of expressing an imperative. And elsewhere in the Bible we see extensive support for this second role of the future-tense forms.

Because of the nature of the Bible, these imperatives are frequently used when God addresses people. It is therefore reasonable to ask if the form *lo* with a future-tense verb is solely for that purpose, and if so, whether we might need a special way of translating it into English. But it turns out that when people talk to each other in the Bible, they use the same form. For example, in Leviticus 10:6, Moses addresses Aaron and his sons, telling them not to bare their heads and not to tear their clothes. For "do not tear [your clothes]," we find the Hebrew phrase *lo tifromu*. We already know that *lo* means "don't." The verb *tifromu* literally means "you will tear."

In short, when Moses tells people not to do something, he uses the construction *lo* with a future-tense verb. This is but one example of many. We conclude that this grammatical form is simply the imperative in Hebrew. So it should be translated as an imperative in English.

Though the KJV usually mistranslates these verb forms as the future tense in English ("thou shalt not . . . ," "ye shall not . . . ," etc.), sometimes it gets the translation right, as in Deuteronomy 1:42, "And the LORD said unto me, Say unto them, Go not up, neither fight." While the KJV fails here by using "Go not up" and "neither fight"—two very different forms in English for the same form in Hebrew—in this case it does correctly render the combination of *lo* and a future-tense verb as an imperative.

At any rate, we are confident that the construction is imperative in nature. The obvious translation choice is "Do not . . ." "Do not steal," for example. Some English dialects may prefer "Don't steal."

Another intriguing option is "No stealing." But while that is probably the point of the commandment, it's not what it says. So we opt for "Do not steal."

Our next task is to figure out what else is forbidden by the Ten Commandments.

LIFE AND DEATH

The fifth or sixth commandment—as usual, depending on who does the counting—is "Don't *r'tsach*." Two common translations for that verb are "kill" and "murder," and they mean very different things. Other reasonable possibilites are "commit manslaughter," "put to death," "slay," and so forth. Let's find out what *r'tsach* really means.

As it happens, the first place we find the verb *r'tsach* in the Bible is in the Ten Commandments themselves, but because the context is sparse, we have almost no information about the verb. All we know from Exodus 20:13 is that *r'tsach* is something not to do. It could be anything.

Numbers 35, however, gives us a wealth of information. That section talks about different kinds of killing.

Numbers 35:6 sets the stage by introducing what are generally called "cities of refuge," a name that reflects the refuge people could find in such a city in one of two circumstances, as we will see next.

The practice in antiquity was for a killing to be avenged by a family member. If a person was killed, that person's brother or father would be expected to kill the killer. The practice is frequently called "blood vengeance," and almost every translation calls the one who does this— the killer who kills the first killer—the "blood avenger." The actual Hebrew suggests "blood redeemer" (*go'el hadam*), however, reflecting the notion that killing the killer is a step toward redemption, not vengeance.

The first function of the cities of refuge is to make sure that the blood redeemer doesn't kill people without due process. Anyone who kills another may flee to a city of refuge, and, once there, the killer is considered beyond the reach of a blood redeemer.

The second function of the cities of refuge is to make sure that the blood redeemer only kills people who are actually guilty of capital crimes. According to Numbers 35, the penalty is death (at the hands of a blood redeemer) only for some kinds of killing. Just to take one example, a blood redeemer is required to kill a man who kills intentionally, but in the case of an accidental killing "the congregation" (also translated "assembly," and perhaps akin to a jury) decides between the blood redeemer and the killer. The congregation has the option of deciding that the killer should die or, alternatively, that the killer should be allowed to live. If the killer is allowed to live, he is returned to the city of refuge, where he is beyond the reach of the blood redeemer.

The cities of refuge thus served both functions of modern jails (and prisons). Suspected criminals are put in jails while awaiting sentencing, and convicted criminals who are allowed to live are punished by having to stay there. Unlike modern jails, however, the cities of refuge required no bars or guards. People didn't want to escape. For once outside the cities of refuge, they were subject to death at the hands of a blood redeemer. Also unlike modern jails, the cities of refuge seem to have been used only for killers.

Details of the cities of refuge are fascinating: Who lived in them? Were they real cities? Was the plan ever implemented? And so forth. But here we will focus on the rules about who went to these cities, using language to help us understand the different categories of killing in the Bible and the words used to denote them.

We ultimately have four words to consider: *hikah*, *heimit*, *harag*, and *ratsach*. (As we usually do, we use the past-tense forms of the verbs when we talk about what they mean. We've already seen the imperative of the last one: *r'tsach*.) What the verbs have in common is that they all represent a situation that results in death.

For example, when Cain kills Abel in Genesis 4:8, the verb is *harag*. When Moses kills the Egyptian taskmaster in Exodus 2:12, the verb is *hikah*. In Genesis 18:25, Abraham pleads with God not to kill the people of Sodom, arguing before God that God should not kill the righteous along with the wicked. There the verb is *heimit*. In Psalm 94:6, *ratsach* is parallel to *harag*, suggesting that they have much in common.

The verb *ratsach*, however, is used primarily in two places. One is the verb in the Ten Commandments. The other is in the discussions of the cities of refuge and the laws regarding the various kinds of killing that accompany them.

So we jump into the book of Numbers, looking at the various words used there as stepping-stones to understanding what *ratsach* means in the Ten Commandments.

Strike

Our first verb, *hikah*, seems to have the general meaning of "strike," for which the KJV generally uses "smite" (or "smote," etc.). Many people's modern understanding of "smite" is "kill," but both that English verb and the original Hebrew *hikah* appear in situations that are more general.

Just to get started, we note that the word for "plague" in Hebrew is *makah*, a noun clearly related to *hikah*. Nouns and verbs, even when they are related, need not mean the same thing, but we note the fact for two reasons. First, it at least suggests that *hikah* might have a broader meaning. And second, we sometimes find the verb *hikah* used, perhaps on purpose, in the narrative about the plagues.

In Exodus 7:17, Moses *hikah*s the water to create the first plague, in which the water turns to blood. In Exodus 9:25, the seventh plague of hail *hikah*s the plants of the field. Perhaps "kill" is the point in the seventh plague, but equally likely the hail just hits the plants. In the first plague, it's hard to imagine Moses "killing" the water. The end result may involve death, because perhaps the now-bloody Nile can no longer support life. But even so, it's the creatures in the Nile that are killed, not the water. And at any rate, in Exodus 8:17, the third plague is brought about when Aaron strikes (*hikah*) the dust of the earth, turning it into lice (or perhaps some other sort of vermin).

We might think that the text in Exodus purposely uses the verb *hikah* because of its relationship to the noun *makah*, "plague." But we find that *hikah* means "hit" elsewhere, as well.

In Numbers 22:23, Balaam hits the donkey that is bringing him to King Balak. We know that the donkey doesn't die, because it keeps walking (and, later, starts talking, joining the snake in Genesis as the only two animals in the Bible that talk). The verb there is *hikah*.

Similarly, after God asks Moses to speak to a rock and get water, Moses in Numbers 20:11 *hikah*s the rock twice instead. Moses clearly didn't kill the rock. He hit it.

For that matter, Exodus 35:16 contains the phrase "if someone *hikah*s someone else and the someone else dies . . . ," making it almost certain that a person can *hikah* another without killing.

On the other hand, as we just saw, Moses *hikah*s a taskmaster in Exodus 2:12 and then buries him. We have to assume that the taskmaster was dead. In the tenth plague in Exodus 12:29, God *hikah*s the firstborn of Egypt, killing them, not merely hitting them.

So it looks like *hikah* means "to hit," and sometimes it means "to hit so hard as to cause death."

Kill

The next verb is *harag*, and it very clearly means "to kill." We have already seen that when Cain kills Abel, the verb is *harag*. It is not always easy to know entirely from context what the verb *harag* means. Even though there is universal agreement that Cain killed Abel and didn't, say, merely wound him or put him into a coma, it's hard to rule out these lesser possibilities from the text in Genesis.

Fortunately, we sometimes find that *harag* is the opposite of "let stay alive." For example, in Numbers 31:17–18, every male gets *harag*ed, but the women and children get to live. *Harag* is incompatible with "let live."

Cause to Die

Next we have *heimit*. The word for "die" or "dead" is *met*, and *heimit* is closely related. Its internal word structure suggests that it might mean "cause to die," and even though we know from Chapter 2 that internal word structure does not always tell us what a word means, we also know that it can sometimes suggest useful avenues of inquiry.

Fortunately, context here is pretty clear. We've already seen that the word is used in connection to God's killing the people in Sodom.

Similarly, in Genesis 37:18–20, we see a connection between *heimit* and *harag*. Joseph's brothers see him coming from afar, and the narrative uses the verb *heimit* to tell us that they conspire to kill him. Then the text puts the words "let us kill him" into the mouths of the brothers. There the verb is *harag*. So it looks as if *harag* and *heimit* mean the same thing.

Deuteronomy 13:10 offers instruction regarding an idolater. Specifically, "You must kill him. Your hand will be the first to kill him." The first verb "kill" is *harag*, and the second is *heimit*. Again, *harag* and *heimit* look like at least near synonyms.

So we see that *hikah* means "hit," perhaps causing death, while both *harag* and *heimit* mean "kill."

What about *ratsach*?

Legal and Illegal Killing

All of this brings us back to Numbers 35.

In 35:11, we find that someone who *ratsach*s another "by accident" may flee to a city of refuge. The next line tells us that one point of the cities of refuge is that the *ratsach*er can stay there until he goes before the congregation, rather than dying at the hands of a redeemer.

Just from 35:11 we don't know what *ratsach* means, but we know that it can include doing something by accident.

Numbers 35:16 gives us more direct information. "If someone hits [*hikah*] another with an iron tool and he [the other] dies, he [the first] is a *ratsach*er." (One problem we have with the text is that it involves two people, both of whom are called "he." In modern English, particularly in legalese, we might prefer "If the party of the first part hits the party of the second part with an iron tool and the party of the second part dies, the party of the first part is a *ratsach*er." Instead what we have, literally, is, "If he hit him with an iron object and he dies, he is a *ratsach*er.")

The point of Numbers 35:16 is that there are lots of kinds of *hikah*-ing, and only some are *ratsach*ing. The first case is someone who *hikah*s another with an iron tool so that the other dies. What we have is a category of "killing" that is considered *ratsach*ing. As is typical in the Bible, the category is defined by examples, and the first example is the case of killing by iron tool.

The next line expands the category to one who strikes another with a "stone that will kill"—that is, a "deadly stone object." (In English, we would say "stone object that can kill" or "stone object that might kill," not "stone object that will kill." Hebrew typically uses fewer modals—words like "can," "might," etc.—than English. Additionally, the text reads "hand stone," not just "stone." We can ignore these minor matters for now to help us better focus on the verb *ratsach*.)

Numbers 35:18 adds "deadly wooden object" to the list.

So we have three actions that are considered *ratsach*ing: killing with an iron object, killing with a deadly stone object, and killing with a deadly wooden object.

Numbers 35:19 offers a brief interlude about what to do with the *ratsach*er. The blood redeemer must kill him, and here the verb for "kill" is *heimit*. That is, what the blood redeemer does is *heimit*, as opposed to *ratsach*, which is what the guy with the iron, deadly stone, or deadly wooden object did.

The text then adds three more cases of people who are *ratsach*ers: Someone who pushes another in hatred and the other dies, someone who purposefully throws something at another and the other dies and someone who hits another with his fist in anger and the other dies. All three are *ratsach*ers, and the blood redeemer must *heimit* them—though, as is frequently the case, the details are not clear. Some translators think that "purposefully" in the second instance refers to lying in wait.

(The "hatred" clause in the first instance is particularly intriguing, because it suggests an ancient parallel with modern hate crimes, a topic that has been hotly debated in modernity. According to the FBI, a "hate crime" is a "criminal offense . . . which is motivated . . . by the offender's bias against a race, religion, disability [etc.]"—in other words, a crime whose motivation is hatred of a particular group to which the victim belongs. Proponents of augmented penalties for hate crimes point to the particularly insidious nature of attacking people for what they represent. On the other side of the debate are those who don't think the law should legislate what a person thinks or feels. They note that it's not illegal to hate someone in America. The Bible seems to take the position that what someone thinks or feels—specifically, hatred—can be an indication of the severity of a crime.)

In contrast to the first group, the text continues with a second category: someone who pushes another spontaneously and not in anger, or throws something inadvertently, or doesn't see another person and throws a nondeadly stone on the other and the other dies, so long as the first person was not the other's enemy and didn't want to harm the other guy. In this second category, the assembly has to judge between the *makeh* (the first guy, or the assailant, as we might say in English) and the blood redeemer.

The punishment for this second category is that the assailant must return to the city of refuge until the death of the high priest. This contrasts with the first category, the punishment for which is death at the hands of the blood redeemer. In both cases, though, the assailant is a *ratsach*er.

What we have seems remarkably similar to the terms "murder" and "manslaughter" as they are frequently used in modernity. The laws of the State of New York, for example, define murder and manslaughter such that the former is a more serious offense than the latter, though the details do not match Numbers.

The laws of the State of New York also reconfirm what we already know—namely, that we cannot rely on the literal meanings of words if we want to know what they really mean. Article 125 of the New York State penal code defines "homicide" to mean illegal killing. Legal killing, in New York State, is not homicide, even though both the etymology and common use of the term suggest otherwise. In fact, Article 125 actually declares that, among other things, "homicide means . . . criminally negligent homicide," using "homicide" to define 'homicide" (and probably causing English teachers all over to cringe)

We should not be misled by similar ties between Biblical law and modern law. In modernity, accidental killing is neither murder nor manslaughter. It is not a crime. In this country, if a person accidentally kills another through no fault of his own—if, say, following the example in Numbers, someone throws a nondeadly object by accident and it just happens to kill another—the thrower is generally not guilty of a crime at all. By contrast, in the Bible the thrower is guilty and sentenced to a city of refuge until the death of the high priest. (Priests in ancient Israel were the guardians of the religion and the ones tasked with performing sacred rites such as sacrifice. The leader of the priests was designated the "high priest." It is not clear why the death of the high priest was connected to letting people out of a city of refuge. Apparently, though perhaps surprisingly, this connection doesn't seem to have created any significant incentive to kill the high priest.)

In short, unforeseeability is no defense in the Bible. (This difference is worthy of a book in itself. Guilt in America has to do with intent. Guilt in the Bible, at least here, has to do with the result.)

In other words, Numbers 35 is about two different kinds of illegal killing. It seems that Biblical law, like our modern law, recognized two different degrees of illegal killing. In some regards, modern codes agree with the Bible: Premeditated killing in both legal systems falls into the more severe category. Both systems also require the handler of a deadly object to exercise care. And both systems take hatred into account as a complicating factor. (At least, some modern systems do this—as we noted earlier, debate continues about hate crimes.)

In addition to the two levels of illegal killing in the Bible, there's a third, legal sort. The blood redeemer who kills a killer is not committing a crime. (Also one interesting point of view lets Cain off the hook. He didn't break any laws because there weren't yet any laws to break.) Killing an idolater, as we saw in Deuteronomy 13:10, is not only legal but required.

Most of the uses of *ratsach* are in connection to the cities of refuge, the laws of which are repeated in Deuteronomy and then again in the Book of Joshua.

We also find the verb in I Kings, where Elijah uses it, quoting God, to rebuke King Ahab for wrongly killing Naboth. The Book of Job (in 24:14), as part of a litany of evils in the world, notes the existence of "*ratsach*ers" who kill the poor and needy, like thieves at night. (As it happens, we have yet another word for "kill" here: *katal*. It's a rare word that means the same thing as *harag*.) Proverbs 22:13 warns that a lazy man worries that there might be a lion outside, and if he goes outside he might be killed—that is, *ratsach*ed. Jeremiah and Hosea both use the verb, but clearly to quote the Ten Commandments. And that's it.

We are finally in a position to understand what *ratsach* means, because in all of these instances (save perhaps the case with the lion, where we assume poetic license), *ratsach* is used for *illegal killing*. The most general word is *hikah*. It means "to hit." Frequently, such hitting will result in death. If so, the words *harag* ("kill") and *heimit* (also, "kill") apply. Those are less general than *hikah*. But they are still more general than *ratsach*, which only applies to illegal killing.

So the Ten Commandments do not forbid all acts of killing, and the KJV translation ("Thou shalt not kill") is wrong because it overreaches. According to the Bible—and, in particular, to the Ten Commandments, certain kinds of killing are OK.

Because of this glaring error in the KJV, the NRSV changed the translation to "You shall not murder." (But the translators hedged, adding a footnote: "or kill.") The NRSV translation is better, because it doesn't leave the reader with the mistaken notion that any killing is forbidden. But it still misses the mark, because it's not strong enough. The Ten Commandments forbid murder, but also what we call manslaughter in this country. So perhaps the less concise "Don't commit homicide" would be better. But, in fact, because the details of the two illegal categories of killing in the Bible differ from modern notions, even "Don't commit homicide" is too weak.

The concept is really, "Don't break the law and kill," a translation that brings us back to the point of the Ten Commandments. If the Ten Commandments were part of a legal code, there would be no point in saying "Don't kill illegally." But the Ten Commandments highlight the fact that some laws (such as the laws against killing) are more important than others (tithing, for example). Even if you'd be happy to live in a city of refuge, and even if you can contrive to make your murder look like an accident, you don't get to kill whomever you want.

We don't have a perfect translation for this in English. But surely "Don't kill" is wrong. In the end, "Don't murder" is the best we have.

We also learn a more general lesson. While "Don't murder" is closer than "Don't kill," it still misses much of the original point, particularly because the Hebrew prohibition includes manslaughter, while "murder" in English sometimes specifically excludes lesser forms of illegal killing. The more general point is that, in isolation and without context, some passages of the Bible don't have any perfect translation. Or, to look at the matter from the other direction, no English translation perfectly conveys the Hebrew.

Sometimes a translation that's almost right is good enough. If we misrepresent the shade of a color (as with the "red heifer" from Numbers 19:2 that we used as an example of Hebrew word order in Chapter 3), it probably doesn't matter too much. Or if we misrepresent a variety of tree in a story, we can probably still understand the story's point. But other times—as here, where we're talking about a fundamental moral framework—almost correct is not "good enough" but "wrong."

This doesn't mean we shouldn't try to find the best translation we can. But we should recognize that sometimes translation can only go so far.

WANTING AND TAKING

So we've seen that one of the most important commandments is often seriously misquoted. The commandment against murder is interesting because it is among the most universal. Most well-meaning people never murder, yet legal killing is more widespread—among soldiers, in self-defense, etc. In other words, while many people violate the common but wrong mistranslation of the commandment, most people follow what it really means.

Another commandment, the tenth or both the ninth and tenth, follows the same pattern. The summary in Table 2 of the tenth commandment (or the ninth and tenth commandments) is purposely vague so as not to prejudice the issue. The commandment is about one's neighbor's wife and property and so forth. What isn't one supposed to do to them?

The familiar answer from the KJV version is "Thou shalt not covet." But what exactly is "coveting"? Unlike "stealing," "killing," "murdering," etc.—which are all common verbs—"coveting" in English is hardly ever used outside of the context of the Ten Commandments themselves.

For example, the U.S. Code—the sum total of the set of federal laws—doesn't contain the word "covet." That extensive legal system uses other words—"steal," "kill," "take," "murder," and so forth—dozens or sometimes hundreds of times. But "covet" doesn't appear.

Most people have only one reference point for "covet," and that's the Ten Commandments. People know what, say, "stealing" is. So when they read "Don't steal" (or "Thou shalt not steal"), the Ten Commandments form a bridge between an ancient commandment and something they already understand. They know that the Ten Commandments forbid something that exists elsewhere in their lives. "Covet" is different. Because people don't use the word elsewhere, when they read that word in the Ten Commandments, they just know that the Ten Commandments forbid something that is forbidden by the Ten Commandments. It takes an additional step to fill in the gaps of what is otherwise nearly circular.

Yet because the Ten Commandments are so widespread, that one appearance of the word is enough to make "covet" much more common than it otherwise might be, and most people have a sense that it means "desire," "want," "crave," "lust," etc.

The English word "covet" does mean that, but the original Hebrew does not.

The Hebrew verb is *chamad*, and we know by now how to figure out what it means. We look at how it is used.

The root Ch.M.D is a fairly common one in Hebrew, and, in addition to the simple verb form we see in the Ten Commandments, the root appears in a variety of other words. But we know from Chapter 2 that using related words might lead us astray.

The first time the verb *chamad* appears in the Bible is in the Ten Commandments themselves. All we know from there is that *chamad* is something not to be done. It could be anything.

The next time we see the verb is in Exodus 34:24, and here we get a very clear sense of what the word means—or at least, what it does not mean. Exodus 34:23 sets the stage by referring to the pilgrimage holidays (the Feast of Matzot, Feast of Weeks, and Feast of Booths) during each of which Jews—or, in Exodus 34:23, just the men—were to leave their homes and ascend to Jerusalem. In that context, Exodus 34:24 promises that ". . . no one will *chamad* your land when you go up [to Jerusalem] three times a year."

Clearly, the verse is meant to tell people that it's OK to leave their land, that nothing bad will happen while they are gone. A variety of meanings seem reasonable, but "covet" is not among them. Surely, when the people left their land untended, they were not afraid that other people would simply desire it. Other people could desire the land whether the landowners were around or not. There is nothing about the temporary absence of the men that would make the land more desirable from afar.

On the other hand, the landowners might reasonably have feared that during their pilgrimage other people would *take* their land. Perhaps *chamad* means "take"?

This verse doesn't do much to narrow down the meaning, unfortunately. Perhaps *chamad* means "destroy," for all we know from just this one verse. So we keep looking.

We see the verb again in Deuteronomy 5, of course, in the repetition of the Ten Commandments.

Then we see it yet again in Deuteronomy 7:25: "Burn their god statues in fire; do not *chamad* the silver and gold on them and take it. . . ." Surprisingly, the KJV has "desire" here, not "covet," even though it's the same verb that the KJV translates as "covet" elsewhere.

The line is tantalizing, because it makes it clear that there's a connection between *chamad* and taking, but we don't immediately know what the connection is.

One reasonable possibility is that *chamad* means the same thing as "take." We frequently find information repeated for clarity or for emphasis. The first part of the line instructs the Israelites to "burn" them "in fire." What else could burning involve but fire? Similarly, *chamad* may be included next to "taking," as if to indicate "*chamad*, by taking," just like "burn, in fire." This would accord perfectly with Exodus 34, where it looked like the word meant "take."

Unfortunately, the other possibility, still based on Deuteronomy 7:25, is that *chamad* is a precursor to taking or is related to taking in some other way. If so, the line would mean something like, "Don't prepare to take the silver and gold, and certainly don't actually take it."

We don't have a verb in English for "prepare to take" or "prepare to acquire," but that doesn't mean that there is no such process. People who are planning to buy a new car will frequently imagine what it would be like to have the car. They might keep a brochure at home. They might talk about it with their friends. Or they might make a project out of buying the car, enjoying the process of looking at colors, optional equipment, etc. Maybe this is what *chamad* means? From Deuteromy 7:25, it's possible. That verse might mean "Don't imagine your life with the silver and gold, because then you'll be tempted to take it."

But does that meaning work in Exodus 34? Not quite. Exodus 34 is so helpful because it tells us that people are more likely to *chamad* someone's land when the landowner is not around. It doesn't seem reasonable that people would be more apt to imagine owning someone's unoccupied land than occupied land. It's unlikely that the people leaving for Jerusalem on their pilgrimage would worry, "I hope no one imagines what it's like to have my land while I'm gone."

A third possibility lies in the middle. Perhaps *chamad* means "take temporarily." The Hebrew verb we just translated as "take" in Deuteronomy 7:25 is *lakach*. Perhaps Hebrew had two kinds of taking, temporary and permanent, and perhaps *lakach* was the latter while *chamad* was the former. In English, "take" normally means "take permanently," but it can, in fact, be either one. "I only took it for an hour and I gave it back" is a perfectly reasonable English sentence. If Hebrew had verbs for both kinds of taking, it would make sense that *chamad*ing could lead to *lakach*ing. "Don't take it home and enjoy having it" could be the point of Deuteromony 7:25, "because then you'll be tempted to take it permanently."

This meaning also meshes with Exodus 34:24. The landowners might have feared that another person would try out their homes while they were away.

Other passages in the Bible reinforce a close connection between *chamad* and *lakach*. Joshua 7:21 and Proverbs 6:25 both juxtapose *chamad* and *lakach*, either one after the other (as in Deuteronomy) or in parallel.

Proverbs 6:25 is particularly interesting, because it starts off with "Don't *chamad* a beauty in your *levav*," which might make it seem as though *chamad* is something that happens as part of the intangible internal process of being human. After all, we saw in Chapter 4 that *levav* represents the aspects of life like thoughts, emotions, etc. But the next half of Proverbs 6:25, parallel to the first, reads, "Do not be taken by her eyelids." Both halves of the line are poetic, and both in the same way. They put overt actions into metaphoric parts of the body. The *levav* ("heart," but not really) is an organ with poetic impact, as we saw in detail in Chapter 4. And the eyelids are used poetically to represent beauty. (We don't know for sure if the Hebrew word means "eyelashes," "eyelids," or some other eyelike body part.)

Proverbs 12:12 lends further support to the idea that *chamad* has something to do with taking, through the use of parallel opposites. The first part of the line has "wicked/*chamad*," and the second part, "righteous/give." The details of the line are a little more difficult to get right, so we'll leave it untranslated, but pretty clearly, *chamad* is the opposite of "give."

In Psalm 68:17, it is God who *chamad*s a mountain. Surely the mountain stays where it is, so this doesn't look like physical taking. It could be that God loves the mountain or that God has taken the mountain in some figurative sense, along the lines of "choose."

Finally, we have Proverbs 1:22: "How long, ye simple ones, will ye love simplicity? And the scorners *chamad* in their scorning, and fools hate knowledge?" (KJV). We have three verbs—"love," "hate," and, between those two, *chamad*. So it might seem that *chamad*, like the other two, is a verb of intention, not of action. That's why the KJV translates it as "delight" here (not "covet").

But the entire line is poetic, with two parallel phrases followed by a third one that contrasts with the first two, conveying the same meaning but breaking the pattern: "simple ones love simplicity"/"scorners *chamad* in scorn"/"fools hate knowledge" (KJV). Though disagreement abounds about the exact meanings of the words translated as "simplicity" and "scorn," we can use those translations to look at the rhetorical style of the passage.

The line has three parts. The first two are of the form "X verb X." "Scorn" appears twice. Then "simple" appears twice. It's the third part that breaks this pattern, with "fools" and "knowledge," using opposites instead of nearly identical words. In this regard the first two parts are the same and the third one different.

But in another regard, it's the middle part that's different. The first and last parts use the words "love" and "hate," which form a familiar pair of opposites. From this point of view, *chamad* is the odd one out. We can't conclude from this fact that *chamad* isn't a verb of intention, but neither can we conclude from the line that *chamad is* a verb of intention. The threefold structure in which *chamad* differs from the other two verbs makes it hard to draw any conclusions at all. So Proverbs 1:22 is interesting in its own right and a useful example of Biblical poetry, but it doesn't help us much with *chamad*.

Fortunately, we don't need Proverbs 1:22 to figure out what *chamad* means. We already have a pretty good idea. Everywhere we have seen it, the verb is either clearly or potentially "take." That is, in some passages hardly any other meaning seems reasonable, while in other passages, even though some other meanings seem possible, "take" is possible, too. So the only question is how the verb *chamad* relates to *lakach*. Are they two kinds of taking? Or are they essentially synonyms?

Unfortunately, these nuances are beyond our reach. As a reasonable guess, *chamad*ing is a precursor to *lakach*ing—that is, a person who wants to *lakach* might first *chamad*. But we have only weak evidence to support that guess. Another possibility is that *chamad* and *lakach* differ in technical legal ways. Perhaps it is not always illegal to *lakach*, but *chamad*ing is always forbidden (though this possibility would need to be refined to account for Psalm 68:17, in which God is the *chamad*er). Or maybe the two verbs tend to accompany different methods of taking. Maybe the two are even near synonyms, like "sofa" and "couch" in English. We have no way of knowing.

But we do know that *chamad* basically means "take."

The last commandment, therefore, should read, "Do not take your neighbor's wife." We don't know if the point is "take with the intent to return" or "take and not plan to give back," but either way the commandment is surely about taking, not about wanting. Wanting may or may not be OK, but the Ten Commandments don't address the issue.

This also solves another potential problem in the Ten Commandments and the way they are usually translated. The Ten Commandments seem to define which *actions* are right and wrong. Keeping the Sabbath is right. Using the Lord's name in vain is wrong. Honoring parents is right. Murdering, stealing, and falsely testifying are wrong. Finally, taking your neighbor's wife or his stuff is wrong. With the usual translation, the Ten Commandments end with a quite clearly out-of-place prohibition against *feeling* a certain way. We now know that the Ten Commandments take no position on how you feel, only on what you do.

In particular, the Ten Commandments tell us that some actions are wrong. They may also have consequences, they may also be illegal, but even if they didn't they would still be wrong. Modern Western society has steadily developed a more refined sense of the legal aspects of behavior and of the consequences that accompany undesired behavior. But the reasons for doing these things have not received similar attention. If anything, the underlying wrongness of illegal behavior has become less and less of a focus in modern society. Perhaps this is why so many people cling to the Ten Commandments.

Whatever the reasons, the Ten Commandments may be the most widespread statement that some things are wrong. And we now have a clearer understanding of what those wrong things are.

8

VIRGINS AND OTHER YOUNG PEOPLE:
HOW WE MARK OUR YEARS

הִנֵּה הָעַלְמָה הָרָה

Behold, a virgin shall conceive

ἰδοὺ ἡ παρθένος ἐν γαστρὶ

Isaiah 7:14, quoted in Matthew 1:23, predicts that the Lord shall give a sign in the form of a "virgin" (KJV) who shall conceive. This virgin has been widely interpreted to be Mary, mother of Jesus, and Isaiah's prophecy is therefore a cornerstone of Christian theology.

But the word doesn't mean "virgin," so the prophecy isn't what is seems.

The Hebrew in Isaiah is *alma*. We now know how to figure out what the word really means. As we follow the same path we did in previous chapters, we'll also need a bit of general background about words that are used to mark age and societal roles.

TEENAGERS

There were no teenagers in antiquity.

Of course, on their way to their twenties people stopped off at thirteen years old, then fourteen, etc., but "teenager" wasn't a stage of life the way it is now.

The famous King Tutankhamun, for example, died before he was twenty, so technically he was a teenager, but he wasn't what we think of now as a "teenager." He was what we now would call an "adult."

Along similar lines, researchers such as David Tracer believe that crawling—a defining stage of childhood in modern Western countries—may be only a couple hundred years old as a widespread human behavior. Tracer also notes that to this day, parents in many cultures carry their children until they are old enough to walk. This illustrates how difficult it can be to imagine cultures vastly different than our own.

Estimates vary, but it seems that the average adult in ancient Egypt died before age forty. The life expectancy was considerably lower—by some estimates as low as twenty—because life expectancies are expressed as averages, and when roughly one-third of people die before their first year, often before their first week, the average drops considerably. But even among the probably 50 percent of people who were lucky enough to live past infancy, most were dead by the end of their fourth decade.

Accordingly, people didn't have time as they do now to spend their first decade as carefree children, then find themselves in their teen years, explore the world as twentysomethings, and settle down as thirtysomethings. They'd be dead before they ever really started living.

Rather, people were "children" and then they were "adults." (And then they were dead.)

Girls in ancient Egypt married around age twelve to fourteen, and boys just a little later. What we now call "middle schoolers" were, back then, newlyweds or even proud new parents.

We have less concrete evidence for ancient Israelite society, and numbers vary widely depending on the approach. If we take the Five Books of Moses literally, life spans near 1,000 years were not uncommon in the days before Abraham. In the time of the patriarchs and matriarchs, people often lived well into their second century (imagine a midlife crisis at age 100). Moses lives to 120. And only in the rest of the Bible did people usually die at ages that are now considered common.

But this very pattern suggests that more is going on than meets the eye. Of these three groups of ages, the first is wildly exaggerated by modern standards: No one lives to be 950, as Noah did according to Genesis 9:29. Nor do people live to be 180, as Isaac did. Moses' life of 120 years is possible but rare, right on the border between possible and impossible. And after Moses, in the time of Kings and so forth, life spans drop considerably.

This threefold division according to ages mirrors three types of distinctly different content in the Bible.

The text from Adam to Abraham seems primarily to address the entire world—how the world came to be, the invention of music, the Neolithic Revolution (that is, the move from a hunter-gatherer society to one built on farming, and the accompanying change from a nomadic and poorly fed culture to a more sedentary one with a surplus of food), the diversity of languages and culture, and so forth.

The text from Abraham through Moses addresses the formation of the Israelite nation, including the patriarchs and matriarchs, the laws of ancient Israelite society, etc.

And the text thereafter deals with Israelite life in ancient Israel.

The fact that people's ages are so different in these three sections (many hundreds for the part about the entire world, a few hundred for the part about forming the Israelite people, and generally less than one hundred for the part about Israelite society) suggests that the authors of the Bible knew and perhaps wanted to highlight the differences among these three parts. They may even have wanted to underscore the historical nature of the third part.

Furthermore, it is probably no coincidence that historians (using evidence from history) believe that the historically accurate section of the Bible begins precisely with that third part. In other words, internal evidence (ages) and external evidence (history) both point in the same direction. The third part is mostly history.

If so, we can look at the detailed history of Israelite kings to get a general sense of how long people lived in ancient Israel. Kings tended to start their reign around age twenty-two and they died in their mid-forties. Kings probably lived longer than the average man, and by almost any calculation lived longer than the average woman, because childbirth was frequently lethal in antiquity. These figures match the Egyptian figures closely and, quite obviously, differ starkly from modern norms. By U.S. law, for example (Article 2, Section 1 of the Constitution), the president must be at least thirty-five years old. At age forty-three, John Kennedy became the youngest man elected president. Theodore Roosevelt (who was sworn in after his predecessor, William McKinley, was assassinated), served at age forty-two. But in ancient Israel they both would probably have already been dead.

It's harder to figure out when ancient Israelites married, but as a rough guess we can assume that girls married around age twelve to fourteen, and boys later, perhaps as late as their twenties.

So a twelve-year-old girl—now considered a "preteen" or "middle schooler," among other options—could have been a bride. On average, women in this country today have their first child around age twenty-seven. The same twenty-seven-year-old could well have been a grandmother in ancient Israel. If she was lucky enough to live to forty-five, a woman in antiquity would probably have been a great-grandmother many times over. At that same age, a woman in the United States stands a reasonable chance of giving birth to her first child. A "young mother" today is nearly double the age of an ancient "young mother."

All of this is important because, as we will see next, we tend to intermix terms that denote age, behavior, and social role.

AGE AND STATUS

Status

We just saw that a twelve-year-old might be called either a "preteen" or a "middle schooler." These terms represent two different ways of expressing almost the same thing.

The theoretical inexactitude of using a role to indicate age, or vice versa, isn't generally a problem. Both "preteen" and "middle schooler" almost always mean the same thing, even though an adult can, at least theoretically, be in middle school, and even though a twelve-year-old can (illegally, in this country) drop out of school. These terms demonstrate an important point. Age can be measured by category ("preteen") or by something associated with that category ("middle schooler").

Similarly, the phrase "giddy as a schoolgirl" uses "schoolgirl" to mean "a girl of the age at which she would be in primary school," whether or not she is actually in school.

People who speak the language and who are familiar with the culture don't usually have any difficulty knowing if a word refers to status or to the people who generally have the status—that is, people who are at the age where the status is typical.

By way of a third example, "grandpa" (or "gramps") can be used to address any old man—that is, any man who is at the age where he might reasonably be a grandfather.

And here we start to see how tied to a particular culture these terms are. We might imagine a denizen of ancient Israel somehow reading a story in modern American English. That ancient Israelite, seeing "gramps," might reasonably draw one of two wrong conclusions about the word. The reader might think that "gramps" refers to someone whose children have had children. While that is one meaning of the word, it is not the only one, or even the most common one.

Or the ancient reader might correctly recognize that "gramps" is an instance of using status to represent age. But here too, without a solid understanding of America, the reader would think that "gramps" means a man in his early forties.

So we see that the notion of status, which we might also refer to as "societal role," can be used instead of age.

It works the other way around, too. "Teenager" refers to age, but, more often, it refers to status. "Teenagers" are people in their teens, but equally people in high school. A teacher might say he "teaches teenagers," even though "high schoolers" would be more accurate.

The term "coed," originally an abbreviation of "coeducation," at first referred to the phenomenon of coeducational college education. Then it became an adjective describing the state of having men and women together. But because women joined previously all-male institutions much more frequently than the other way around, "coed" eventually took on the meaning of the people—that is, the female students—who joined the hitherto male institution. A "coed," then, was a female student. But, in fact, a "coed" doesn't have to go to school at all.

The "American Coed Pageants," for example, are for girls and young women, regardless of whether or not they go to school. The three oldest categories are "Jr. Teen," "Teen," and "Coed." Though they are technically a mixture of ages and roles, no one is confused. That's because, as we have seen, ages can be used for roles and roles for ages.

This is one of two ways in which age terms are ambiguous. To understand similar words in the Bible, we have to appreciate the other way as well.

Behavior

In addition to referring literally to age or to societal role, both age words and role words can refer to people who typify what is expected of a particular age or role.

For example, a grown man who is "being a child" is acting in a way that children often do. Certainly the man is not actually a child, nor do all children act the way he does. Instead, "child" is used as an abbreviation for "a person who acts the way children often act."

Obviously, this sort of usage is particularly sensitive to cultural norms. There used to be a standard that children should be "seen and not heard." But "being a child" in America does not mean being "seen and not heard." For that matter, children are generally shorter than adults, but "being a child" doesn't mean "being short." Rather, it generally means acting immaturely, a term that is only slightly less relative to culture, because one culture's "mature" behavior might well be what another calls "immature."

"She's such a twelve-year-old" in modern America might mean a girl who plays with makeup and is experimenting with defying her parents. A similar expression in ancient Israel might have meant a newlywed. That's because different things express the essence of "twelve-year-oldness" in different cultures.

VIRGINS AND YOUNG PEOPLE

With this background we are in a position to return to Isaiah 7:14 and, therefore, Matthew 1:23. Most of the line is mostly clear: "Therefore the Lord himself shall give you a sign; Behold, *ha-alma hara*, and bear a son, and shall call his name Immanuel" (KJV). The KJV translates *ha-alma* as "a virgin" (even though *ha-* means "the," not "a," as we will discuss) and *hara* as "shall conceive," giving us the familiar translation and the dominant theme of Matthew 1:23. ("Immanuel" in Hebrew literally means "God is with us.")

To understand the line, we have to know what *alma* and *hara* mean. In terms of the former, we will have to look at the word *alma* and also at the similar words *na'arah* and *b'tulah*, all three of which have related meanings. Then to figure out the correct translation, we'll have to incorporate the difference between age and status that we just saw. After that, we'll see that it's not hard to decode the word *hara*. Then we can deal with "the" and "a."

We'll start with a diversion through German that helps illustrate the issues involved.

A German Diversion
In 1534 Martin Luther published a Bible commonly called the *Luther Bibel*, or, in English, the "Luther Bible." More accurately, the version is called

the *unrevidierte Luther Bibel*, or "unrevised Luther Bible," in contrast to a 1912 version that enjoys the name "revised Luther Bible." We'll look at the 1912 version, which is basically written in modern German.

The translation of Isaiah 7:14 uses the word *Jungfrau* for the Hebrew *alma*. *Jungfrau* is clearly a compound of *jung* ("young") and *frau* ("woman"). It seems, therefore, that *Jungfrau* would probably mean "young woman." But it does not. It means "virgin."

We already know that etymology and internal word structure are unreliable indicators of what a word means, so we shouldn't be surprised if looking at *jung* and *frau* in isolation leads us astray here. (In this case, it's hard to know if we're looking at etymology or word structure.)

Nonetheless, the form of the word highlights a fairly obvious point: There's a conceptual connection between youth and virginity. The form also suggests that, at the time the word was coined, the stereotypical role of young women was that they were virgins. Once again, we know better than to use the form of a compound to figure out its meaning, but even so, what we have is suggestive of a particular connection between age and role, the same sort of thing that we saw with "middle schooler" and "preteen" in English. In this case, we find the literal "young woman" used to mean "virgin." "Young" measures age, and "virgin" measures societal role. This pairing is hardly surprising. But it serves to emphasize both the obvious connection and the difficulty in translating these sorts of words accurately.

As it happens, the German *Jungfrau* is used to translate not only *alma*, but also the common Hebrew words *b'tulah* and *na'arah*, even though other German words are also used for *na'arah* and *alma*. In short, there is only partial correspondence between the original Hebrew and the German terms: *Jungfrau*, as we have seen, and also *Dirne* and, rarely, *Mädchen*, two more German words that roughly mean "young woman."

To make matters worse, an even more updated 1984 version of the *Luther Bibel* (also called *revidierte*, that is, "revised") sometimes uses *Mädchen* where the 1912 version has *Dirne*.

The reason we look at these German translations is that we have other ways of figuring out what the words mean. For example, "the virgin Mary" is called *Jungfrau Maria*, and we know that the point of that phrase is that Mary (*Maria*) was a virgin, not merely that she was young.

In the end, we see exactly what we expect: a variety of German words are used to represent age and role. There is significant overlap among the words. The meanings of the words cannot be deduced from their etymology or structure. And the words change meanings over time.

We will see exactly the same pattern in the original Hebrew and in the influential third-century B.C. Greek translation known at the Septuagint.

Hebrew

So we return to *alma*, *na'arah*, and *b'tulah*. We know how to figure out what they mean. We look at the contexts in which the words are used.

We'll start with *na'arah*, but we'll quickly end up looking at the three words all at once, because they are so frequently used together.

Before we actually look at the word *na'arah*, a caution is in order. The word *na'arah* is the feminine version of *na'ar*. As such, we would expect it to be spelled with a final *heh* in Hebrew, following the pattern of most masculine/feminine pairs. Frequently, however, that final letter is missing in the Bible. There are so many possible reasons for this spelling anomaly that it doesn't help us understand the word. For example, it could be that a *na'arah* and a *na'ar* were so close in meaning that they were sometimes spelled the same way. Or, contrarily, perhaps the words were so different in meaning that there was usually no chance of any confusion, so there was no reason to spell the words differently. We note the fact only because readers who want to find the word *na'arah* in the original Hebrew should be aware of it.

The word *na'arah* first appears in Genesis 24:14. Abraham's servant, at Abraham's request, has traveled to the place called Aram-naharaim, where he is to find a wife for Abraham's son Isaac. The servant prays for a sign in the form of a *na'arah* who will come to draw water. The servant will ask the *na'arah* to lower her water jug, and the *na'arah* will oblige.

In the next verse, Rebekkah appears with a water jug on her shoulder.

And in Genesis 24:16, Rebekkah is described as "a *na'arah* who looks very good, a *b'tulah*, and no man had had sex with her." So it seems that a *b'tulah* is a kind of *na'arah*.

Based on Genesis 24:16, though, two possibilites for *b'tulah* present themselves.

The first possibility is that there are two kinds of *b'tulah*, one who has had sex and one who has not. And to make the matter clear, Genesis 24:16 explains that this is the second kind of *b'tulah*. Just as *b'tulah* explains what kind of *na'arah* Rebekkah was, so too the next phrase might explain what kind of *b'tulah* she was.

The other possibility is that "no man had known her" is in parallel to *b'tulah*, and that it explains what *b'tulah* means. That is, the phrase is for emphasis or poetic force.

Other contexts, give us a clearer picture of what *b'tulah* means.

Leviticus 21:14 explains whom a priest can marry. He cannot marry "a widow, divorcée, or profaned whore." Rather, he must marry a *b'tulah*. (We use the word "divorcée" for the Hebrew word *grusha* with some caution. As we saw in Chapter 6, we don't know enough about divorce in the Bible to know that the ancient practice created what we now call "divorcées." The word literally means "one who is cast away.") Ezekiel repeats the same basic idea in different language. There, priests shall not take a "widow or divorcée" as a wife, but rather a *b'tulah*.

In both cases, it's clear that *b'tulah* is the opposite of "widow," "divorcée," and "whore." In other words, a *b'tulah* is a woman who has never had sex—that is, a virgin.

Other contexts support this interpretation.

Deuteronomy 22, starting with verse 13, contains laws about what happens if a man marries a woman, decides he doesn't like her, and spreads rumors about the state in which he found her. In particular, according to the text, the case in question is if the man says that he didn't find *b'tulim*. Clearly the word *b'tulim* is related to *b'tulah*, and most translations render the word as "virgin," or "signs of virginity." But we know that the similarity of form is not enough to demonstrate that *b'tulim* means almost the same thing as *b'tulah*.

Fortunately, Deuteronomy 22:19 makes the connection explicit. After a discussion about the woman's parents and proof of *b'tulim*, the text explains what happens if it is demonstrated that the man made up the accusation about the woman. He is to be fined "because he spread rumors about a *b'tulah* of Israel." So we know that a woman who has *b'tulim* is a *b'tulah*.

Deuteronomy 22:21 explains what happens if the man's claim turns out to be true—that is, if she wasn't really a *b'tulah*. She gets stoned to death "because she . . . was a whore." Again we see that a whore cannot be a *b'tulah*. (As an aside, we might note that the punishment seems overly harsh to some, and there are those who think that it was never implemented. But the nature of the punishment doesn't change how we interpret *b'tulah* and *b'tulim* here.)

Deuteronomy follows up with laws about an engaged *b'tulah* who has sex with a man. If the sex is consensual, they both get killed, while if she was raped only the rapist is killed. (Again, the details of the punishments don't concern us now.) The passage is important for understanding what *b'tulah* means because we see a regulation about what happens if a *b'tulah* has sex. While just in this very limited context we might imagine a variety of options for what *b'tulah* means, the most obvious is "virgin." If a virgin has sex, she is no longer a virgin.

Elsewhere we see the same concern about what happens if a *b'tulah* has sex. Exodus 22:15–16 (frequently numbered 16–17, because traditions about verse divisions sometimes differ), for example, describes what happens if a man has sex with an unengaged *b'tulah*. The man has to marry her and pay a dowry. However, if her father refuses to let her go, the man still must pay the dowry "of *b'tulah*s." Once again, we see that the woman was worth the price of a *b'tulah* until she had sex.

Other contexts are less clear, but they do not contradict what we have seen. For example, Deuteronomy 32:25 juxtaposes *bachur* with *b'tulah*. Isaiah 62:5 uses the imagery of a *bachur* who marries a *b'tulah*. Assuming *bachur* means "young man" or even "(male) virgin," we don't know for sure what *b'tulah* means from either of these contexts, but neither do they present evidence that we are on the wrong track.

We see the word again at the beginning of I Kings, which starts with the story of the aged King David, who in his old age cannot keep warm. So a *b'tulah* is found to lie with him—though not have sex with him—to keep him warm. Again, we don't know for sure from this passage that *b'tulah* means "virgin," but it could.

In short, we see the word *b'tulah* used frequently in the Bible, and in every case it either might mean or it pretty clearly does mean "virgin." So we conclude that that's what the word means.

All of this brings us back to *na'arah*, which we saw in Genesis 24. There a *b'tulah* was a kind of *na'arah*. If *b'tulah* means "virgin," we conclude that *na'arah* does not, because, it seems from Genesis 24:16, only some *na'arah*s are *b'tulah*s.

In Genesis 24:28, as part of the continuation of the same story, we once again find the word *na'arah*. This time the word is used not to describe Rebekkah but rather simply as a convenient way of referring to her. "And the *na'arah* ran off, and told" people what had happened.

The story in Genesis 24 seems to be written from two points of view: the limited point of the view of the servant and the omniscient point of view of the narrator. Sometimes the text tells us things as the servant would see them, yet other times we are given information that none of the characters could know.

In Genesis 24:14, the servant hopes to find a *na'arah*. That is all the text says. This is the limited servant-oriented view.

Then in 24:16 we get information that the servant does not have: The *na'arah* was a *b'tulah*. In addition to providing more confirmation that we are on the right track in translating *b'tulah*, we learn from this contrast that an observer (the servant, in this case) can tell by looking who is a *na'arah* but not who is a *b'tulah*. (The narrator knows, but the servant does not.)

This is why 24:28 uses the word *na'arah*. It seems akin to something like: "The servant saw a young woman . . . and the young woman ran off."

We next find the word *na'arah* in Genesis 34:3, where it refers to Dinah. In Genesis 34:1 we learn that Dinah goes out "to see the daughters of the land" (KJV). Then in 34:2 Shechem has sex with her. (This is commonly assumed to be a case of rape, and this story is generally known as "the rape of Dinah.") But in 34:3, Dinah is still a *na'arah*. This further confirms our observation that only some *na'arah*s are virgins—that is, *b'tulah*s.

Elsewhere, we find the word *na'arah* used in reference to female servants. In Esther 4:4, we read of Esther's *na'arah*s and her male servants of some sort, perhaps eunuchs. Similarly, Proverbs 31:15 teaches that a good wife provides for her house and for her *na'arah*s, presumably female servants.

According to Exodus 2:5, Pharaoh's daughter has *na'arah*s with her as she goes down to the Nile to wash.

And going back to Abraham's servant finding Rebekkah, we read toward the end of the story in 24:61 that Rebekkah "and her *na'arah*s" followed the servant. So Rebekkah is a *na'arah* and she has *na'arah*s.

So now we've seen that *na'arah* is a woman of some sort, and that *b'tulah* means "virgin." Knowing what these two words mean will help us understand *alma*.

We also find the word *alma* in the story about Abraham's servant and Rebekkah. Rebekkah has a brother, Laban. Inside Laban's house, Abraham's servant tells Laban (and Rebekkah and their father, Bethuel) about his journey, repeating what the reader already knows. He explains that he hoped for a sign from God. In Genesis 24:14, when the text explains to the reader what Abraham's servant did, the language we find is that the servant hopes for a *na'arah*. But in Genesis 24:43, when the servant explains to Rebekkah and her family what he did, the servant uses the word *alma*.

The two passages are not phrased identically, but they contain many of the same words, and they certainly are meant to convey the same idea. Genesis 24:15 and Genesis 25:44, which both continue Abraham's servant's hope for a sign, are even more similar.

As is frequently the case, two vastly different interpretations present themselves here. Either *na'arah* and *alma* are so similar that they are interchangeable, or they are different, and part of the cleverness of the text is the way Abraham's servant phrases his hope one way in his own head and another when reporting to the family.

We find the word *alma* again in the story about Pharaoh's daughter (Exodus 2:8), as she discovers the stranded baby Moses in the basket. Pharaoh's daughter goes down to the Nile to wash. Her *na'arah*s, as we just saw, accompany her. In the meantime, Moses' sister is watching to see what will happen to Moses. After Pharaoh's daughter discovers Moses and concludes that this baby in a basket must be an abandoned Hebrew boy, Moses' sister asks the daughter if she, the sister, should go get a Hebrew to nurse the child. Pharaoh's daughter agrees. Then the text tells us that the *alma*—that is, Moses' sister—goes to get Moses' mother.

Once again, we see a connection between *na'arah* and *alma*, and once again the connection is unclear. Perhaps the two words mean the same thing, and the text uses *alma* just to make it clear that it wasn't one of Pharaoh's daughter's *na'arah*s who went to get Moses' mother. Or perhaps *alma* is similar to *na'arah* but different. For example, maybe *alma* is a more polite way of saying *na'arah*. If so, we would also understand why Abraham's servant uses *na'arah* in his own mind but *alma* when speaking aloud of Rebekkah. But there are myriad other possible ways the words might be related, too.

We must note, however, that the passage in Exodus has nothing to do with sex or marriage or courtship. There is no reason to refer to Moses' (at this point anonymous) sister as a "virgin." In fact, it seems like the only reason not to just use "she" here is that, in the sentence, "she" could mean "the sister" or "Pharaoh's daughter." In other words, instead of "And Pharaoh's daughter said to her, Go. And she went and called the child's mother," which might be confusing, the text gives us, "And Pharaoh's daughter said to her, Go. And the *alma* went and called the child's mother." So one possibility is that, for reasons we haven't uncovered, *alma* cannot be Pharaoh's daughter here. On the other hand, the Bible frequently uses "he" and "she" when the referent is not entirely clear. In the end, then, we learn from Exodus 2:8 that our best guess for *alma* is some kind of young woman, perhaps with connotations of politeness or loftiness, but with no reference to virginity.

Proverbs 30 gives us another use of the word *alma*, though the context is poetic and obtuse. In Proverbs 30:18 we read, "Three things too wonderful for me; four I do not understand" (NSRV). The phrases "too wonderful for me" and "I do not understand" are almost certainly in parallel, suggesting that "three" and "four" are also in parallel, even though they do not mean the same thing. Such, apparently, was the poetic effect, an effect repeated in Proverbs 30:21: "Under three things the earth trembles; under four it cannot bear up." (We find the "three/four" pattern elsewhere as well. The prophet Amos describes a litany of the sins committed by various peoples, using very similar language. In Amos 1:3, the prophet quotes God as refusing to hold back punishment on account of "three transgressions of Damascus, even four. . . ." Then three verses later, it's on account of "three transgressions of Gaza, even four. . . ." After listing four other evil places, God finally promises to exact punishment on account of "three transgressions of

Judah, even four . . ." and, after that, "three transgressions of Israel, even four. . . ." Amos's message is typical of the prophets, who call Israel to task for behaving as badly as other nations.)

The four things alluded to in Proverbs 30:18 are listed in Proverbs 30:19: "The way of the eagle in the sky, the way of a snake on a rock, the way of a ship in the heart of the sea, and the way of a man with an *alma*." We have to assume that the "way of a man with an *alma*" is sex, but beyond that the passage offers little more. Is this, like "the eagle in the sky," the sort of repetitive behavior that is part of the natural course of things, in which case *alma* cannot possibly mean "virgin"? Probably.

But Proverbs 31:20 offers a fifth thing, seemingly out of place after a reference to "four things." The fifth is "the way of an adulterous woman. . . ." Some people see this fifth thing as part of the list, while others disagree. If it is part of the list, we again have two options. Either it is meant to clarify the fourth list item—in which case the "way of a man with an *alma*" would be like the way of an adulterous woman—or it is meant to augment the fourth item. Whatever the case, the section is complicated enough and vague enough that with very little twisting it can point in almost any direction.

So Proverbs 31, while interesting, doesn't help us much. Still, people who have an agenda frequently refer to Proverbs 31, confusing consistency with proof. Proverbs 31 is consistent with a lot of meanings for *alma*. But that doesn't prove what *alma* means.

Psalm 68:26 gives us a different look at *alma*s. Psalm 68:25 sets the stage by introducing the concept of God's processions, which the next line describes as "singers in front, players [of music] behind, among *alma*s drumming." Debate rages over the exact meanings of the words we translate as "sing," "play," and "drum," but consensus is universal that we have three types of music-making going on here. One kind involves *alma*s doing something. (As yet another example of how English has changed and how minor differences in phrasing can alter the meaning of a passage, it is interesting to note that the KJV translates the last bit as "[damsels] playing *with* timbrels." In modern English, if they are playing timbrels they are making music, while if they are playing *with* timbrels, they are just having fun.)

If *alma*s are to be involved in God's procession, at the very least we know that *alma* is not a derogatory word. From Psalm 68:26, we suspect that it may be a fancy word or even specifically a musical one. (Psalm 46:1 also connects *alma*s with music in a way that is so vague that most translators don't translate the word. It's hard to know for sure, but I Chronicles 15:20 may do so, too.)

Finally, we have Song of Songs. The word *alma* appears twice, once in 1:3 and once in 6:8.

The first time, we learn that the hero is anointed and "therefore *alma*s love" him. The second time, the text tells us that there are "sixty queens, eighty concubines, and countless *alma*s," but only one heroine who is the hero's "dove . . . whom daughters see and delight, queens and concubines praise."

While Song of Songs doesn't tell us precisely what *alma* means, it confirms what we already know and provides information about what the word *doesn't* mean, because we see a very clear context for *alma* here. The *alma*s are like queens and, crucially, like concubines. They are women who have had sex. That doesn't mean *alma* means "woman who has had sex," but quite clearly the word doesn't mean "virgin."

Indeed, we have seen no reason in any of the examples to think that *alma* means the same thing as *b'tulah*, and we saw that *b'tulah* means "virgin." Rather, *alma* means something like *na'arah*, and only some *na'arah*s are *b'tulah*s. We also suspect that *alma* is a poetic word. Perhaps the word implies musicality, or maybe music is just one way a *na'arah* becomes an *alma*. There are lots of possibilities, and, as usual, we have no way to know the details of the nuances for sure. But one thing is clear. We have no evidence to suggest that *alma* means "virgin" and lots of evidence to suggest that it does not.

Why, then, does the King James Version, paving the way for future translations, sometimes translate *alma* precisely as "virgin"?

To find an answer, we turn to King Ptolemy II of Egypt, whose reign lasted from 287 to 247 B.C. According to legend, in the middle of the third century B.C., King Ptolemy commissioned seventy-two Israelites—six from each of the twelve tribes—quizzing them with seventy-two questions and asking them to translate the Five Books of Moses from Hebrew into Greek. After seventy-two days, the seventy-two Israelites, working independently and in isolation, all produced exactly the same Greek text, proving that it was a God-inspired translation.

As it happens, it was a God-awful translation, as we will soon see (in particular on page 217). In addition to the text of the translation itself, though, there are aspects of the legend that call its veracity into doubt. For example, the story comes from a letter sent from someone who calls himself Aristeas and claims to be a Greek pagan. Yet from the content of the letter (which we know about from the Roman writer Josephus), it is almost certain that the writer was Jewish. Also, the twelve tribes had been disbanded centuries earlier.

Scholars now believe that the translation dates from the third century B.C. onward, and that it comes from Egypt, probably Alexandria. The first versions of the Septuagint included only the Five Books of Moses, and other parts of the Bible were translated later. (Even though scholars no longer believe the legend about the seventy-two people, questions, and days, the version still goes by the name "Septuagint," which is Greek for "seventy." In a bit of academic cleverness, scholars frequently abbreviate this Greek name with the Roman numeral "LXX.")

Because of the centrality of Greek in the Church, and because this is one of the oldest translations of the Bible, the Septuagint is frequently consulted in matters concerning translation and, more broadly, the text of the Bible.

Greek

Deuteronomy 31:1 starts with the Hebrew word *vayelech*—that is, "he went." The sentence is "Moses went [*vayelech*] and spoke these words to all of Israel." It appears after one of Moses' finest speeches, in which he calls on heaven and earth to witness, exhorting the people of Israel to choose life over death.

The Hebrew phrasing seems odd. Where, exactly, was Moses going? Why does it say "Moses went"? As it happens, we have an English expression: "go and . . ." For example, "You had to go and open your big mouth again. . . ." In English, the verb here doesn't have anything to do with actually going anywhere. By contrast, Biblical Hebrew had no such expression. The English expression masks the oddity of the original Hebrew.

The Septuagint, however, has a completely different translation here. The Septuagint reads, "Moses finished speaking these words . . ." That would make a lot more sense as a segue. First Moses speaks the monumental words of his speech, and then, when he had finished speaking the words, the next thing happens.

The Hebrew for "he went" consists of four letters: *vav-yud-lamed-kaf*, or, in transliteration, V-Y-L-K. The verb for "he finished," however, is V-Y-K-L. And, in fact, it is V-Y-K-L that appears in the Dead Sea Scrolls where the Hebrew Bible has V-Y-L-K. In other words, this looks like what scholars call haplography ("wrong writing") and what everyone else calls a typo.

It looks like the original text read V-Y-K-L, "he finished," and somewhere along the line a scribe mixed up two letters. The mix-up happened, it would seem, after the Dead Sea Scrolls were written sometime after the year 200 B.C., and after the Septuagint was written. This case and others like it prompt people to look to the Septuagint as at least an aid in understanding the Hebrew.

There are, of course, problems with that strategy. We don't always know what the Greek meant. And we must allow for the real possibility that the authors of the Septuagint weren't very good translators. None-theless, it's often at least interesting to know how the Septuagint renders a particular Hebrew phrase.

And here we get to the source of the problem. The Septuagint is fairly consistent in using the Greek word *parthenos* for the Hebrew *b'tulah*. The word *b'tulah* and the related *b'tulim* appear dozens of times in the Bible, and in almost each case the Greek translation is *parthenos*. And of the times where the Greek is another word, there is usually a good reason.

Sometimes the reason is that the Greek text is just different from the Hebrew, so the Greek doesn't have the word at all. (In addition to cases of haplography and other errors, the Septuagint and the Bible that we use differ because they reflect different traditions.) For example, Esther 2:19 in the Hebrew Bible reads, "And when the virgins were gathered together the second time, then Mordecai sat in the king's gate" (KJV). But the Septuagint is shorter. It just says, "But Mardoch-aeus served in the palace." The Septuagint version of Esther frequently differs from the Hebrew text, so we are not surprised at this divergence here. We also find a few instances in Jeremiah where the Greek differs enough from the Hebrew text that it doesn't contain the word *b'tulah* at all.

Other times, as in Ezekiel 23:3, the Greek uses a verbal related to *parthenos* (sort of like *parthenos*ized) where the Hebrew has an expression. Either way, the point is probably "become a nonvirgin." Five verses later, the Greek has "sexual immorality" instead of "virgin" for the same reason.

Taking into account some additional, complicated reasons why the Greek might differ, we end up with only a few cases where the Hebrew *b'tulah* seems like it should be *parthenos* but isn't.

So we are on very solid ground in deducing the widely accepted fact that *parthenos* means "virgin" and is the Greek translation of *b'tulah*. (Because we have other evidence from outside the Septuagint, we have other ways of knowing what *parthenos* means. So this is fur-

ther evidence that we are correct in our translation of *b'tulah*, though
the additional evidence here is based on the dubious Septuagint translation, so it's not as solid as it would be if we had more faith in the fidelity of that translation.)

The Septuagint had more trouble finding a translation for *alma*. In
Genesis 24:43, the Greek is *thygatir*, "daughter." In Exodus 2:8, Song
of Songs, and Psalm 68, the Greek is *neanis*, which means "young
girl" or something like it. (In Psalm 46, where we have noted that the
reference to *alma*s was difficult to interpret, the Greek assumes that
the word is not *alamot*, the Hebrew plural of *alma*, but rather *alamut*,
which means "secret." The Septuagint may be more accurate here. If
so, the Psalm would begin, ". . . a Psalm about secret things.")

We perhaps shouldn't be surprised that the translators of the Septuagint didn't know exactly how to translate *alma*. The word is uncommon and, as we just saw, it's not easy to figure out exactly what it
means. Probably it was a word that English doesn't have and that
Greek didn't have, either.

So there are probably a handful of ways to translate *alma* that are
fine—or, at least, not terrible. Anything that roughly means "young
woman" is probably pretty good.

Unfortunately for us, in most cases in antiquity, "virgin" was a word
that also meant "young woman." Whereas today the words have very
different meanings, in antiquity using "virgin" for "young woman"
was exactly the same as using "coed" for "woman" or "middle schooler"
for "young woman." As we have seen, ages can be used for roles and
vice versa.

In a society where twelve-year-olds married, there was very little
room for nonvirgin young women. Certainly some girls must have
married late (or not at all). Some must have remained virgins past their
early teens. And we must allow for the unfortunate possibility that
some girls lost their virginity at a much younger age.

This ancient situation with age and sex mirrors the modern one
regarding age and school. And because ages and roles are usually

interchangeable, there was usually no reason not to use "virgin"—that is, *parthenos*—in translating a word that literally meant "young woman." It was like using "high schooler" for "teenager."

This is why the Septuagint uses *parthenos* not only for *b'tulah* but for other words as well. In Genesis 24:14, the Septuagint renders *na'arah* as *parthenos*. It was a translation error, but not a serious one. Rebekkah was probably both a "young woman" and a "virgin." But we see the consequences of the error two verses later, where the Septuagint uses *parthenos* both for *na'arah* and for *b'tulah*, yielding the fairly silly translation, "the virgin was . . . a virgin." (It should be, "the young woman was . . . a virgin.")

Any careful translator would have noticed the error at this point. While there are frequently a variety of equally good choices for translating a particular word, when one language has two different words, it is almost always wrong to translate them as the same word. Doing so destroys the effect of having two words in the first place. The Greek in Genesis 24:16 is a classic example of what can go wrong. But rather than find another word for *na'arah*—*neanis* ("young girl"), for example, or even *thygatir* ("daughter")—the Septuagint blindly translates *na'arah* as *parthenos*, its authors perhaps not even noticing the inconsistency of using *parthenos* for *na'arah* right next to *parthenos* for *b'tulah*.

This is actually typical of the Septuagint. While it has value, particularly when it reflects a text that seems to differ from what we expect, the Septuagint is not by and large a very good translation. The authors of the Septuagint seem to have known very little about translating. They had not read Chapters 2 and 3 of this book, or any of the other modern books that explain translation. Rather, they mechanically translated the Hebrew, sometimes word by word, into Greek. Frequently, the only question the translators seem to have asked themselves is how to say a particular Hebrew word in Greek. They didn't ask if it was the right word *in context*. This is what led to the awful rendering of Genesis 24:16.

This is also what led to the awful rendering of Isaiah 7:14. The

Hebrew reads: "The *alma*" shall conceive. (That's a rough translation. We still haven't gotten to what *hara*, "shall conceive," means. But we will.) We know that *alma* means something like "young woman," and we know that it does not mean "virgin." The Septuagint, however— following its usual pattern of simply finding a word that's good enough, regardless of context—translates *alma* as *parthenos* here. In other contexts, it's not a terrible choice for *alma*. After all, as we have seen, "young women" and "virgin" meant almost the same thing.

But, of course, there is one time when they absolutely did not, and do not, mean the same thing. And that is when sex is involved. Or, to look at the situation another way, "virgin" implies "young woman"— because it was hard for a woman to get past her early teen years without having sex—but "young woman" does not imply "virgin." There was no reason a woman couldn't have sex before she might otherwise be expected to. A modern parallel, again, would be using "high schooler" for "teenager." Usually it wouldn't be a problem. But the difference becomes relevant when schooling is involved, so "the high schooler had no education" is not at all the same thing as "the teenager had no education," even though both "high schooler" and "teenager" work equally well in many other contexts. *Parthenos* for *alma* is similar.

Based on this sloppy and ultimately faulty translation, the KJV, too, translates *alma* as "virgin," giving us the famous translation: "Therefore the Lord himself shall give you a sign; Behold, a virgin shall conceive, and bear a son, and shall call his name Immanuel."

But this is a mistake. While the woman may have been a virgin, the text does not say "virgin." It says "young woman."

The authors of the KJV must have known better, too. In Exodus 2:8, they use "maid" for *alma*. In Psalm 68, "damsel." In Song of Songs, they again use "virgin." In Genesis 24:14 and 24:16, they use "damsel" for *na'arah* and "virgin" for *b'tulah*. But again they revert to "virgin" in Genesis 24:43.

In other words, when *alma* appeared by itself, the authors of the KJV seemed perfectly happy with "maid," "damsel," or "virgin."

Their reasoning may have been that, in the days of the translation, "virgin" was used not just in its modern sense but also to mean any young woman. So the English of the KJV was similar to the Greek of the Septuagint. "Virgin" (or *parthenos*) meant what it does today, but also referred to any young woman. Unlike the authors of the Septuagint, the authors of the KJV were usually careful to avoid nonsense like "the virgin was . . . a virgin." They took context into account.

But in the crucial case of Isaiah 7:14, apparently, they couldn't resist mucking with the translation to make it mean what they wanted it to for theological reasons. They wanted Isaiah to prophesy the birth of Christ.

Young Men and Women

It turns out that both *alma* and *na'arah* have masculine counterparts, namely, *alam* and *na'ar*. (The connection between *na'ar* and *na'arah* is easier to see for those who don't know the details of Biblical grammar, but the connection between *alam* and *alma* is, in fact, just as clear. It's like *melech* and *malka* for "king" and "queen.")

It is tempting to try to analyze the words *alam* and *na'ar* to help us figure out what *alma* and *na'arah* mean, but it would be a mistake, because we frequently find that gendered words mean different things for men and women. Even though *na'arah* is the feminine form of *na'ar*, the two words might mean different things. The same problem applies to *alam* and *alma*.

As an example, we can compare the English words "master" and "mistress." While they may have once had similar meanings, they certainly don't anymore. "Mistress," as we saw in Chapter 6, is generally a term for a woman in an unmarried relationship. More importantly, "mistress" in this context doesn't imply any power—and, in fact, suggests a lack of power. The man has power over the mistress, not the other way around. By contrast, "master" is, in general, a position of power, or a state of high competency. A "master storyteller," for example, is a storyteller who's very good at storytelling. But a woman isn't a "mistress storyteller."

And even if we wanted to use *alam* to help us understand *alma*, the word appears only twice in the Bible. Both times it appears to mean "young man," but it's hard to know for sure. The KJV translates the word once as "young man" (in I Samuel 20:22) and once as the otherwise unattested "stripling" (in I Samuel 17:56), a rare word that means "young man."

The Youth

It turns out that Isaiah 7:14 doesn't just talk about "an *alma*" but rather "the *alma*." The difference between "a" and "the" is that "the" is usually used only when the reader can be expected to know not only what the word means but also what it refers to.

As an example of "a" versus "the" in English, we might note that this sentence begins with "an example," because the reader doesn't yet know what the example refers to. But the third time "example" is used in the sentence, it is "the example," referring to the example that was introduced in the first part of the sentence.

But the matter is tricky.

Another example of "the" in English might distinguish "cat" from "the cat." "A cat is a feline creature that thinks it runs the world" refers to any cat, in general, not to a particular one. On the other hand, "The cat in my house knows that it runs the world" refers to a specific cat, and the reader is expected to know which one. In this case, it's the one "in my house."

But even so, a researcher might note that "the wolf is returning to Yellowstone Park," which doesn't mean that a particular wolf has been making a long trek from somewhere and is finally near the end of its journey. Rather, it means almost the same thing as "wolves are returning. . . ."

In other languages, too—as we now expect—we find similar complexity and only a partial match to English. Some languages like

Portuguese put "the" before names (for example, "The Chris has a cat"). Others don't even have words for "the," and use syntax where English uses vocabulary.

So in Isaiah when we read "the *alma*," we have to be careful. It may refer to a specific *alma*, but, if so, the text doesn't tell us who she is. (In Exodus 2:8, by contrast, we see "the *alma*" only after the preceding verses tell us about Moses' sister.) Or the use of "the" may refer to a general phenomenon in Isaiah, as if to say the sign is that "*alma*s will get pregnant and give birth." Sometimes the Bible reads "the God" (*ha-elohim*) and sometimes just "God" (*elohim*), but the point is always the same, and most translators know better than to mimic the Hebrew word for "the." This may be a similar situation. Or it may even reflect poetic license.

One thing we know. We cannot blindly assume that "the" in Hebrew should be "the" in English.

Youth in General

We have a few loose ends to address, including where the notion of "young" comes into play and, finally, a short discussion of the Hebrew *hara*, wrongly translated as "shall conceive" in the KJV. We'll start by returning to *alma* and *na'arah*.

We have translated those two words so far as "young woman." It's clear that they refer to women or girls of some age, but where does the notion of "young" come from?

Here we have to be particularly careful, too, because "young" and "old" mean different things in different contexts. A young woman is older than an old girl, for example (just like a big mouse is smaller than a small elephant). For that matter, a ninety-five-year-old might call her fifty-one-year-old granddaughter a "young woman," while that woman's children probably would not. Ten-year-old children sometimes talk about "when they were young," to the amusement of adults who think the ten-year-olds still are. And when the average life expectancy was forty, a forty-five-year-old was, generally speaking, pretty old. She no longer is.

So our real question is twofold: How old, and in what stage of life, were these *na'arah*s and *alma*s? And do we have a way to express that in English?

We don't have any direct information to help us answer the first question. We certainly don't know how old they were. We do know that *na'arah* and *alma* include women of marriageable age, which, back then, was roughly twelve and onward.

We can guess that *na'arah* did not refer to the elderly, though, based on unreliable evidence from the word *na'ar*. We just saw that we have to be careful using a masculine word to determine what a feminine word means; with this in mind, we note that the phrase "from *na'ar* to old" appears in the Bible, at least suggesting that *na'ar*, and perhaps *na'arah*, have something to do with youth.

Similarly, we can guess that *na'arah* was not limited to older children or younger adults. In Exodus 2:6, Moses, having just been discovered by Pharaoh's daughter and about to get a wet nurse, is called a "crying *na'ar*." (The KJV uses "babe" for *na'ar* here.) If *na'ar* meant "any young (male) person," we might guess that *na'arah* meant any young female person, from infancy up to some age that we cannot determine.

At first glance, this might seem troubling. If *na'arah* can mean an infant, why would Abraham's servant have been looking for a *na'arah*? The answer, of course, is that *na'arah* is broader than just "infant," just as it is broader than just "virgin" (or "nonvirgin"). The word *na'arah* seems to be a very general term. In colloquial English, we use the word "girl" for this. A "girl" is a baby, a child, a date, a secretary, etc., though some populations frown on using "girl" in some of these contexts. (And yet again, we see a difference between masculine and feminine words. A boss might refer to a female secretary as "my girl," but usually not to a male secretary as "my boy.")

Information about *alma* is even more difficult to discover because the word is used so rarely. We know that an *alma* can be at least some of the ages of a *na'arah*, so we can probably exclude old women, but we can't even be sure of that. Our best clue is the way Abraham's servant uses the word in the presence of the people he wants to impress. So *alma* probably doesn't mean "hag" or any other insulting term.

But even though we don't have evidence from the text, we have anthropological evidence about the culture. Once we remember that all of these people getting married and having children were in their teens, we realize that the most accurate description of *na'arah* is "teenager," or simply "teen." Both are the wrong translation, but before looking at why, another look at the word "teenager" is helpful, because it reemphasizes an important point about words and how they work.

A "teenager" can be a boy or a girl (or, perhaps, a man or a woman). But a "teenager who gets pregnant" must be a woman in English. In other words, "teenager" is usually ambiguous as to gender, but context sometimes renders it specific. In Modern Hebrew, there are two words for "teenager"—one masculine, one feminine. Context tells us which Hebrew word to use for the English.

Similarly, the words we have seen—*alma* and *na'arah*—are sometimes ambiguous, but context tells us which words to use for them in English.

And an *alma* can be—in fact, usually was—a teenager. Still, we don't want to refer to a "pregnant teenager" in our translation because a pregnant *alma* was a common occurrence in antiquity. The age of an *alma* was the usual age for childbirth, and *alma*s were expected to get pregnant. The same is not true of "teenager." We frequently use different words to describe the same phenomenon when we wish to make our attitudes about it clear. (Earlier, we noted that a "teen" could be a "girl" or a "woman," but once she's pregnant, we prefer "woman.") More importantly, "teen," while chronologically accurate, is completely misleading because, as we noted at the beginning of the chapter, there were no teens in antiquity, at least not as we generally use the word.

"Teen" most naturally refers to a stage of life, and that stage of life wasn't part of antiquity.

So we make a list of our clues about the word *alma*. Though it was compatible with "virgin," there's no reason to think that it meant that. It was the natural age for childbirth. And it was, at the very least, not a derogatory word. We actually have a word for that in English: "woman."

We don't use "young woman," because in English that implies a woman younger than one might expect, or, at least, at the young end of some spectrum. While an *alma* was chronologically young, she was older than a child and ready to bear children.

So we've translated *alma*: "woman." To translate the line, we have to take a quick look at *hara*.

Pregnant

Fortunately, unlike *alma*, *hara* is easy to decipher. The word occurs more than a dozen times in the Bible, and every single time it means "pregnant."

For example, in Genesis 16:11, Hagar is told, "You are *hara*, and you will give birth to a son." The KJV translates it as "with child." The NRSV prefers "You have conceived." And the NAB gets it right with "You are now pregnant."

Talking about pregnancy is taboo in some circles, so new words to describe pregnancy keep popping up in the language. Once "with child" was a common expression. Then that became too common, so people started using "pregnant," Latin for "expecting," as in "expecting a child." Then *that* became too common, and now some people prefer the English "expecting." In yet another move away from talking about the woman and her womb and so forth, many people use "pregnant" and "expecting" for both members of a couple, so in some dialects it's not just the woman who's "pregnant" or "expecting," it's the couple.

We have no reason to think that a similar taboo existed in the Bible and we have no reason to use a euphemism in translating *hara*.

If the point is "You are with child," the right English is "You are pregnant."

Genesis 38:24–25 is equally clear. Tamar gets pregnant (after "playing the whore"). She is *hara*.

Exodus 21:22 is also clear. If someone hits a woman who is *hara* and she loses her baby, the offender must pay a fine.

Accordingly, "the *alma* is *hara*" can only mean a woman who is pregnant.

WORDS AND SIGNS

So Isaiah 7:14 reads, "Therefore the Lord himself will give you a sign. A pregnant woman will give birth to a son, and call him Immanuel." Because the name "Immanuel" means "God is with us," so we might equally translate, ". . . call him Godiswithus."

At first glance, one might wonder—and people have wondered, vocally and vehemently—what kind of sign "a pregnant woman" giving birth might be. After all, they (wrongly) argue, only a "virgin" giving birth would be worthy of "sign"-ship. That would be a fitting introduction for "Immanuel," for God being with us. But just any woman of childbearing age bearing a child would not properly set the stage.

They are completely wrong, and they have missed the entire point.

The sign here is a reminder that extraordinary things can come out of the ordinary. That is Isaiah's point. If a virgin gave birth, we would hardly need the text to tell us how amazing that was. Surely we would know it on our own. But, Isaiah is apparently concerned, some people might forget that signs come from daily events, too; that Immanuel can come from a perfectly plain woman of childbearing age; that life itself can be miraculous.

When we look carefully at Isaiah, we see the sign hidden in plain sight and we know that God is with us.

Conclusion

THE POWER OF WORDS
(OR GO MARRY A HARLOT)

קְחוּ עִמָּכֶם דְּבָרִים

Take with you words

λάβετε μεθ ἑαυτῶν λόγους

Hosea 14:1 (numbered 14:2 by Jews) calls on us to "return to the Lord."

Hosea is one of the "minor prophets," as they are sometimes called by modern scholars, or simply "the Twelve Prophets," as they are somewhat more reverently referred to in verse 49:10 of the 2,200-year-old Book of Sirach.

The Book of Hosea is hard to date. It begins with a preamble that puts itself in "the days of Uzziah, Jotham, Ahaz, and Hezekiah, kings of Judah" and "the days of Joash's son, Jeroboam, King of Israel." So the book dates to the divided monarchy, when what we now call "Israel" was divided into a northern kingdom called "Israel" and a southern kingdom called "Judah." (Historians, being nothing if not clever, sometimes call the northern kingdom "The Northern Kingdom" and the southern kingdom "The Southern Kingdom," rather than using the terms "Israel" and "Judah.")

Unfortunately, according to II Kings 15:8, Jeroboam died while Uzziah reigned, so there was no period of time during both "the days . . . of Jotham" and "the days . . . of Jeroboam."

One possibility is that the author, perhaps knowing the history of one kingdom better than the other, was confused about who reigned when; or maybe II Kings 15:8 is imprecise. We shouldn't be surprised, though, because dating conflicts such as these are common, even appearing in the most authoritative copy of the Hebrew Bible, the Leningrad Codex. (According to a prologue similar in style to Hosea, the Leningrad Codex dates variously to A.D. 1008, A.D. 1009, A.D. 1010, or, to judge by a reference there to King Jehoiachin, to A.D. 846, a date that historical evidence cannot support.)

The *Jewish Study Bible* raises the intriguing possibility that the dates in Hosea are symbolic, representing both Israel's strength (under King Jeroboam) and its approaching demise (under King Hezekiah). Hosea may refer to a time when the Northern Kingdom's strength was unchallenged but about to end.

A more daring interpretation suggests that the dating is purposely vague, perhaps even arbitrary, because Hosea wanted to underscore the timeless nature of his message.

Hosea's story begins when God tells him to marry a harlot. He does. When he and his harlot wife have a son, God tells Hosea to call him Jezreel, after the Jezreel Valley where Naboth was murdered. (For a modern parallel, it's like an inhabitant of New Orleans naming a daughter Katrina, after the hurricane that destroyed the city.) Hosea has two more children, a girl, Lo-Ruhama, and a boy, Lo-Ami. Lo-Ruhama means "unloved" and Lo-Ami means "not my people." A reasonable English approximation of Hosea's family, then, is that he is married to a harlot, has one kid named after a disaster, and two others called, essentially, Unloved and Unwanted.

In case the reader misses the hardly subtle allusions in the names, the text expands on each one. In Hosea 1:6, we read, "Call her Unloved, for I will no longer love the House of Israel. . . . But I will love the House of Judah." Hosea 1:9 deals with the third kid: "Call him Not-my-people, for you are not my people, and I will not be your God."

But most translations relegate the imagery of the names to footnotes or, worse, hope that the reader knows enough Biblical Hebrew to know what they mean. The KJV reads (Hosea 1:6), "Call her name Loruhamah: for I will no more have mercy upon the house of Israel." It hardly makes sense. (The translation "mercy" instead of "love" is a more complicated issue. The Hebrew word implies both.) The NRSV is similar, changing "mercy" into "pity," but still leaving the English-speaking reader unaware of the symbolic name: "Then the LORD said to him, 'Name her Lo-ruhamah, for I will no longer have pity on the house of Israel.'" Only a footnote explains the meaning of "Lo-ruhamah."

Even though it is Hosea who is married to the harlot, Hosea specifically calls God the "husband," using two Hebrew words for the metaphor. The first word is *ishi*—literally, "my man." (Remember from Chapter 6 that the suffix *-i* means "my." The word *ish* means "man.") The second is *ba'ali*—literally, "my lord." But *ba'al* is also the name of a pagan god, which we spell with a capital letter: Baal. So the two names for God are "my husband/man" and "my husband/pagan god"!

(The word *ba'al* meaning "lord" appears in II Kings 1:2, where *ba'al zvuv* is the false god to which messengers of the King of Samaria turn for advice. The prophet Elijah insists that they should not consult *ba'al zvuv* but rather the God of Israel. The KJV simply transliterates *ba'al zvuv* as "Baalzebub," but *zvuv*, a word of onomatopoetic origin, means "fly," and the phrase means "Lord of the Flies." This is where William Golding got the name of his famous allegorical tale.)

Hosea's imagery depends closely on the words he chooses. Things will right themselves when (Hosea 2:1, numbered 2:3 by Jews) people will call their brothers "My-people" (as opposed to "Not-my-people"), when they call their sisters "Loved" (as opposed to "Un-loved"), and when their God (2:16, 2:18 for Jews) is *ishi*, "my husband," with no connotations of pagan worship, instead of *ba'ali*, "my husband," who shares a name with the pagan god Baal.

Hosea has other poetic imagery that depends on a close reading of the Hebrew. The *emek achor*, the "Valley of Achor" (KJV) will become a *petach tikvah*, a "door of hope" (KJV). Taken as it is in translation, the passage hardly seems poetic. But the Hebrew word *achor* means "trouble" or "darkness." A similar wordplay in English might have a weeping willow tree laughing. Once again, Hosea demands that we look carefully at his words. (The phrase *petach tikvah* was used in 1878 to name a settlement in Palestine. In 1937 it became a city, and today it is a suburb of Tel Aviv. This is yet one more way that Hosea's words continue to thrive.)

Throughout his writing, Hosea insists that we look deeply at what words mean. Only then do the names make sense and the images come to life.

For the past couple hundred pages, we have seen that it's not easy to look at the Hebrew carefully and accurately. Just knowing what the words mean is a difficult task. Knowing how to translate them into English is even harder. But thanks to modern linguistics and translation theory, the difficult task is not impossible.

And the work is worth the effort.

By trying to understand sometimes complicated theory and then striving to learn what the original text really meant, we've gained considerable insight not only into the Bible but into ourselves as well.

We've seen that Jesus' most important commandment is an instruction not only about how to relate to God but also about who we are. We have a tangible, physical existence (*nefesh*) and also intangible qualities (*levav*) like thoughts, emotions, aspirations, and the like. The mind-body connection is real and relevant, but the usual translation of "heart" and "soul" for this pair of words destroys the original message.

We've learned that Psalm 23—surely one of the best bits of poetry ever penned—is not really about sheep or modern-day shepherds. Sheep are only the background to the much more powerful image of a valiant protector who is with us, who keeps us safe from enemies, lets us enjoy the beauty of the world, and gives our lives higher purpose as we strive to dwell in God's House.

We were hardly shocked to discover that the Bible's only foray into romantic and erotic poetry was not about incest, as common translations would suggest. But many readers were probably pleasantly surprised to learn that the point of the poetry was to emphasize the importance of equality in a loving relationship.

In Chapter 7 we moved away from poetry toward what looked like a legal treatise, but learned that instead it was the world's first and most lasting code of morality. Furthermore, for generations the Ten Commandments have been severely mistranslated, sometimes by accident and sometimes on purpose to push an agenda. Some things are wrong, the Bible teaches, like taking what is not yours (though you can desire whatever you wish). Some laws are purely legal, like, in modernity, paying for parking or filing taxes on April 15 instead of April 17. But some laws, such as those condemning murder, have moral content. Those who violate them have done much worse than merely break the law. This vital distinction—the observation that our world is filled with right and wrong—is lost in modern legal compilations, so it is all the more important to make sure we preserve the original Hebrew one.

And in Chapter 8 we saw a beautiful and subtle reminder that daily life is full of signs and miracles—or, as Israel's first prime minister, David Ben-Gurion, posited, believing in miracles is part of being a realist.

These are, of course, only the tip of the proverbial iceberg. (And we know now that the tip of the iceberg has nothing to do with tips or icebergs.)

Modern resources like interlinear translations and computer programs—see the Appendix for details—put context-based analysis, once possible only for those who had mastered Hebrew, into the hands of laypeople. No longer can antiquated approaches to language or purposeful mistranslations conceal the original meaning of the Bible.

All of this brings us back to Hosea and his timeless message. In 14:1 (14:2 for Jews), he commands the people to "return to the Lord." We don't know exactly when the Book of Hosea was written, but it's easy to narrow it down to the first millennium B.C.—probably the first half of the first millennium—which puts it firmly in the era of animal sacrifice. The Old Testament model of service to God through serving God food was still well established. (It wouldn't be abandoned by Jews until after the destruction of the Second Temple in A.D. 70.) Do something wrong, and you offer a sacrifice of atonement.

But Hosea has another idea. In 14:2 (14:3 for Jews), he demonstrates the same appreciation of language that we saw in his imagery, only he takes the power of words to new heights. Anticipating the future by several hundred years, he rejects animal sacrifice and in its place calls on us to "take words" in order to "return to God."

More than at any time since the Hebrew was first composed, the ancient words are ours for the taking.

APPENDIX:
A GUIDE TO TRANSLATIONS
AND FURTHER READING

ENGLISH TRANSLATIONS

We have already seen that the **King James Version (KJV)** of the Bible set the standard for English translations. It turns out, though, that in spite of all it has to recommend it, the **KJV** is a fool's-gold standard, for the reasons we have seen. The translators knew almost nothing about linguistics or translation theory. They wanted to create a homogenized text where the original was heterogeneous. And even when they got the translation right, the four centuries that have passed since its publication have turned some of their successes into outdated relics. Still, for its historical value and because so many translations use the **KJV** as their starting point, you will want to have a copy of it on your bookshelf. The text at this point is in the public domain, so you have literally dozens of published compilations to choose from. You can also find it on the Internet and in the computer program called Bibleworks (which I describe on page 237).

The **New Revised Standard Version (NRSV)** remains the best translation available, though it, too, suffers from significant shortcomings. The path from the **KJV** to the **NRSV** includes an 1885 version called the **English Revised Version (ERV)**, the 1901 **American Standard Version (ASV)**, and the 1952 **Revised Standard Version (RSV)**. (The **RSV** was the first version to try to take into account what scholars were learning about the Bible from the Dead Sea Scrolls. If you're interested in reading about the Dead Sea Scrolls, I have some suggestions coming up.) To use the terminology from our discussion of levels in Chapter 3, the **NRSV** stops somewhere between words and phrases, usually missing the concepts and affect, and even getting some of the words wrong (like "heart," "soul," "covet," and many more). Still, of all the publications, the **NRSV** does the best job of presenting a readable text that usually doesn't stray too far from the original. More important, where the **NRSV** fails, there is seldom a better option. It achieves better success with the prose than with the poetry, so for readers who want to read the basic stories, the **NRSV** is often sufficient. For the poetry, the **NRSV** is a fine starting point, but it's hardly enough. Like the **KJV**, the **NRSV** is available in dozens of published compilations, on the Internet, and from Bibleworks.

The closest Catholic equivalent to the **RSV** and the **NRSV**—in the sense that they are all intended as a way to bring the ancient Biblical texts to modern audiences—is the **New American Bible (NAB)**. The project—a direct result of a 1943 encyclical by Pope Pius—was begun in 1944. But its publication came in fits and starts over three decades, with some Biblical books being published, revised, and republished as part of the final 1970 edition. (A newer version is in the works as this book goes to press.) Unlike the **(N)RSV** and in keeping with Pope Pius's encyclical, the **NAB** purports to augment translation with literary criticism, presenting the "sense of the biblical text in as correct a form as possible" (according to the Preface to the **NAB**). In this sense, the **NAB** is an openly Catholic translation. And though the translators claim to have created "a completely new translation throughout" (again from the Preface), the claim is hardly credible in light of the widespread and significant overlaps with the errors in the **KJV**. The **NAB** goes one step further than the **NRSV** in that it not only takes the Dead Sea Scrolls and other ancient manuscripts into account, sometimes it prefers those manuscripts to the otherwise authoritative versions. So the text of the **NAB**, even before being translated into English, is not always the same as the **KJV**'s. The **NAB** also steps one degree further away from the original than the **NRSV** does. Although this often results in more readable English, the English is not necessarily closer to the original. It is, however, not nearly so distant as, for example, **The Living Bible**, which I describe below. The **NAB** is widely available in bookstores, on the Internet, and as part of Bibleworks.

In 1973 an international group of scholars published a new translation of the New Testament called the **New International Version (NIV)**. In 1978 they added the Old Testament and published the two together under the same name. The **NIV** sometimes relies on a better understanding of the text than other translations, and the translators had an appreciation of how translation really works. For example (from their Introduction), the translators say about themselves, "They have striven for more than a word-for-word translation." This is good. But even so, they wrongly translate *achoti kalah* as the incestuous "my sister, my bride." Further in support of the **NIV** (and still from the Introduction), the translators "endeavored to avoid a sameness of style." Yet even so, "they have consistently aimed at simplicity of expression." It's good to be clear, but sometimes the Bible's expression is not simple. The **NIV** has much to recommend it, but, unfortunately, sometimes it doesn't live up to its own standards. Still, this is a very close second to the **NRSV**. While, like the **NRSV**, it doesn't progress past a word- and phrase-level translation, it at least does a pretty good job with the words and phrases.

The **Jewish Publication Society (JPS)** published its first translation in 1917. While it was widely accepted among Jews—it used the traditional Jewish Hebrew text, which sometimes differs from the Christian Bible—and while, like any new translation, it offered a few improvements (and introduced a few setbacks) compared with other editions, it was created before the advent of modern translation theory and linguistics. So at this point, it doesn't have much to recommend it beyond its role in history. This version, sometimes called "JPS" and sometimes the "old JPS translation," is in the public domain, so it's available on the Web and as part of Bibleworks.

In 1962 the Jewish Publication Society published a wholly new translation, and in 1973 it published a revised version of that translation. Dr. Harry M. Orlinsky (whom I was lucky enough to know briefly) oversaw the translations. Dr. Orlinsky, the only Jew to work on the **NRSV** (and the **RSV**), was a trailblazer in Bible translation, striving for accurate, modern, and readable renderings. As such, his translation (like the **NRSV**) is vastly better than the **KJV**, though it falls short in some of the same ways that the **NRSV** does. In addition, Judaism has a long-standing tradition that each word of the Bible has intrinsic meaning. (Indeed, traditionally each letter has meaning, as do the serifs on the letters and even the spaces between them!) Orlinsky's translation walks a middle ground, respecting his Jewish tradition and also trying to adhere to his sense of modernity. The 1973 translation, variously called the "JPS" translation or the **New JPS (NJPS)**, offers an interesting mix of accuracy and traditional Judaism. Like the **NRSV**, the **NJPS** falls somewhere between the word and phrase level, but because of its Jewish orientation, it hews a little closer to the words than the **NRSV**. Its prose is therefore a little harder to read. The 1973 translation is available in a variety of formats from the Jewish Publication Society and through Bibleworks. It is also included in the *Jewish Study Bible*. If you're buying the **NJPS**, you may as well get the study Bible, which includes a wealth of scholarly and Jewish information about the text of the Old Testament.

Another Jewish translation—so far limited to the Five Books of Moses—comes from Dr. Everett Fox. Dr. Fox has a keen understanding of the Hebrew, but his translations are a step backward in that they seldom include more than word-level renderings.

Fox essentially skips right through Table 1, mimicking the Hebrew rather than translating it. As such, his 2000 book *The Five Books of Moses* is an interesting way to study Hebrew, but it does not give the English reader a sense of what the Hebrew means or represents. (Like the **KJV**, though, it has other useful purposes. Because Fox's English is so arcane, odder even than the **KJV**'s, it imparts a sense of loftiness to the text, even though that loftiness is often not part of the original.)

Dr. Robert Alter also penned a Jewish translation of the Five Books of Moses (published in 2004, released in paperback in 2008) and of Psalms (2007) as well. Alter knows better than to stop translating at word level, and he understands—better than most other translators—that prose should be translated as prose and poetry as poetry. His brave translation of Psalms undertakes an almost impossible task: rendering in modern English the brilliant Hebrew poetry of the book of Psalms. (Remember how much trouble we had just with Psalm 23!) And while Alter's methodology falls short in some regards—he doesn't always appreciate the role of function as it relates to poetry (remember Table 1?)—his copious footnotes combined with his translations offer considerable insight into the Bible. If you're interested in the Psalms, you will want to have his translation of them.

Kenneth Taylor's **The Living Bible (TLB)**, published in 1971, also represents a move away from word-level translation. Unfortunately, in his work, Taylor moves away from the Bible itself. The work is not a translation but rather a paraphrase. While it sometimes gets the concepts right, it fails completely regarding register and effect. The **KJV**, too, usually gets the register and effect wrong, but at least that older translation does a better job with the words and phrases. The good news is that the English in the **TLB** is accessible. The bad news is that it does not usually accurately represent what the Bible says. For example, its translation of Psalm 23 begins, "Because the Lord is my Shepherd, I have everything I need." That translation, like many others, gets "shepherd" wrong. But then it veers away from the Bible even further, spelling out the notion of causality that is only implied in the original. In other words, lyric poetry has become mundane prose. (This is like taking Shakespeare's "Oh, that I were a glove upon that hand," which Romeo utters about his desire for Juliet, and turning it into "I like Juliet.") Similarly, the original "let him kiss me with the kisses of his mouth" becomes "kiss me and kiss me again"; it is perhaps acceptable poetry, but it is not Song of Songs. (Continuing the Shakespeare example, this time it would be like taking Romeo's image of the glove and turning it into "I want to be a glass, placed on Juliet's lips." The idea is roughly the same, but it's not a translation.) For *achoti kalah*, we find "my treasure, my bride," with a footnote that "treasure" is really "sister." These are typical of **TLB**. It is a good read, but it's not what the Bible says.

In a similar vein we find the **Good News Bible (GNB)**. In 1966 the American

Bible Society published a colloquial version of the New Testament. It proved so successful that a decade later it published the **GNB**, containing both the Old and New Testaments. The **GNB**, like the **TLB**, is colloquial and chatty, and therefore easy to read. Many people think that because they can actually understand the **GNB** (unlike the **KJV**), the **GNB** must be closer to what the Bible really says. It is not. For example, it translates the beginning of Genesis, "In the beginning, when God created the universe, the earth was formless and desolate." We have already seen that the point of Genesis 1:1 was to answer the question "when?" and affirm God's role in creation. The **GNB** shifts the focus away from God and highlights instead the state of the earth. Song of Songs in the **GNB** begins, "Your lips cover me with kisses"; again, perhaps nice poetry, but it's not Song of Songs. For *achoti kalah*, the **GNB** offers "my sweetheart, my bride." We have already seen that "bride" is wrong. "Sweetheart" is a lovely thought, but it, too, misses the essential point of equality. In short, while the text of the **GNB** is easy to read, it is usually less accurate than other translations.

Going even farther away from the original Bible is **The Message**. Published in 1994 by Eugene Peterson, that rendition is essentially a rewrite loosely based on the themes of the Bible. For example, Genesis 1:1 in **The Message** reads, "First this: God created the Heavens and Earth—all you see, all you don't see." Peterson adds the phrase "all you see, all you don't see," which is (perhaps) interesting, but it does not come from the Bible. His version of Psalm 23 begins, "God, my shepherd! I don't need a thing." By turning "my shepherd" into a way of addressing God rather than a statement of what God is, Peterson destroys the connection between the two. The original point is that "I don't need a thing" only because "God is my shepherd." Peterson's line implies that regardless of what God is, "I don't need a thing." So whereas the **TLB** gets the idea right but destroys the poetry, **The Message** destroys both, in this case actually reversing the point of the Psalm. As a final example, **The Message** translates *achoti kalah* from Song of Songs as "dear friend." It's no longer incest (as it is in so many other translations), but neither it is still the text of the Bible.

The success of **The Message** and other rewrites based loosely on the Bible mirrors the continued success of the **KJV**. All of those make the Bible into something people want, rather than presenting what the Bible is. There's nothing wrong with that, but you should know what you're reading.

The Septuagint

There is only one translation of the Septuagint widely available, and that's the 1851 Brenton edition, reprinted in 2001 along with an overview of the history and nature of the Septuagint. Obviously, the nineteenth-century translation is outdated. It is also imperfect. But it's all there is. If you're interested in how the Septuagint translates the

Bible, you either have to master ancient Greek or pick up Brenton. The Septuagint is also available from Bibleworks.

Books Summarizing Bible Versions

There are many other English translations of the Bible. A good guide to them is Dr. Philip Comfort's *Essential Guide to Bible Versions*, published by Tyndale House Publishers in 2000. While the time line that starts the book on page xi mixes myth with history, and while the sections describing the modern versions talk more about the English than about their fidelity to the Hebrew, the book covers the history of all of the translations, including almost all of the important modern English ones and the historically important Greek and Latin translations. The book does a better job describing where the translations come from than it does with the nature of the translation itself. Similarly, the eighteen pages Comfort devotes to "the theory and practice of Bible translation" are hardly enough to do justice to the topic.

Another overview of Bible translations can be found in Bruce M. Metzger's *The Bible in Translation*, published by Baker Academic in 2001. Metzger's book, a little more rigorous and also a little harder to read than Comfort's, similarly describes the history behind the many Bible translations. And like Comfort, Metzger does a better job with the publication details and stories behind the translations than he does analyzing the translations themselves. For example, he criticizes the **NIV**: "It is surprising that translators who profess to have 'a high view of Scripture' should . . . [add] words that are not in the manuscripts." In so doing, Metzger shows a limited understanding of the nature of translation.

Zondervan has a publication called the *Comparative Study Bible*. It presents four translations, including the **NIV** and the **KJV**, side by side, so you can get a sense of how modern translations like the **NIV** differ from the older and less accurate **KJV**. Zondervan has also published a version with the **NIV** and **The Message** side by side. If you don't get Bibleworks (which I'm about to describe), you may want to look into these much cheaper, though more limited, options, to help you appreciate how far **The Message** has strayed and how archaic the **KJV** really is.

To help you understand the original Hebrew words of the Old Testament (and the Greek of the New Testament), as well as the grammars of both languages, Hendrickson Publishers offers what's called an interlinear translation, putting the English translations of each Hebrew or Greek word underneath the original. This is purely a word-level translation, and its main goal is to help you learn more about Hebrew or Greek. For example, instead of "In the beginning, God created," this text reads, "In the beginning created God," matching English with the Hebrew word for word. (Bibleworks, which I'm finally about to describe, will do this, too.)

Software

A wonderful program called Bibleworks contains many of the English translations of the Bible, the English translation of the Septuagint (along with the Greek), the complete Hebrew of the Old Testament, and literally dozens of foreign-language translations, including, for example the various versions of the *Luther Bibel*. One of the nicest features of the program is that it offers built-in Greek and Hebrew dictionaries. You move the mouse over a Greek or Hebrew word, and the program tells you what it means. In other words, it does the word-by-word translation for you. The program also has an advanced search feature that makes it easy to research words in context. The program is not cheap, but it's well worth it.

EXPANDING YOUR KNOWLEDGE

In the Beginning

If you are interested in the **KJV**, and of course you are, you will want to read Allister McGrath's *In the Beginning*, published in 2001 by Doubleday. It walks the perfect line between academic accuracy and readability. The book covers King James himself, the culture that produced the **KJV**, English of the time, the way the two influenced each other, printing technology, and much more. It's highly recommended.

Another book by the same name is also highly recommended, because I wrote it. My NYU Press publication *In the Beginning: A Short History of the Hebrew Language* (2004) was released in paperback in 2006. As the title suggests, it covers the history of Hebrew, starting with the invention of the alphabet, then describing what we know about the sounds of Biblical Hebrew, where the current writing system comes from, dialects of Hebrew in the Bible, how Modern Hebrew is related to Biblical Hebrew, the Dead Sea Scrolls, and more. Some of the text is dense, but (I hope) it's worth it. As you plod through, look for the jokes in the footnotes.

I have also contributed to a ten-volume multiauthor series on the Jewish prayers called *My People's Prayer Book*, published by Jewish Lights Publishing from 1997 to 2007 and edited by my father, Rabbi Lawrence A. Hoffman, Ph.D. My role was translator and linguistic commentator. (Other people contributed commentary from liturgical, Biblical, mystical, modern, and many other points of view.) Because the Jewish liturgy contains significant Biblical material, you may want to look at that series to get a sense of how I translate Biblical, and other, Hebrew. The book is generally accessible and easy to read.

Advancing

If my NYU book hasn't convinced you to stop studying Hebrew, you may want to take a chance on Angel Sáenz-Badillos's *A History of the Hebrew Language*, published by Cambridge University Press in 1993. (Sáenz-Badillos wrote the book in Spanish; the 1993 book is John Elwolde's translation into English.) The almost seventy-page bibliography in small type is representative of the book. It references almost everything written on the topic. However, as is typical of the European world of scholarship in which the book was written, it frequently presents the various scholarly opinions equally, rather than helping the reader decide among them. That these opinions are sometimes in German or Latin makes things even harder. But for those who can read it, it's a great source of information about Hebrew.

Also in the realm of scholarly books, though not as difficult, is *The Cambridge Companion to Biblical Interpretation*, edited by John Barton and published in 1998 by Cambridge University Press. It's a collection of scholarly essays, and, as such, some parts are easier to read than others. Chapters 7 and 9 of that book (on theoretical hermeneutics and linguistics, respectively) address some of the issues I cover in here, offering a little more depth in the first case and a little less in the second. Other chapters, such as the one on feminist interpretation, may prove interesting even if not directly related to what you've read here.

Similar in nature though not content is *The Challenge of Bible Translation*, edited by Glen Scorgie, Mark Strauss, and Steven Voth and published in 2003 by Zondervan. For readers who want to understand the field of Bible translation, this is an excellent place to start. Some of the issues are important if narrow, like the chapter on capital letters in translations. But if you're interested in learning more about the field of Bible translation, youll at least want to read Chapter 2 ("Bible Translation Philosophies with Special Reference to the New International Version"), which describes both the approach I've adopted here and a variety of methods that I reject; and Chapter 3 ("The Limits of Functional Equivalence in Bible Translation—and Other Limits, Too"), which offers more background about the approach I present here. General readers may find the prose in some chapters difficult and dense, and the book lacking focus. On the other hand, scholars (for whom the book was written) will appreciate its depth, detailed discussions, and copious notes.

You may decide you want to learn Biblical Hebrew for yourself. If so, you have two options. You can get a modern tutorial or an older one. I actually recommend the older approach, for example Weingreen's *A Practical Grammar for Classical Hebrew*, published in 1939. The step-by-step tutorial will take you through almost everything you need to know about Biblical Hebrew, starting right at the beginning. It will take you about half a year to work your way through Weingreen, and by the end you'll be able to read most of the Hebrew Bible in Hebrew.

Be careful to distinguish between Biblical Hebrew and Modern Israeli Hebrew. The former is what most of the Old Testament is written in. The latter is one of the three official languages of the modern State of Israel (Arabic and English are the other two). Learning Modern Hebrew will not help you very much with Biblical Hebrew, and it may even confuse you. Still, it can be a lot of fun. If you want to learn Modern Hebrew, Lewis Glinert's books are by far the best way to go. His *Modern Hebrew: An Essential Grammar*, for example, published in paperback in 2005 by Routledge, describes Modern Hebrew grammar, and it does so accurately. Many other "Modern Hebrew" grammars mix Modern and ancient Hebrew, leaving readers with a mistaken understanding of the modern language.

If you're really serious about Biblical Hebrew, you'll also want a few reference works. Bibleworks, the computer program, comes with a fairly accurate dictionary of Hebrew based on James Strong's work (and it has the added benefit that you don't have to know Hebrew to look up a word—you just use the mouse). If you don't get the computer program, Strong's dictionaries are available in print format, too. Though they don't contain a lot of detail, most of the information is accurate. If you see a Hebrew word in the Bible and you want a starting point for understanding it, go with Strong. (And then use the techniques of Chapter 2 to investigate the word for yourself.)

Ernest Klein's *A Comprehensive Etymological Dictionary of the Hebrew Language for Readers of English* is a mostly accurate and enjoyable book to have. In addition to serving as a dictionary for Biblical and Modern Hebrew, the etymology is the book is interesting (even though, as we know from Chapter 2, the etymology doesn't tell you what a word means).

In order to learn more about a word, you'll want a concordance. Once again, Bibleworks has this built in (and more), but if you want a print version you have a few options. Strong's concordance is best if your Hebrew skills are weak. If you are comfortable reading Hebrew, the classic reference work is by Shlomo Mandelkorn, and used copies are widely available. Even Shoshan, an Israeli publishing company, has a more modern-looking volume with essentially the same information.

Translation

If you're interested in translation in general, I highly recommend Douglas Hofstadter's *Le Ton Beau de Marot: In Praise of the Music of Language*. It's in English, despite the French pun that forms the title, and you don't have to speak French to read and love the book. (The title means "the sweet tone of Marot," after Clément Marot, who wrote the poem that forms the uniting thread of the book. But the French sounds like *le tombeau de Marot*, "Marot's tomb," reflecting the fact that Marot died in 1544.) Hofstadter's creation is a marvelous if meandering investigation into translation in general. Most of the book centers around several dozen English translations of the same obscure French poem, which Hofstadter uses to look at the nature of language and translation. His book does not specifically address the Bible, and it's not a treatise on translation, but it will really get you thinking about translation. (Two other books by Hofstadter, *Metamagical Themas* and *Gödel, Escher, Bach*, both contain discussions about translation here and there. They are few and far between, but they're great.)

More rigorous treatments of translation are widely available. To get a sense of the field, you might start with André Lefevere's *Translating Poetry* (published in 1975) and *Translating Literature* (1992), or with Peter Newmark's *Textbook of Translation* (1988).

The Text of the Bible

To learn more about where the text of the Old Testament comes from, two books are worth having on your bookshelf. The first is Würthwein's *The Text of the Old Testament* (1995), translated by Erroll Rhodes and published by William B. Eardmans. The book has fifty pictures of various historical manuscripts at the end, and even without anything else those pictures justify the purchase price. The rest of the book is a reference about the history of the text in the Old Testament. The second book is Emanuel Tov's *Textual Criticism of the Hebrew Bible* (2001), published by Fortress Press. It goes into more detail and offers a little more analysis than Würthwein's book.

For the text of the New Testament, Bart Ehrman's popular *Misquoting Jesus*, published in paperback by HarperSanFrancisco, is a good place to start. Ehrman's point—widely acknowledged by scholars but less appreciated by lay audiences—is that the text of the New Testament has changed over two millennia. The book explains where our current version comes from and how we know about the changes, and suggests some reasons the text might have changed. *Misquoting Jesus* is a fun, easy read that does for the New Testament what Würthwein and Tov do for the Old Testament.

The Dead Sea Scrolls

Since their accidental discovery in 1947 by two Bedouin, the Dead Sea Scrolls have captured the popular imagination more than any other historical find. The two-thousand-year-old scrolls are nearly intact, and in addition to offering a wealth of other material, they contain parts of every book of the Old Testament except Esther. So they present concrete evidence of what the Bible was like two thousand years ago. For this reason alone, anyone interested in the Bible eventually becomes interested in the Dead Sea Scrolls.

In addition, the story behind their discovery, authentication, and eventual publication is nothing short of riveting. (Just for example, a goat and a partridge were involved. So was a hidden cache in a Bethlehem house, and an archaeologist who just happened to be in charge of the Israeli army in 1967.) The saga is documented in many places, including Chapter 7 of my *In the Beginning*. Another good source is the introduction of Martínez's *The Dead Sea Scrolls Translated*, published in 1996. The popular *Scrolls from the Dead Sea*, by Sussman and Peled (1993), contains some wonderful full-color photographs.

Unfortunately, books on the content of the Dead Sea Scrolls vary widely in their quality and accuracy, so you probably want to read the originals yourself. The best way to do that is in Martínez and Tigchelaar's *The Dead Sea Scrolls Study Edition*, published in 2000. It comes in a convenient two-volume paperback edition and contains the most complete summary of transcriptions and translations of the non-Biblical Dead Sea Scrolls. You'll find the original Hebrew (or Aramaic) text alongside a fairly good word-level English translation.

You can get the Biblical material from the 2002 paperback edition of *The Dead Sea Scrolls Bible*, by Martin Abegg, Peter Flint, and Eugene Ulrich. That book doesn't contain the original Hebrew, but the authors' translation indicates where the Dead Sea Scrolls differ from the modern version of the Old Testament.

If you really get interested in the Dead Sea Scrolls, plan on a trip to Jerusalem where they are on display in the Shrine of the Book at the Israel Museum.

Life in Ancient Israel

If you're interested in what life was like in ancient Israel—marriage habits, for example, or how people earned a living—you'll want to read Philip King and Lawrence Stager's *Life in Biblical Israel*, published in 2002 by Westminster John Knox. Relying on archaeology, the Bible, and general history, the book covers everything from daily individual life to societal norms, musical instruments to clothing, food to shelter. (My discussion in Chapter 8 about the most likely average age of marriage, and my conclusion, is taken largely from their work.)

You'll also want to read one of the best books I've ever encountered: Saggs's *Civilization Before Greece and Rome*, published in 1989 by Yale University Press. Better than almost any other author, Saggs knows how to mix scholarly research and accuracy with popular accessibility. The result is an informative book that's also a page-turner. Though not specifically about the Bible or life in ancient Israel, his book covers those topics and puts them in the broader context of what we know about preclassical civilization.

Archaeology

Much of our information about life in the time of the Bible comes from archaeological evidence. Two books will help you learn more about this exciting field: Mazar's

Archaeology of the Land of the Bible, published in 1992 by Doubleday, and Dr. Harry Orlinsky's *Understanding the Bible Through History and Archaeology*, published in 1972 by Ktav Publishing. (This is the same Dr. Orlinsky who contributed to the **NRSV** and the **NJPS**.) Mazar's book is a compendium of information gleaned from archaeology about life in ancient Israel from 10,000 B.C. up to the First Exile in 586 B.C. Orlinsky's book cleverly compares Biblical passages with archaeological information. We have learned a lot in the nearly four decades since Orlinsky published his volume, so it's less complete, but it's more fun to read. If you're really interested in the topic, you'll want both books.

Linguistics

One of the most exciting advances of the twentieth century was what linguists learned about the mind, language, and the intersection of the two. Perhaps the best introduction to the new field of linguistics is Steven Pinker's *The Language Instinct*, published by Perennial in 2000. It is fascinating, accurate, and easy to read. If you found yourself wanting to know more about language as I discussed how linguistics helps us understand Bible translation, Pinker's book is the place to start.

Specifically regarding what it means for a word to mean something, you may want to read Hilary Putnam's *Representation and Reality* (1988), which bridges linguistics and philosophy. It's a little dense but well worth the effort, and after reading it you'll never think about words the same way again.

My Ph.D. thesis, available online, offers some insight into word order and how it relates to meaning. The title, "Syntactic and Paratactic Word Order Effects," offers a fair sense of the writing style, which is technical and not especially entertaining. But I included an appendix, "For the Non-Linguist," that explains the main points of the work.

George Lakoff has made a career of investigating metaphor—how it works, both in individual languages and across languages. His *Woman, Fire, and Dangerous Things* (1987) will open your eyes to one approach for understanding how metaphor and symbolic language work. (The title is provocative, but the text is not misogynistic. Rather, the book gets its name from one of Lakoff's observations: We traditionally use the pronoun "she" in English for things that we want to control, like boats and cars, and things that we wish we could control, like fires and hurricanes. His is an observation about language, not a suggestion for social roles.)

Umberto Eco has a 1992 book called *Interpretation and Overinterpretation* about the notion of "what a text really means": whether there is such a thing, and whether we can know what it is. The book—based on a series of lectures and responses to them—is dense but informative, and addresses some important theoretical issues that I didn't have space for here.

Eco also wrote the fantastically funny collection of essays *How to Travel with a Salmon*. If you're going to read *Interpretation and Overinterpretation*—or, for that matter, Putnam's or Sáenz-Badillos's books—do yourself a favor and get *How to Travel with a Salmon*, too, for when you need a break.

Happy reading.

INDEX

INDEX OF BIBLICAL REFERENCES

OLD TESTAMENT

NEW TESTAMENT